U0935973

《云南少数民族非纸质典籍聚珍·竹木简牍类二》编委会名单

学 术 顾 问：吴贵飙　普学旺　谢沫华

编委会主任：起国庆

主　　　编：和六花

副　主　编：杨筱奕　依旺的

编　　　委：岩叫满　李克忠　龙江莉　艾　芳　保俊萍　王向松

李国琼　李玉琴　申洁妆　王先安

文 字 撰 稿：和六花　杨筱奕

民 文 翻 译：依旺的

英 文 翻 译：和六花

本卷资料提供：云南省少数民族古籍整理出版规划办公室

国家民文出版项目库项目
民族文字出版专项资金资助项目

云南少数民族非纸质典籍聚珍

云南省少数民族古籍整理出版规划办公室◎编

竹木简牍类二

和六花◎主编

云南出版集团
云南人民出版社

图书在版编目（CIP）数据

云南少数民族非纸质典籍聚珍．竹木简牍类．二：汉文、傣文、英文 / 云南省少数民族古籍整理出版规划办公室编；和六花主编．-- 昆明：云南人民出版社，2020.10

ISBN 978-7-222-19080-1

Ⅰ．①云… Ⅱ．①云… ②和… Ⅲ．①少数民族－古籍－汇编－云南－汉、傣、英 Ⅳ．① K280.74

中国版本图书馆 CIP 数据核字 (2019) 第 287335 号

出 品 人： 赵石定
责任编辑： 金学丽　田大余　姚　云
英文编辑： 赵明珍
民文审稿： 岩满叫
封面设计： 马　滨
责任校对： 王以富　周　彦
责任印制： 代隆参

云南少数民族非纸质典籍聚珍·竹木简牍类二

YUNNAN SHAOSHU MINZU FEIZHIZHI DIANJI JUZHEN · ZHUMU JIANDU LEI ER

云南省少数民族古籍整理出版规划办公室◎编
和六花◎主编

出版　云南出版集团　云南人民出版社
发行　云南人民出版社
社址　昆明市环城西路 609 号
邮编　650034
网址　www.ynpph.com.cn
E-mail　ynrms@sina.com
开本　889mm × 1194mm　1/16
印张　28.5
版次　2020 年 10 月第 1 版第 1 次印刷
印刷　昆明精妙印务有限公司
书号　ISBN 978-7-222-19080-1
定价　560.00 元

云南人民出版社
微信公众号

如有图书质量及相关问题请与我社联系
审校部电话：0871-64164626　印制科电话：0871-64191534

概说

我国是一个统一的多民族国家。在漫长的历史发展进程中，各民族创造并积累了丰富多彩的历史文化，留下了浩如烟海的古籍。这些古籍资料，从不同的角度记录中华各民族的社会进程、历史走向和文化内涵，从不同侧面反映各民族祖先的智慧、文明成果和气质风貌，是中华文化的重要组成部分，是文化传承的独特载体，是中华民族多元一体格局的真实映射。少数民族古籍是其中不可或缺、独具特色的重要部分。云南素有“民族文化博物馆”之美誉，各民族先民创造了卷帙浩繁的书面文献和难以计数的口传文献。这些少数民族古籍涉及的语言文种多种多样，记录的内容博大精深，载体形态更是纷繁复杂，有记载历史时期官方盟誓、功绩、先贤德行、颁赏、封诰等的金石铭刻，有描绘先民生产生活景致和认知的岩画，有刻写了经书、经文和神灵造像的石刻，有绘制于麻布之上的民族神灵造像，有用铁笔刻写在贝多罗树叶上的贝叶经，等等。这些便是本套丛书所要收集、采录的少数民族非纸质典籍。

一

中国少数民族古籍（以下简称“少数民族古籍”），是指中国55个少数民族在历史上用各自的语言文字形成的文献典籍、碑刻铭文和口头传承资料等。其内容涉及政治、哲学、法律、历史、宗教、军事、文学、艺术、语言、文字、地理、天文、历算、经济、医学等领域。本套丛书收集、采录的少数民族古籍的时间范畴一般以1911年为下限，但由于各民族的历史特点和古籍存世情况差异，根据各民族古籍的实际情况，有的适当延至1949年。

少数民族古籍是中国传统文化的重要组成部分，是古籍学、文献学的重要研究对象。过去，传统研究未对此作出全面、系统的阐述，直到20世纪80年代，随着各级各类民族古籍工作部门的建立，民族古籍工作迎来了春天。1981年中共中央在《关于整理我国古籍的指示》中指出：“整理古籍，把祖国宝贵的文化遗产继承下来，是一项十分重要的、关系到子孙后代的工作。”1984年，国务院在转发《国家民委关于抢救、整理少数民族古籍的请示》的通知中强调：“少数民族古籍是祖国宝贵文化遗产的一部分，抢救、整理少数民族古籍，是一项十分重要的工作。”根据指示精神，从国家到地方都建立了相应的民族古籍工作部门，全面开展少数民族古籍的抢救保护、整理出版工作。我国少数民族古籍工作以“救书、救人、救学科”为己任，取得了丰硕的成果。然而，这项工作也面临着重重困难，走得异常艰难。随着社会日新月异的发展，少数民族古籍资源和古籍人才流失态势日趋严峻，少数民族古籍学科的发展又相对滞后，基础理论研究十分薄弱。诸如，中国各少数民族古籍种类众多、卷帙浩繁，对于少数民族古籍的分类至今仍无定论。对“民族古籍”的界定，是一个非常重要的问题，观点众说纷纭。[1] 这里，我们无意对此作系统梳理，只为明确少数民族非纸质典籍收录的范围。

在少数民族古籍抢救保护、整理出版工作中，特别是1997年以来，围绕《中国少数民族古籍总目提要》开展的全国范围内的少数民族古籍整理工作中，我们习惯性地将民族古籍主要分为两大类：一是有文字类；二是无文字类。有文字类的民族古籍又包括三个子类：一是用各少数民族文字（包括少数民族古文字）记载的历史文书和历史典籍；二是用汉文记载的有关少数民族内容的古代文献典籍；三是用少数民族文字和汉文记载的有关少

---

① 李国文在《云南少数民族古籍文献调查与研究》（民族出版社2010年版）一书的前言中对学界关于“民族古籍”的理解和界定做了较为系统的回顾。近年，也有相关研究做了一些讨论，观点几乏善可陈。

数民族内容的碑刻铭文。无文字的民族古籍主要是指各少数民族在历史上口头传承下来的具有历史和文化价值的各种资料。[①] 在《中国少数民族古籍总目提要》实施过程中，鉴于少数民族古籍文献载体形式的不同，又将少数民族古籍细分为书籍类、铭刻类、文书类和讲唱类四类予以收录。[②] 其中，书籍类全面收录少数民族在历史上形成的具有古典装帧形式的书册。铭刻类收录石碑、摩崖石刻、墓志、鼎彝、哀册、金属刻、竹木刻等碑刻铭文。文书类收录各类告示、契约、传单、函告、函件、账单、抄件、公约、规章、执照、档案、书信、柬帖等文献资料。讲唱类则收录少数民族口头传承的有关民族起源、民族迁徙、文明起源等具有历史文化价值的神话、传说、故事、歌谣等。依据少数民族古籍文献载体产生的四分类法，用于《中国少数民族古籍总目提要》各民族卷的编撰是符合客观实际且行之有效的。与此同时，因此项工作涉及面广、持续时间较长，这个分类法影响力较大。但是，依据古籍的载体形式对民族古籍加以分类，可否将“文书类”单独归为一类尚可斟酌。何谓“文献载体”？《辞海》中对于“载体”一词给出了五层解释，其中一个“指承载知识或信息的物质形体”。顾名思义，“文献载体”就是文献的物质载体，纸、绢帛、布匹、木头、树叶、兽骨、石头、金石器物、兽皮等等都可作为文献载体。“文书”一词起源甚早，早在汉晋时期的史籍中即已出现，是指以文字为主要方式记录信息的一种书面文书，按其性质可分为对公文书和对私文书，各类告示、契约、传单、函告、函件、账单、抄件、公约、规章、执照、档案、书信、柬帖等皆属文书。从这个层面来说，文书是依照文献内容界定的概念。在云南少数民族古籍中，同为文书，也有不同的物质载体形式，有书写在纸上的，有凿刻在砖石上的。

此外，乌谷先生《民族古籍学》一书对民族古籍的概念及其分类颇具代表性，他认为：“民族古籍就是指曾经在中华人民共和国疆域范围内生活过的各少数民族或正在生活着的各少数民族在历史上遗留下来的一切用文字、具有某种文化含义的符号（文字的雏形）及口头语言记录下来的文化载体。这种文化载体可分为四大类型，即原生载体古籍、金石载体古籍、口碑载体古籍和书面载体古籍。”[③] 按照乌谷先生的分类，各民族在历史上流传下来的以竹简、布帛、纸张为载体的各种历史文献，包括用各种民族文字书写出来的书籍、

① 国家民族事务委员会全国少数民族古籍整理研究室：《中国少数民族古籍总目提要·纳西族卷》序言，中国大百科全书出版社 2003 年版。

② 国家民族事务委员会全国少数民族古籍整理研究室：《中国少数民族古籍总目提要·哈尼族卷》序言，中国大百科全书出版社 2008 年版，第 10 页。

③ 乌谷：《民族古籍学》，云南民族出版社 1994 年版，第 6 页。

档案、文书、诏令、户籍、契约、谱牒、信札、告示、乡规民约等都归为书面载体古籍。而在众多的分类法中，铭刻类（或称“金石载体古籍”）、讲唱类（或称“口碑古籍”）按载体形式作为单独的一类没有太多的争议。但“铭刻类”和“金石载体古籍”因提法不同，内涵和外延产生了很大的差异，铭刻类涉及的物质载体更为宽泛、全面，不局限于金石器物，涵盖了石刻、竹木刻、骨刻、摩崖刻、器物刻等，铭刻类实质上已涵盖乌谷先生所界定的书面载体古籍和原生载体古籍的一部分，但“铭刻类”强调的是古籍的书写方式，而非载体形式。“金石载体古籍”这个类目的界定又略显狭隘，未将骨刻、竹木刻等载体形式囊括其中。乌谷先生虽另外界定了“原生载体”这个类目，“原生载体是指在一个民族的文字形成之初，用于记事表意被赋予某种特殊涵义的实物或符号。……我国各民族在自己的历史上都曾先后留下了大量有关刻木记事、结绳记事、实物记事等生动翔实的原生载体古籍”①。从这个概念来看，将骨刻、竹木刻归入原生载体古籍一类显然不合适。

综上所述，因中国各少数民族所处的环境不同、历史发展进程各异，少数民族古籍的载体形式多种多样，有的数量稀少却异常珍贵，有的历史上有过却早已佚失。用一种或者几种载体类别对琳琅纷呈的中国少数民族古籍作分类，难度巨大，难免挂一漏万，概括不够全面。我们选择以“非纸质”作为切入点，除了纸质载体以外的，具有有形实物载体的云南少数民族古籍都是我们收录的对象，意在将散布在各地图书馆、博物馆、档案馆等馆藏机构的以及散藏民间的，长期未公之于众的，又具有重要历史文化价值、文物价值和科学研究价值的云南各少数民族非纸质载体古籍汇编成册，公开出版发行。

二

云南是一个多民族聚居的省份，人口达5000人以上的世居少数民族有25个，除回族、水族、满族3个少数民族已通用汉语外，其余22个少数民族使用着26种语言（有的民族使用2种或2种以上语言），其中14个民族拥有23种文字或拼音方案（有的民族使用2种或2种以上文字），并留下了卷帙浩繁的民族古籍。据统计，云南散藏民间的藏文古籍、纳西东巴古籍、彝文古籍、壮文古籍、傈僳族音节文字古籍、白文古籍、普米族韩规古籍、傣文古籍、瑶文古籍等计有10万余册（卷）。其他如哈尼族、苗族、拉祜族、佤族、景颇族、布朗族、布依族、阿昌族、怒族、基诺族、德昂族、水族、独龙族等虽无本民族的古老文字，

① 乌谷：《民族古籍学》，云南民族出版社1994年版，第10页。

但他们靠口耳相传传承本民族历史文化，口传文献丰富多彩，创世史诗、迁徙史诗、叙事长诗、神话、传说、祭祀歌、劳动歌、生活习俗歌等数以万计。此外，有古老文字的民族中尚有大量口传文献流传。云南少数民族口传古籍达4万余种，内容涉及政治、哲学、法律、历史、宗教、军事、文学、艺术、语言、文字、地理、天文、历算、经济、医学等领域。

云南少数民族古籍储量巨大、历史悠久、载体多样，其中不乏非纸质典籍。依据现有资料来看，云南25个世居少数民族都或多或少拥有一些非纸质典籍。每一个民族都曾经经历过或正在经历着无文字的历史阶段，为便于沟通交流、传辞达意，随之萌芽了一些可用于记事表意的“实物语言”或“符号语言”，如结绳记事、刻木记事、树叶信等原生文化载体。在特殊文化场阈中，这些原生文化载体被赋予不同的象征意义。随着人类社会的发展，特别是文字产生后，原生文化载体在群体中的实用价值逐渐被淡化，有的甚至消失在了历史长河中。但在无文字民族中，这些原生文化载体的实用价值已远超其文化和文物价值。原生文化载体是否能纳入民族古籍的范畴，至今仍众说纷纭。鉴于云南各少数民族留存至今的原生文化载体数量不多，且新近发现者居多，族属难辨、释读不易，本书未作收录。在目前所知的十余万册云南少数民族古籍中，基于各民族分布区自然环境各异，历史发展进程各有轨迹，传统文化各具特色，民族古籍的载体可谓琳琅满目，布匹、竹木、兽骨、兽皮、金石器物等都在不同的历史时期成为不同族群古籍的承载体。这里，我们大体介绍一下非纸质典籍数量较多、载体较具代表性的几个民族的古籍情况：

1. 纳西族典籍

目前已知国内外收藏的东巴古籍有1000余种（内容大体相同的算为一种）3万余册，俗称“东巴经”，多数为图画象形文字写本，部分为图画象形文和哥巴文掺杂写本，极少数为纯哥巴文写本。其以宗教典籍为主，亦包括用东巴文书写的文书、铭刻和纳西族口耳相传的口头文献，内容涵盖社会历史、语言文字、哲学宗教、风俗习惯、文学艺术、天文医学等多个方面，被誉为“纳西族古代社会的百科全书”。按其内容可分为祈福延寿类的《远祖回归记》《献牲》《神鹏和署争斗的故事》等，禳鬼消灾类的《鲁般鲁饶》《董术战争》《创世纪》《白蝙蝠取经记》等，丧葬超度类的《杀猛鬼和恩鬼，高勒趣招父魂》《人类迁徙的来历》《马的来历》等，占卜类的《大地上卜卦之书》《用巴格图占卜》《占梦之书》等，涉及舞蹈、医药、民歌等的《东巴舞谱》《医药之书》《民歌范本》等，以及独具地域特色的丽江市宁蒗彝族自治县油米村的阮可东巴经。

纳西族非纸质典籍中，最具代表性、使用最广泛、储量较多的，有绘制于木头之上的木牌画和布匹之上的卷轴画。木牌画是一种历史悠久的原始绘画艺术，是东巴艺术在萌芽阶段的作品，大多应用于大型祭祀活动。木牌一般长约 60 厘米、宽约 10 厘米、厚约 1 厘米，内容依照东巴画谱所记载的为准，按祭祀功能可分为神牌、鬼牌、门牌、还债牌、诅咒牌等。图像造型奇特，形貌古朴，线条粗犷，笔法豪放，自然流畅，具有先民原始艺术的特点。卷轴画，纳西语叫“普劳幛”，是东巴用矿物质颜料绘制于土布上的神像画，是东巴绘画艺术跨入发达阶段而趋于精熟的作品，有长卷、多幅和独幅等多种。每幅卷轴画主要画一尊大神或护法神，表现某个神祇及其所居的神界，用于东巴教仪式中，悬挂于神坛正上方，不同仪式所挂的神像不尽相同。具有代表性的卷轴画有东巴教教主东巴什罗像、东巴教大神依古窝格、战神优麻、阳神董神、阴神术神、萨依威德、神路图等。其中，神路图是东巴卷轴画中最原始、最有代表性的巨作，一般宽 16~30 厘米、长约 15 米。画卷分段连续描绘地狱、人间、天堂三个部分，绘有 360 多个人、神、鬼及 70 多种奇禽怪兽，被称为“我国美术史上最长的直幅长卷”，享有“古代宗教绘画第一长卷”之誉，具有较高的文化和艺术研究价值。神路图的内容、性质、用途大体一致，但因载体材质、颜料、绘画技法等不同，每一幅神路图都有独特的艺术风格。

2. 壮族古籍

壮族有自己的语言文字，壮语属汉藏语系壮侗语族壮傣语支，分南北两大方言。壮族文字在先秦时期即已萌芽，隋唐时期，壮族先民即用汉字记壮语，效仿汉字六书的构字方法创制了方块壮字，称“土字”或“土俗字”，并用古壮字来记录民间故事，书写经文、家谱、碑文、账务等，一批方块壮字古籍流传至今。古壮文古籍，壮语称“师摩”“师多在”“师雅”等，“师”壮语意为“书籍”，多抄写在用纱皮树树皮制成的纱纸上，或是用嫩竹、构树皮制成的者卡土纸上。壮族古籍种类广、数量多，有记录摩教仪式、经文、教义的《摩经布洛陀》《摩荷泰》《麻仙》《德傣掸登俄》等，有反映朴素世界观和价值观的叙事长诗、古歌，如《盘古歌》《卜伯》《摩则杜》等，有民间七言叙事诗《毛洪》《董永》《舜儿》等，亦不乏展现绘画艺术的《鸡卜经》及宗教绘画“莱摩”，内容涉及历史、语言、文学、艺术、哲学、宗教、天文、历算等众多方面，可谓博大精深、绮丽多姿。

壮族的非纸质典籍以岩画、骨刻书和绘画典籍较具代表性。一是岩画。今壮族分布区尚存数百处摩崖石刻。据现有考古资料，今壮族分布区有众多的原始刻绘艺术遗存，虽难于明确界定这些考古遗存的族属，但壮族先民是这些绘画遗存的创作者、拥有者之一是确信无疑的。分布在文山壮族苗族自治州境内最具代表性的岩画，有麻栗坡大王岩岩画、丘北黑箐龙岩画、砚山卡子岩画、广南弄卡岩画、西畴蚌谷狮子山岩画等 10 余处，占地约 5430 平方米，有 170 幅 400 多个图案。二是骨刻书。云南壮族先民在器物、兽骨甚至身体上刻绘图案的历史由来已久，至今仍在部分地区传承使用，其中以壮族的骨刻历算器最为著名，文山壮族苗族自治州民族宗教事务委员会即在境内发现 58 块骨刻。骨刻，壮语称“甲巴克”“瓦甲巴”，意为刻在骨片上的图纹符号、书籍，是原始先民推算日历、占卜的器具。兽骨上一般刻有人物、桌子、棺材、植物、弓箭、动物、干栏、太阳纹等图像，是一种兼具审美和记事功能的图像文字。三是神像画。壮族神像画众多，类型多样，作品丰富，隐含借“神”避邪的世俗观念，审美态度与情感交织。依据其内容、形制、用途，大体分为摩教神图长卷、宗教挂图和占卜绘画三类。其中，摩教神图长卷是摩教特有的宗教神图之一，由摩教祭司传承使用；绘于壮族自制土麻布上，形制为长卷竖幅，分栏作画，多用于丧葬仪式、祭扫仪式等。

3. 傣族古籍

傣族有本民族文字。傣文古籍多为刻本、写本、稿本和抄本，有贝叶古籍和纸质（绵纸、构皮纸）古籍两种，形制一般为梵夹装、经折装、线装，主要流传于西双版纳、德宏、保山、普洱、临沧、红河等州、市的傣族地区。按内容大致有宗教类的《朗丝奢不仙宰》《杀鸡祭水神祷辞》《祭谷魂词》《招魂词》等，政治历史类的《泐史》《孟连宣抚史》等，文学艺术类的《巴塔麻嘎捧尚罗》《兰嘎西贺》《厘俸》，以及天文历法类、农田水利类、医药类、理论专著类、军事武术类、语言文字类、译著类等。

傣族的非纸质典籍载体多样、数量众多，最具代表性的便是傣族的银器、贝叶经书和绘画典籍。其中，贝叶经是最具代表性的非纸质典籍。贝叶经，傣语称作“坦兰”，是用民间制作的铁笔刻写在经过特制的贝多罗树叶上而成的。此外，傣族的壁画、布画等非纸质绘画典籍也较有特色。

4. 彝族古籍

彝族有自己的语言和文字。语言属汉藏语系藏缅语族彝语支，可分为东部、西部、南部、北部、中部、东南部六大方言区。彝族有自己古老的文字，汉文古籍称其为“夷经”“爨文”“罗罗文”等，现统称“老彝文”，每一个字形代表一个字义，并有不同写法。现存的老彝文有 1 万多字形，常用的有 1000 多字。历史上，彝族先民用老彝文撰写了卷帙浩繁的文献典籍和数量众多的金石铭刻，内容涉及政治、军事、哲学、宗教、历史、地理、语言、文字、文学、艺术、天文、历算、医药、卫生等方面。近现代流行于彝族地区的彝文古籍主要有纸书、皮书、布书、骨书、岩书、瓦书、木牍、木刻、金石铭刻、印玺等载体形制，其中纸书占绝对比例，包括抄本与木刻印刷本两种。现存彝文古籍达2万余册（件），手抄本较多，少数为木刻印刷本。云南彝文古籍可分为滇南彝文古籍、武定禄劝彝文古籍、撒尼彝文古籍、阿哲彝文古籍、宣威彝文古籍、罗平彝文古籍、北部彝文古籍七类。较具代表性的有传统宗教礼仪典籍《吾查》《们查》《指路经》《祭龙经》《祈雨经》《鲁资楠道》《脑斯古》《招魂经》《尼布木司》等，著名文学作品有《阿诗玛》《尼迷诗》等，创世史诗有《查姆》《阿细的先基》《梅葛》《阿黑西尼摩》《尼苏夺节》等，译文文献长诗有《董永与七仙女》《凤凰记》《木荷与薇叶》《唐王游地府》《唐僧取经记》等。

云南彝族非纸质典籍最具代表性的是彝文摩崖。如昆明市禄劝彝族苗族自治县境内便有一通我国西南彝族地区历史较永久、留存较完整的长篇彝文金石铭刻——罗婺盛世史摩崖，刻面高206厘米，宽80厘米，镌刻于明嘉靖十年（1531年），迄今已有480多年，记述了武定凤氏土司14代350多年间的兴盛史。

云南每一个少数民族都拥有或者曾经拥有过或多或少的非纸质典籍。中华人民共和国成立以后特别是20世纪80年代后，很多的非纸质典籍得到了抢救保护，有的收藏于各级各类收藏机构，有的陈列于各类博物馆，有的已有了相关的整理研究成果。但更多的非纸质典籍，如深藏山野的摩崖石刻正经历着风吹日晒、沧海桑田，有的还曾经历过灭顶之灾。如壮族骨刻散布民间、无人释读，研究者有意寻访亦难见其真颜；又如纳西族木牌因仪式物品使用禁忌、用完即毁，难寻旧物……如此种种不只是云南少数民族非纸质典籍面临的生境，也是少数民族古籍所面临的困境。

三

文化是民族的根脉，是人类的精神家园，是一个民族凝聚力、生命力、创造力的源泉，是国家强盛的重要支撑。少数民族古籍真实而生动地记录了少数民族的历史发展进程，蕴含着少数民族特有的精神价值、思维方式和非凡的想象力、创造力，是人类文明的瑰宝，是中国珍贵的文化遗产。在长期的传播交流过程中，少数民族古籍发挥着积极进取的价值取向和经世致用的社会功能。一部优秀的民族古籍作品，其在民族社会中的价值远远超出了一个学科的专业范畴，代表了一个民族在某个专业领域的认知、反映了一个民族的某个历史发展阶段，甚或承载、再现了一个民族的社会事实和历史走向。加强少数民族古籍抢救和保护，对于丰富中华文化宝库，全面了解中华民族的发展历程，构建平等团结互助和谐的社会主义新型民族关系，推动民族团结进步事业，具有重要的历史意义和现实意义。

中华人民共和国成立后，在各级党委、政府的领导下，经过几代古籍工作者筚路蓝缕的努力，云南省少数民族古籍抢救保护和翻译整理出版工作取得了显著成绩。本着“抢救为主，保护第一”的原则，抢救了少数民族文字文献古籍 3 万余册（卷），口传古籍 1 万余种，以《纳西东巴古籍译注全集》《中国贝叶经全集》《彝族毕摩经典译注全集》《云南少数民族古籍珍本集成》《红河彝族文化遗产古籍典藏》《云南少数民族古典史诗全集》《云南少数民族叙事长诗全集》等为代表的民族古籍抢救保护成果引起国内外的广泛关注。但是，于卷帙浩繁的少数民族古籍而言，目前的抢救保护、翻译整理成果不过是沧海一粟。初略估算，除已征集保管的少数民族古籍以外，云南仍有 7 万余册（卷）的少数民族文字文献古籍散存民间。由于保管不善或无人传承等诸多原因，许多散存民间的古籍难以做到活态传承，佚失、损毁现象严重，抢救保护迫在眉睫。就云南少数民族非纸质典籍而言，其生境尤令人担忧。部分可移动的、具有文物价值的非纸质古籍，多数已被各级各类机构、企业、私人征集收藏，这样的抢救保护最大化地彰显了此类古籍的文物价值，但这些民族古籍收而藏之后，原本在民间尚能活态传承的民族智慧结晶极易成为待在深闺无人识的宝贝；少量仍存于民间的，亦不乏寻访之人，各色寻访者在山乡村寨走访寻宝，不幸的是有的已被倒卖流到境外。而诸多不可以移动的非纸质古籍的生境更是让人心生惋惜，这些承载着民族文化的石刻、摩崖多隐匿深山，常年经受着日晒雨淋以致文字符号或字迹模糊、难于辨识，或直接被人为损毁。石刻、摩崖受自然侵蚀逐渐消失，这是事物发展的自然规律，但对于民族文化而言是一个让人痛心的巨大损失。

我们在做这套丛书的过程中，也亲历和见证了数次痛心的时刻。2011 年起，在云南省财政厅、云南省民族宗教事务委员会的支持下，我们一直在持续开展“云南省民族文化百项精品工程”项目《云南少数民族古籍珍本集成》。同时，按照《国家民委关于印发全国少数民族古籍保护工作“十三五”规划通知》的要求，“基本完成全国少数民族古籍普查工作。会同相关部门全力推进普查工作，摸清各地少数民族古籍资源。建立健全普查登记管理制度，构建普查登记平台，对各地少数民族古籍普查情况进行录入、统计、汇总，形成全国少数民族古籍普查登记目录档案”。本着“摸家底、建平台”的目的，我们在云南全省范围内开展了少数民族古籍普查、采录工作。为此，我们访遍云南各州、市的少数民族古籍收藏机构，走访古籍传承人、收藏爱好者，足迹几遍及云南全省。2016 年，我们在迪庆藏族自治州调研时，迪庆藏族自治州藏学研究院的同志为我们介绍了州内非纸质典籍的留存分布情况，提到在维西傈僳族自治县塔城镇附近一个山坡上有很多藏文石刻。我们在电脑里看到了该院数年前实地调研时拍摄的照片，从中可以看到半面山坡都是石刻，都是一些有年代的文化遗存。我们异常兴奋，因为这个石刻分布地和发现唐代藏文碑刻《格子碑》的格子村相距仅数里，又隐匿深山，难保不是一些有价值的非纸质典籍。遗憾的是，因此行我们未携带拍摄设备，心想留待日后再专程前来调研。未想此次擦肩而过，却错失了一睹其风采的机会。2018 年 5 月，我们组织了专业的拍摄、传拓人员前往迪庆州，一行人在迪庆州藏学院相关同志的带领下，经历修路堵车、徒步山林，风尘仆仆地来到那片山坡。可眼前的景象却让我们傻眼了，哪里还见得到石刻，只见坡头有一道高五六米的混着石头的土堆，下方红土里稀稀拉拉种了一些重楼。几经周折联系上村委会的同志，方得知该村为发展农业经济，特地请了推土机来平整土地，这些石刻已经被埋到了土堆下。这只是我们在开展云南少数民族古籍抢救保护工作中经历的几乎不值一提的一件小事，这样的事情不止在迪庆，在全省各地都在发生着；不止石刻、摩崖，纸质文献、丝帛素书、竹木简牍无不面临着这样的生存困境。倾心于民族文化抢救保护的人们痛心疾首，却也深深地感受到，仅凭一个部门、一些群体去抢救保护，确实是势单力薄。基于这样的现状，抢救保护非纸质典籍确实是迫在眉睫。基于经费、人员、技术等各方面的制约，哪怕是采用最简单、最传统的办法，也得先把这些文化遗存的影像留下来，供社会科学研究使用，同时借以呼吁全社会共同关注民族古籍的抢救保护，这可是一件意义深远的事情，也正是本丛书策划之初最真实的出发点。

云南省少数民族古籍整理出版规划办公室于数年前就多次到民族地区征集典籍，了解线索，拍摄图片。经过数年的努力，由丽江市博物院、丽江东巴文化研究院、丽江市玉龙纳西族自治县图书馆等单位和一些民间收藏爱好者收藏的云南非纸质典籍最终得以在此书中整合出版。当然，这也得益于云南人民出版社长期以来对云南少数民族古籍的抢救保护、整理出版工作给予了极大的支持，并于 2016 年将云南少数民族非纸质典籍抢救保护项目申报国家民族文字图书出版资金资助。为收集这些非纸质典籍，相关人员付出了辛勤劳动，足迹几遍及云南全省。大量的原数据采集回来后，我们在典籍的分类整合上却遇到了前所未有的困难。云南各少数民族的非纸质典籍载体可谓琳琅满目，每种载体类型古籍的数量和质量参差不齐，作为丛书汇总出版既要全面涵盖具有代表性的非纸质典籍的载体类型，又要兼顾覆盖各民族的非纸质典籍；既要鉴别甄选各民族非纸质典籍的珍品、精品，又要尽可能地考虑民族古籍在民族社会中的情感价值；既要客观地收录古籍珍品，又要考虑每卷图书的体量和规模。几经求证，严格按照民族古籍学的学科分类对云南的非纸质典籍进行归类，几乎是不可能的。我们只能对倾尽全力收集到的非纸质典籍做个大概的分类，各卷再细分类目。

总的说来，本丛书是云南少数民族非纸质典籍的第一次集成和汇总。它将以往秘不外传的众多少数民族古籍珍品第一次集中展示于世人面前，不论学术价值、史料价值，还是传世、鉴赏、收藏价值等都具有诸多独特性，在保护各民族文化遗产、弘扬各民族优秀文化、增进民族团结、促进中华民族共有精神家园建设等方面具有重要意义。

少数民族古籍的抢救保护是一项长期的工作，不是朝夕之功。我们想全面呈现云南非纸质典籍的精品、珍品，在实际工作中会不断发现新典籍、扩充新类目，所以丛书难免有不当之处，唯有祈求方家海涵、指正。

General Introduction

China is a unified multi-ethnic country. Various ethnic groups have created and accumulated rich and colorful historic culture, while leaving a vast number of ancient books and records in the process of long-term historical development. Recording social process, historical trends and cultural connotations from different perspectives and reflecting wisdom, civilization achievements and the essence style from various sides, these ancient books and records are an important part of Chinese culture, a unique carrier for cultural inheritance, and a real reflection of the diversified but integrated historical pattern in China. Ancient books and records of ethnic groups are an indispensable and unique part. Yunnan has long been enjoying the good reputation as "Museum of Ethnic Culture". Ancestors of ethnic groups have created voluminous written documents and countless oral literature. A great diversity of language record types are involved in the ancient books of the ethnic groups. The contents of the records are extensive and profound, and the carrier forms are more complicated. Besides, there are inscriptions recording the historical events such as the official vows, merits and achievements, virtues of ancient wise men, awarding and imperial mandate appointments. Moreover, there are cliff engravings carved on the cliffs to depict the production and living situations as well as the cognitions of the ancestors. There are also sutras and scriptures carved on stones, stone-carved statues of gods, and Pattra-leaf Scriptures carved on pattra leaves with the stencil pen (a cutting tool used in carving seals, etc.). These are the non-paper ancient books and records of the ethnic groups to be collected and recorded in this series of books.

I

Ancient books and records of the ethnic groups in China (hereinafter referred to as ancient books and records of the ethnic groups) refer to ancient books and records, inscriptions, oral inheritance materials and other documents of 55 ethnic groups in their respective languages in history, contents of which cover politics, philosophy, history, religion, military affairs, literature, art, languages, geography, the celestial almanac, economy, medicine and other fields. Year 1911 is generally taken as the lower limit for the time category of ancient books and records of the ethnic groups. However, due to historical characteristics of the various ethnic groups and differences in the existence of the ancient books and records, some of them may be extended to 1949 in accordance with the actual situation of ancient books of the various ethnic groups.

Ancient books and records of the ethnic groups are an important part of Chinese traditional culture as well as an important study subject of ancient books, records and literature. In the past, there were no comprehensive or systematic explanations on such subject in the traditional research. Nevertheless, with the establishment of various levels and kinds of departments on ancient books of the ethnic groups in the 1980s, work of ancient books and records of the ethnic groups ushered in the spring. In 1981, the Central Committee of the Communist Party of China pointed out in *The Instructions on Sorting-out of Ancient Chinese Books,* "It is a fundamental task that affects later generations to sort out ancient books and records and inherit the precious cultural heritage of the nation." In 1984, the State Council, in forwarding the notification of *The Request from the State Civil Affairs Commission on the Rescue and Sorting-out of Ancient Books and Records of the Ethnic Groups,* stressed, "Ancient books and records of the ethnic groups are part of the precious cultural heritage of the nation, and it is a fundamental task to rescue and sortout them." In accordance with the instructions, corresponding departments responsible for the work on ancient books and records of the ethnic groups were set up at the national and local levels to carry out the rescue, protection, sorting-out and publication of ancient books of the ethnic groups. The personnel responsible for the work on ancient books and records of the ethnic groups have been taking the mission of "rescuing books, the people and the subject" as their mission, and have achieved fruitful goals. However, this task is also faced with numerous difficulties, and it is extremely difficult to push it forward. With the rapid development of society, depletion of ancient book , record resources and the outflow of talents for ancient books and records of the ethnic groups become increasingly severe. Besides, the development of the subject on ancient books and records of the ethnic groups is relatively backward, and the basic theoretical research is very weak. For instance, there are so many voluminous ancient books and records of the ethnic groups in China that the classification of such books is still inconclusive. Moreover, the definition of "ancient books and records of the ethnic groups" is a very important issue, but relevant opinions are divergent. ①Here, we have no intention to make systematical sorting, but just to clarify the inclusion scope of non-paper ancient books and records of the ethnic groups.

During the rescue, protection, sorting-out and publication of ancient books and records of the ethnic groups, especially since 1997, when sorting out ancient books and records of the ethnic groups conducted throughout the country on *Summary of the Catalog of Ancient Books and Records of the Ethnic Groups in China,* we habitually divide ancient books and records of the ethnic groups into two categories: literal and non-literal. Ethnic ancient books and records of literal category can be divided into the following three subcategories: first, historical documents, books and records recorded in the current and ancient languages of the ethnic groups; secondly, ancient literature, books and records relevant to the ethnic groups recorded in Chinese; thirdly, inscriptions related to the ethnic groups recorded in Chinese and ethnic languages. Ethnic ancient books and records of non-literal category mainly refer to various kinds of historical and cultural material handed down orally by the ethnic groups in history.② In view of the different carrier forms, ancient books and records of the ethnic groups were further divided into four categories as books, inscriptions, documents and lectures and songs in the implementation of *Summary of the Catalog of Ancient Books and Records of the Ethnic Groups in China.*③ Among them, the classical binding forms of books and records of the ethnic groups in history are comprehensively included in the category of books; stone-tablet and cliff carvings, epigraphs, inscriptions carved on the sacrificial utensil, the elegy volume, and bamboo and wooden engravings are included in the category of inscriptions. Various kinds of notices, contracts, leaflets, letters of notifications, correspondence, bills, duplicates, conventions, regulations,

---

① In the preface of *Investigation and Research on Ancient Books and Records of the Ethnic Groups in Yunnan* (*Yunnan* Minzu Publishing House, Edition 2010), Li Guowen made a systematic review of the understanding and definition of "ancient books and records of the ethnic groups" in the academic circle. In recent years, there have been some discussions on the relevant research, but the views have nothing to brag about.

② The Research Office of Ancient Books and Records of the Ethnic Groups for National Ethnic Affairs Commission: "Preface" of *Volume of the Naxi Ethnic Group for Summary of Catalogue of Ancient Books and Records of the Ethnic Groups in China,* Edition 2003 by Encyclopedia of China Publishing House.

③ The Research Office of Ancient Books and Records of the Ethnic Groups for National Ethnic Affairs Commission: "Preface" of *Volume of the Hani Ethnic Group for Summary of Catalogue of Ancient Books and Records of the Ethnic Groups in China,* Page 10 of Edition 2008 by Encyclopedia of China Publishing House.

licenses, archives, letters, notes and other documents are included in the document category of ethnic ancient books and records. The myths, legends, stories and ballads with historical and cultural value related to ethnic origin, migration of the ethnic groups and the origin of civilization and other oral inheritance of the ethnic groups are included in the category of lectures and songs. According to the four-classification method of the literature carriers of ancient books and records of the ethnic groups, the compilation of various ethnic volumes in *Summary of the Catalog of Ancient Books and Records of the Ethnic Groups in China* is in line with the objective reality and effective. Meanwhile, the classification method has great influence because of the wide scope and long duration of the task. Nevertheless, since ancient books and records of the ethnic groups are classified according to the carrier forms, whether books and records of "document category" can be taken as an individual category is still to be considered. What is the "literature carrier"? Explanations in five aspects in *Cihai* have been provided for the word "carrier", one of which refers to "the material form carrying knowledge or information". As the name suggests, "literature carrier" is the material carrier of literature. Materials such as paper, silk, cloth, wood, leaves, animal bones, stones, bronze and stone implements, and animal skins can be used as literature carriers. The word "document" can be dated far back in time, which could be seen in the historical records as early as in the Han and Jin dynasties. Besides, it referred to a type of written documents taking the written language as the main method to record information, which could be divided into official and private documents, various kinds of notifications, contracts, leaflets, letter of notification, correspondence, bills, duplicates, conventions, regulations, licenses, archives, letters, notes and other documents by nature. Seen from this aspect, a document is a concept defined by the content of literature. In the ancient books and records of the ethnic groups in Yunnan, there are different forms of material carriers, such as documents written on paper or carved or chiseled on bricks and stones.

Furthermore, the concept and classification of ancient books and records of the ethnic groups mentioned in *Ancient Books and Records* of the Ethnic Groups by Mr. Wu Gu were quite representative. He believed that " ancient books and records of the ethnic groups refer to all the cultural carriers of the ethnic groups who once lived or are living within the territory of the People's Republic of China, which are recorded in words, symbols with certain cultural meanings (prototypes of written language), and in oral languages carried over in history. This kind of cultural carriers can be divided into four major categories, i.e., ancient books and records of original, inscriptions, oral inheritance materials and written carriers."[①] According to the classification by Mr. Wu Gu, various kinds of historical documents passed on by the ethnic groups in history with bamboo slips, cloth and paper as the carriers, including books, archives, documents, imperial edicts, household registrations, contracts, ultimatums, letters, notifications, township rules and folk contracts written in various ethnic languages, are classified as ancient books and records with written carriers. In the numerous classification methods, the category of inscriptions (or known as ancient books and records with ancient bronze and stone tablet carriers) and the category of lectures and songs (or called as oral inheritance materials ancient books and records) can be regarded as separate categories according to the carrier form without many controversies. However, due to the different names, the connotations and extensions of "inscriptions and ancient books and records with ancient bronze and stone tablet carriers" vary significantly. Inscriptions cover a broader and more comprehensive range of material carriers and are not restricted to bronze and stone implements, including stone, bamboo, wooden and bone carvings and cliff engravings, implements and other materials. In essence, the category of inscriptions covers part of the original carriers of ancient books and records as defined by Mr. Wu Gu. However, "inscriptions" emphasizes the writing modes of ancient books rather than the carrier forms. The category of "ancient books and records with carriers of ancient bronze and stone tablets" is narrowly defined, which does not include such carrier forms as bone and bamboo carvings. Although Mr. Wu Gu further defined the category of "original carrier", "it referred to material objects or symbols provided with a certain special meaning and used to record events or express meanings at the beginning of formation of the written language of an ethnic group... Each ethnic group has left over a large number of vivid and detailed original ancient books and records relevant to record keeping of events through wooden carving, knot tying and record keeping with material objects." [②] Seen from this concept, it is obviously improper to classify bone, bamboo and wooden carvings into the ancient books and records with original carriers.

In conclusion, due to the different environments and historical development process of the ethnic groups in China, the carrier forms of ancient books and records of the ethnic groups are diverse. Some are rare but extremely precious, while some have disappeared in history. It is extremely difficult to classify the numerous ancient books and records of the ethnic groups in China with one or several carrier forms. Besides, it is hard to make comprehensive generalizations. We choose the "non-paper" carrier forms as the point of penetration. In addition

① Wu Gu: *Studies on Ancient Books and Records* of the Ethnic Groups, Edition 1994 by Yunnan Minzu Publishing House, P6 .

② Wu Gu: *Studies on Ancient Books and Records* of the Ethnic Groups, Edition 1994 by Yunnan Ethnic Publishing House, P10 .

to paper carriers, ancient books and records with tangible physical carriers of the ethnic groups in Yunnan are all the objects to be included by us, for the purpose of compiling and publishing the ancient books with non-paper carriers of the various ethnic groups in Yunnan, which are scattered in libraries, museums, archive centers and other collection institutions in various regions, as well as the scattered folk collections, which have not been made public for a long time and have significant historical and cultural value, as well as value of cultural relics and scientific research.

II

Yunnan is a province where multiple ethnic groups live in compact communities. 25 ethnic groups with a population of more than 5,000 people have been living there for generations. Chinese is generally used in the three ethnic groups (the Hui ethnic group, the Shui ethnic group and Manchu). However, the other 22 ethnic groups use 26 languages (some ethnic groups even use two or more languages). Among them, 14 ethnic groups have 23 kinds of writing or spelling systems, and some of them use two or more written languages. Moreover, they have left over voluminous ancient books and records of the ethnic groups. According to the statistics, there are more than 100,000 books (volumes) of ancient books and records scattered in Yunnan, including those in Tibetan, Naxi Dongba, Yi, Zhuang characters, Lisu and Bai characters, Hangui characters in the Pumi ethnic group, and Dai and Yao characters. As for other ethnic groups such as the Hani, the Miao, the Lahu, the Wa, the Jingpo, the Bulang, the Buyi, the Achang, the Nu, the Jinuo, the De'ang, the Shui and the Dulong ethnic groups, although they don't have their own ancient languages, they pass on their historic culture orally, with rich and colorful oral documents. Moreover, there are tens of thousands of creation epics, migration epics, narrative poems, myths, legends, sacrifice songs, labor songs, living custom songs, etc. Furthermore, there are still a large number of oral literatures passed down among the ethnic groups with ancient languages. There are over 40,000 kinds of oral ancient records passed on in the ethnic groups in Yunnan, covering politics, philosophy, law, history, religion, military affairs, literature, art, language, writing, geography, astronomy, calendar, economy, medicine and other fields.

The ancient books and records of the ethnic groups in Yunnan have been provided with the characteristics of huge reserves, long history and various carriers, among which there are lots of non-paper ancient books and records. All the ethnic groups once experienced or are experiencing a period of history without written languages. In order to facilitate communication and convey meanings, some "material languages" or "symbol languages" that can be used to record events and convey meanings were created, for instance, the original cultural carriers such as record-keeping through knots tying, wood carving and with leaf letters. Under the special cultural circumstances, these original cultural carriers were provided with different symbolic meanings. With the development of human society, especially after the creation of the written languages, the practical value of the original cultural carriers in the groups is gradually diluted, and some even disappeared in history. However, the practical value of these original cultural carriers has far exceeded their cultural and historical-relic value. Whether the original cultural carriers can be included into the category of ancient books and records of the ethnic groups is still controversial. In view of the fact that the number of original cultural carriers retained in the various ethnic groups in Yunnan is limited, the majority of the carriers were discovered recently, and that it is difficult to distinguish their ethnic classification and make interpretations, they are not included in this book. Based on the different natural environment in the distribution areas of the various ethnic groups, the distinctive historical development process, and the unique traditional culture, it can be said that there are a wide variety of the carriers for the over 100,000 discovered ancient books and records of the ethnic groups in Yunnan. Cloths, bamboos, animal bones and skins, ancient bronzes and stone tablet implements and other materials have become the carriers of ancient books and records of the various ethnic groups in different historical periods. Here, we generally introduce the ancient books and records of several ethnic groups with a large number of non-paper ancient books and records as well as the representative carriers.

1. Ancient Books and Records of the Naxi Ethnic Group

Currently, there are more than 1,000 kinds (over 30,000 volumes) of Dongba ancient books and records collected at home and abroad (books of roughly the same contents are taken as one kind), commonly known as "Dongba Scriptures". Besides, most are pictorial hieroglyphic-writing transcripts; some are mixed with pictorial pictographs and Geba scripts; a very few are pure Geba scripts. There are mainly ancient religious books and records, and documents and inscriptions in Dongba characters, and oral documents passed down from mouth to mouth by the Naxi ethnic group are also included. Contents of the Dongba ancient books and records cover social history, language, philosophy, religion, customs, literature and art, astronomy, medicine and other fields, which can be regarded as "the encyclopedia of the ancient Naxi ethnic group". According to the contents, the ancient books and records can be divided into the category of praying for prolonged life including *The Return of Remote Ancestors, Animal Sacrifice,*

Battle between the Great Roc and the Shu Synopsis, the category of ghosts and disaster elimination such as *Luban Lurao, The War between the "Dong" and "Su"Tribes, The Creation, White Bat's Collection of Scriptures*, the category of the release of the souls from suffering in the funerals such as *Killing the Devil Ghost and Helpful Ghost, Gao Lequ Recall of Father's Soul, The Origin of Human Migration*, and *The Origin of Horses*, the category of divination such as *The Book of the Divination of the Earth, Divination with Hatem Bagato*, and *The Skills of Divination by Interpreting Dreams*, and the category concerning dance, medicine and folk songs such as *Dongba Dance Notation, The Book of Medicine*, and *the Model of Folk Songs*, as well as the Ruanke Dongba Scripture with unique regional features at Youmi Village in Ninglang County of Lijiang City.

Among the Naxi non-paper ancient books and records, the most representative, the most widely used and the most abundant ones are the wooden-plaque paintings on wooden plaques and the scroll paintings on cloth. As a kind of primitive painting art with a long history, the wooden-plaque paintings are a work of Dongba art in its infancy stage, which is mostly used in large-scale sacrificial activities. Generally, the wooden plaques are approximately 60 cm in length, 10 cm in width and 1 cm in thickness, and the contents are in accordance with the records of Dongba picture copybooks. According to the sacrificial functions, they can be divided into god and ghost plaques, door plates, debt-collecting, cursing and other plaques. The picture is peculiar in shape, simple in appearance, straightforward in line, and bold, natural and fluent in brushwork, which is provided with the primitive art characteristics of the ancestors. Scroll paintings, known as "Pulaozhang" in the Naxi language, are statues of gods painted on homespun cloth by the Dongba people with mineral pigments, and are all works tending to be sophisticated when the Dongba paintings have entered a developed stage, including multiple types such as long scrolls, multiple and single pieces. A great god or a guardian god is mainly depicted in each scroll painting representing a certain god and the divine circle where he/she lived. The painting is used in Dongba religious rituals and directly hung above the altar. Different statues of gods are hung in different ceremonies. Representative scroll paintings include statues of Dingbashiluo (founder of the Dongba Religion), Yiguwoge (great god of the Dongba Religion), Youma (god of wars), God Dong (god of Yang), God Shu (god of Yin), Sayiweide and road maps of Gods. Among them, Road Maps of Gods are the most original and representative masterpiece in Dongba scroll paintings, with a width of 16–30 cm and a length of approximately 15 meters. Three parts of the hell, the world of mortals and heaven are successively depicted on the scroll paintings, with more than 360 individuals, gods, ghosts and over 70 kinds of odd birds and monsters. It is known as the longest straight scroll in the history of the Chinese art, and enjoys the reputation of "the first long scroll of the ancient religious painting", which is provided with high cultural and artistic research value. The contents, nature and use of road maps of gods are basically consistent. However, due to different carrier materials, pigments and painting techniques, each of the road map has its unique artistic style.

2. Ancient Books and Records of the Zhuang Ethnic Group

The Zhuang ethnic group has its own language and characters, and the Zhuang language is a category of the Zhuang-Dai language branch of the Zhuang-Dong Group of the Sino-Tibetan languages, which is divided into two big dialects of the north and south. The Zhuang language was already in the embryonic stage in the Pre-Qin Period. In the Sui and Tang dynasties, ancestors of the Zhuang ethnic group recorded the Zhuang language with Chinese characters, and invented the square Zhuang characters, called as "Tuzi" or "Tusuzi". Besides, they used the ancient Zhuang characters to record folk stories, and record scriptures, genealogy, inscriptions, accounting, etc. Besides, a batch of ancient books in square the Zhuang characters has been handed down. The ancient Zhuang books and records are known as "Shimo" "Shiduozai" "Shiya", etc. in the Zhuang language. "Shi" in the Zhuang language refers to "books", which are mainly transcribed on the gauze paper made of barks of the Shapi trees, written on the Zheka paper made from fresh bamboos or tapa. The ancient books of the Zhuang ethnic group are in a wide variety and a large number, including books recording the rites, scriptures and doctrines of the Mo Religion such as *Buluotuo Lection*, *Mohetai*, *Maxian*, and *De Dai Shan Deng E*, narrative poems and ancient songs reflecting simplicity world view and values such as *Pangu Song*, *Bubo*, and *Mozedu*, folk seven-character narrative poems such as *Maohong*, *Dongyong* and *Shun'er*. Moreover, there are also quite a few *Jibu Scriptures* representing art of painting as well as the religious paintings "Laimo", contents of which cover history, language, literature, art, philosophy, religion, astronomy, calendar and many other fields and can be said to be extensive and profound and gorgeous.

The non-paper ancient books and records of the Zhuang ethnic group are represented by cliff engravings, bone carvings and drawing books and records. The first category is cliff engravings. There are hundreds of cliff engravings in the current distribution area of the Zhuang ethnic group. According to the existing archaeological data, there are many original carved and painted art relics in the distribution area of today's Zhuang ethnic group. Although it is difficult to clearly define the ethnic group of these archaeological relics, it is certain that the ancestors of the Zhuang ethnic group are the creators and owners of these paintings. The most representative cliff engravings are distributed in the Zhuang and Miao Autonomous Prefecture of Wenshan. There are more than 10 places, including the cliff engravings on the Dawang Cliff in Malipo, Heiqinglong in Qiubei, Kazi in Yanshan, Nongka in Guangnan and the Shizi Mountain in Benggu of Xichou, covering an area of approximately 5,430 square meters, with more than 170 engravings and over 400 designs. The second type is bone-carved books. The ancestors of the Zhuang ethnic group in Yunnan had a long history of carving patterns on utensils, animal bones and even human body, which are still passed on and used in some areas. Among them, the most famous one is bone-carved almanac calculator in the Zhuang ethnic group. The Committee of Ethnic and Religious Affairs of Zhuang and Miao Autonomous Prefecture of Wenshan discovered 58 bone carvings within its territory. Bone carvings, known as "Jiabake" and "Wajiaba" in the Zhuang language, refer to graphic symbols and books engraved on the bone pieces, which were the utensils used by the primitive people for calculating calendars and divination. Animal bones were usually engraved with figures, tables, coffins, plants, bows and arrows, animals, stilts, sun patterns and other images, which are pictographs with both aesthetic and recording functions. The third type refers to the statues of gods. Majority of the engravings in the Zhuang ethnic group are statues of gods, with diverse types and abundant works, implying the secular concept of avoiding evil by the power of "god". The aesthetic attitude and emotion are intertwined. According to the content, shapes and use, it can be roughly divided into three categories: long-scroll statues of gods in the Mo Religion, religious wall pictures and divination paintings. Among them, long-scroll statues of gods in the Mo Religion are among the unique religious images of the religion, which is inherited and used by the priests in the Mo Religion. Painted on the homespun linen, the statues are in long vertical-scroll form. Besides, column painting is made, mostly used for funeral and tomb-sweeping ceremonies.

3. Ancient Books of the Dai Ethnic Group

The Dai ethnic group has its own ethnic written language. Most of the ancient books and records in the Dai language are carving and writing copies, manuscripts and transcripts. There are two kinds of ancient books and records, i.e., pattra-leaf and paper (tissue and vellum paper) books. The shape and structure are generally composed of the form of two plaques sandwiched together, folding and traditional thread binding, which are mainly spread in the Dai areas of Xishuangbanna, Dehong, Baoshan, Pu'er, Lincang, Honghe and other prefectures and cities. According to the contents, ancient books of the Dai language can be divided into the religious category such as *Lang Si She Bu Xian Zai, Prayer for Chicken Sacrifice to the Water God, Prayer for the Soul of the Rice Sacrifice*, and *The Conjuring Words*, the political and historical category such as *The Le History* and *Xuanfu History of Menglian*, the literature and art category including *Batamaga Pengshangluo*, *Lan Ga Xi He*, and *Li Feng*, as well as the categories of astronomy and calendar, farmland water conservancy, medicine, theory monograph, military martial arts, languages and characters, translation work and other categories.

Non-paper ancient book carriers of the Dai ethnic group are provided with the characteristics of a variety of forms and large quantities, the most representative of which are the silverware, pattra-leaf scriptures and ancient painting books of the Dai ethnic group. Among them, pattra-leaf scriptures are the most typical non-paper ancient books and records. The pattra-leaf scriptures, known as "Tanlan" in the Dai language, are carved on specially-made pattra leaves with the stencil pen (a cutting tool used in carving seals, etc.) by the local people. Furthermore, wall and cloth paintings and other non-paper painting books and records are also quite distinctive.

4. Ancient Books of the Yi Ethnic Group

The Yi ethnic group has its own language and writing system. Yi Language is a category of the Yi language branch of the Tibeto-Burman Group of Sino-Tibetan Languages, which is divided into six big dialects of the east, west, south, north, central and southeast regions. The Yi ethnic group has its own ancient writing system, which was called "Yi Scriptures" "Cuan characters" "Luoluo characters", etc. in ancient Chinese books and records. Currently, they are collectively known as the "ancient Yi language". Each character pattern represents a literal meaning, and there are various ways of writing. There are over 10,000 character forms in the existing ancient Yi characters, with over 1,000 words in common use. In history, ancestors of the Yi ethnic group used the ancient Yi language to write voluminous literature and books as well as numerous inscriptions, covering politics, military affairs, philosophy, religion, history, geography, language, writing system, literature, art, astronomy, calendar, medicine, health and other fields. The ancient Yi books and records popular in the Yi ethnic group in modern times mainly include paper, leather, cloth, bones, cliffs, wooden slips, wood engraving, inscriptions, seals and other carrier forms, of which paper books account for an absolute proportion, including transcripts and wood-carving printed copies. There are over 20,000 volumes (pieces) of ancient books and records in the Yi language in existence, most of which are transcripts and a few are wood-carving printed copies. Ancient Books and records in the Yi language in Yunnan can be divided into seven categories of ancient books and records in the Yi language in South Yunnan, Luquan and Wuding, Sani, Azhe, Xuanwei, Luoping and the north. The more representative books include the traditional religious ritual ancient books such as *Wucha, Mencha, The Scripture for Guiding Passage,* The *Scripture for Dragon Worship, The Scripture for Prayer to the Heavens for Rain, Lu Zi Nan Dao, Nao Si Gu, The Scripture for Recalling the Soul of the Dead,* and *Ni Bu Mu Si,* the famous literary work such as *Ashima* and *Nimi Poem,* the creation epics such as *Chamu, Axi's xianji, Meige, Ahei Xinimo,* and *Ni Su Duo Jie,* and the literature long poems in translation such as *Dong Yong and Qi Xiannü Celestial, The Phoenix, Muhe and Weiye , Tangwang's Wandering to the Nether World,* and *Tang Monks' Journey for Buddhist Scriptures.*

The most representative non-paper ancient books and records of the Yi ethnic group in Yunnan are cliff engravings in the Yi language. For instance, the Cliff Engraving Depicting History of the Flourishing Age of Luowu (the carved area is 206 cm in height and 80 cm in width) is the long-piece inscription in the Yi language with a relatively large history and retained relatively complete in the Yi ethnic group in the southwest region of China within the territory of Yi and Miao Autonomous County in Luquan of Kunming City, which was engraved in the 10th year during the reign of Emperor Jiajing of the Ming Dynasty (1531 AD). It has a history of over 480 years, recording the prosperous history of 14 generations of Feng's hereditary headmen in Wuding in more than 350 years.

Each ethnic group in Yunnan has or once had more or less non-paper ancient books and records. Since the establishment of the People's Republic of China, especially after the 1980s, many non-paper ancient books and records have been rescued and protected. Some are preserved in various collection institutions at all levels, some are displayed in various kinds of museums, and some have received relevant research results. Nevertheless, a great many non-paper ancient books and records, such as cliff engravings hidden in the deep mountains and exposed to the weather, have been changed a lot, or even have disappeared. For instance, bone carvings of the Zhuang ethnic group were scattered here and there, and no one has interpreted them. The researchers intended to seek and discover the profound mysteries, but they failed. For another example, due to the taboo of using ritual items, wooden plaques were destroyed immediately after use. It is difficult to find the ancestors' utensils... All these are not only the existing situation faced by the non-paper books and records of the ethnic groups in Yunnan, but also the dilemma faced by the ancient records of the ethnic groups.

III

Culture is the root of the ethnic groups, the spiritual home of mankind, the source of a nation's cohesion, vitality and creativity, and an important support for a strong and prosperous country. The ancient books and records of the ethnic groups are true and vivid records of the historical development process of the ethnic groups, which contain the unique spiritual values, ways of thinking and extraordinary imagination and creativity of the ethnic groups. They are the treasures of human civilization and the precious cultural heritage of China. Ancient books and records of the ethnic groups have been playing an active value orientation role and a social function of practical application in the long process of spreading and communication. The value of an excellent work of ethnic ancient books and records in the national society goes far beyond the professional scope of a subject, representing the cognition of a nation in a certain professional field, reflecting a certain historical development stage of a nation, or even bearing and representing the social facts and historical trend of a nation. It is important historical and practical significance to strengthen the rescue and protection of ancient books and records of the ethnic groups for enriching the treasure house of Chinese culture, comprehensively understanding the development course of the Chinese nation, building a new socialist ethnic relationship of equality, solidarity, mutual assistance and harmony, and promoting the cause of ethnic unity and progress.

After the founding of the People's Republic of China, under the leadership of party committees and governments at all levels, remarkable achievements have been made in the rescue, protection, translation, collation and publication of ancient books and records of the ethnic groups in Yunnan Province through unremitting efforts of several generations of relevant working personnel on ancient books and records. Based on the principle of "rescue orientation, and protection first", more than 30,000 ancient books (volumes) of written literature and over 10,000 oral ancient records of the ethnic groups have been rescued. Moreover, *Complete Works of Translations and Annotations on Ancient Books and Records of Naxi Dongba, Complete Works of Chinese Pattra-leaf Scriptures, Integration of Rare Editions of Ancient Books and Records of the Ethnic Groups in Yunnan, Reservation of Ancient Books and Records of Cultural Heritage of the Yi Ethnic Group in Honghe, Complete Works of Classical Epics of the Ethnic Groups in Yunnan, Complete Works of Narrative Poems of the Ethnic Groups in Yunnan* and other representative ethnic ancient book and record achievements have attracted extensive attentions at home and abroad.

However, the current achievements of the rescue, protection, translation and compilation are not worth mentioning for the voluminous ancient books and records of the ethnic groups. It is roughly estimated that in addition to the collected and preserved ancient books and records of the ethnic groups, there are still more than 70,000 ancient books (volumes) of the ethnic group literature scattered in Yunnan. Due to the numerous reasons such as improper preservation or no inheritance, it is difficult to carry out active-state inheritance for many ancient books scattered among the people. Moreover, many ancient books are lost or damaged, so the task rescue and protection task is urgent. The specific regional conditions of the non-paper ancient books and records of the ethnic groups in Yunnan are especially worrying. The majority part of the movable, non-paper ancient books with cultural relic value have been collected and preserved by the institutions at all levels, the enterprises and the people. The rescue and protection work maximizes the cultural value of such ancient books and records. However, after the collection and preservation of ancient books of the ethnic groups, the national wisdom crystallization, which could have been passed down in the folk in active state, can easily become the treasure in the private book cabinets that no one else knows. There are still various kinds of people paying visits to the mountains and villages to search for the small number of ancient books and records of the ethnic groups, some of which have been resold overseas at a profit. Meanwhile, the specific regional conditions for many immovable non-paper ancient books and records are even more regrettable. These stone carvings and cliff engravings bearing ethnic culture are mostly hidden in deep mountains, which are exposed to the weather all the year round. Therefore, the writing symbols or handwriting are so blurred that it is difficult to identify them, or they have directly been damaged by human beings. Natural erosion and gradual disappearance of the stone carvings and cliff engravings is the natural law of development, but it is a huge loss for the ethnic culture.

We have experienced and witnessed several painful moments during the preparation of this series of books. With the support of Yunnan Provincial Department of Finance and Yunnan Provincial Commission of Ethnic and Religious Affairs, we have been consistently pushing forward the project of *Integration of Rare Editions of Ancient Books and Records of the Ethnic Groups in Yunnan*, which is among one hundred excellent cultural projects in Yunnan Province. Meanwhile, according to the requirements specified in *Notification on the 13th Five-year Plan for the Protection of Ancient Books and Records of the Ethnic Groups issued by National Ethnic Affairs Commission of the People's Republic of China*, "the national census on ancient books of the ethnic groups have been basically completed; the census work has been fully promoted together with relevant departments to find out the resources of ancient books and records of the ethnic groups in the various regions. Moreover, the census registration management system shall be established and improved; and a census registration platform shall be constructed to enter, calculate and summarize the census information of ancient books and records of the ethnic groups in various regions, so that the national census registration catalogue of ancient books and records of the ethnic groups can be established." In line with the purpose of "understanding the basic condition and building a platform", we have conducted a general survey and collection of ancient books and records of the ethnic groups in Yunnan. For this purpose, we have visited the collection institutions of ancient books and records of the ethnic groups in every prefecture and city of Yunnan, and paid visits to the inheritors of ancient books and records and the collectors. Our footprints have almost covered all the regions of Yunnan. When we conducted research in Diqing Tibetan Autonomous Prefecture in 2016, the Research Institute of Tibetan Studies in Diqing Tibetan Autonomous Prefecture introduced the preservation and distribution of non-paper ancient books and records in the prefecture, and mentioned that there were many Tibetan stone carvings on the hillside near Tacheng Town of Weixi County. We found the pictures taken by the institute during the field research in the computer several years ago. We could see that half of the hillside was covered with stone carvings, which were all age-old cultural relics. We were so excited. Since there were only a few miles between the distribution location of the stone carvings and Gezi Village where the *Grid Tablet Inscription* engraved in the Tibetan language in the Tang Dynasty, and the stone carvings were hidden in the deep mountains, there may be some valuable non-paper ancient records. Unfortunately, we didn't bring the shooting equipment with us, so we decided to go there for investigation later. We didn't expect that we had missed the chance to see its elegant style and features. In May 2018, we organized professional photo-taking, transferring and rubbing personnel to visit Diqing Tibetan Autonomous Prefecture. Led by relevant comrades of Tibetan Institute of Diqing Tibetan Autonomous Prefecture, the group went through the road repair and blocking, trekking in the mountains and came to the hillside tirelessly. However, the scene shocked us, there was no stone carvings at all, but a mound mixed with a stones of 5–6 meters in height on the slope. A few Paris polyphylla were planted in the red earth below. After several twists and turns, we got in touch with the comrades of the village committee, and learned that the village had specially assigned bulldozers to level the land so as to develop agricultural economy, and these stone carvings were buried under the mound. This is just a trivial matter we have experienced in the process of the rescue and protection of ancient books and records of the ethnic groups in Yunnan. Such things are happening not only in Diqing, but also in all the regions all over the province. All the stone carvings, cliff engraving, paper literature, silk books, bamboo slips and wooden engraving are all confronted with such living dilemma. Personnel devoted to the rescue and protection of the ethnic culture felt deeply distressed, but deeply understand that the force of a department and even some groups is so weak to carry out the rescue and protection task. Based on such situation, it is urgent to rescue and protect non-paper ancient books and records. In view of the restriction of funds, personnel, technology and various other aspects, it is suggested that pictures of these culture heritages should be kept for the use of social science research even using the simplest and the most traditional way. Meanwhile, we call on the whole society to attach importance to the rescue and protection of ethnic ancient books and records, which is a profound cause, and also the most actual starting point at the beginning of planning this series of books.

Yunnan People's Publishing House has offered vigorous supports to the rescue, protection, collation and publication of ancient books and records of the ethnic groups in Yunnan. The project of the rescue and protection of non-paper ancient books and records of the ethnic groups in Yunnan was funded by the publication fund for ancient books and records in the ethnic languages through application in 2016. Several years ago, Yunnan Provincial Planning Office of Sorting and Publishing Ancient Books of the Ethnic Groups collected ancient books and records from the ethnic areas for many times, trying to obtain the clues and take pictures. Yunnan non-paper ancient books and records collected by Lijiang Museum, Lijiang Dongba Culture Research Institute, the Library in Yulong Naxi Autonomous County of Lijiang and Yunnan non-paper ancient books and records collected by folk collectors are finally integrated and published in this book after years of efforts. In order to collect these non-paper ancient books and records, relevant personnel have made great efforts and their footprints almost covered the whole regions of Yunnan Province. After collecting a great deal of original data, we encountered unprecedented difficulties in the classification and integration of the ancient books and records. Carriers of the non-paper ancient books and records in the various ethnic groups can be said to be in a great variety, and the quantity and quality of each carrier type of ancient books and records are at different levels. Since it is taken as the carrier form of a series of books that are summarized and published and comprehensively cover the representative non-paper ancient books and records, it should also take the non-paper ancient books and records covering all the ethnic groups into account. Not only shall the precious and fine works of non-paper ancient books and records of the various ethnic groups be identified and selected, but also the emotional value of ethnic ancient books in ethnic society shall be taken into consideration as much as possible. The precious ancient books shall be objectively collected and included, and the volume and scale of books shall be also taken into consideration. Through several confirmations, we find that it is almost impossible to classify the non-paper ancient books and records in Yunnan in accordance with the discipline classification of the ethnic ancient books and records. We can only make a general classification of the non-paper ancient books and records that we have collected with all our efforts, and then classify each volume into different subcategory.

In conclusion, this series of books are the first large-scale integration and collection of non-paper ancient books and records of the ethnic groups in Yunnan. It is for the first time that numerous ancient books and precious records of the ethnic groups, which have been kept secret in the past, are shown to the public. They have been provided with many unique features in terms of academic, historical, inheritance, appreciation and collection value. Moreover, it is of great significance in protecting the cultural heritage of the various ethnic groups, carrying forward their excellent culture, enhancing ethnic unity and promoting the construction of the common spiritual homeland of the Chinese People.

The rescue and protection of ancient books and records of the ethnic groups is a long-term painstaking task, which cannot be completed in a short period. We were expected to present the high-quality and precious works of Yunnan non-paper ancient books and records comprehensively, but we are constantly discovering new ancient books and records and expanding new categories in our practical work. Therefore, there are inevitably some improper aspects in the series of books, so we can only hope for the forgiveness and corrections of the experts earnestly.

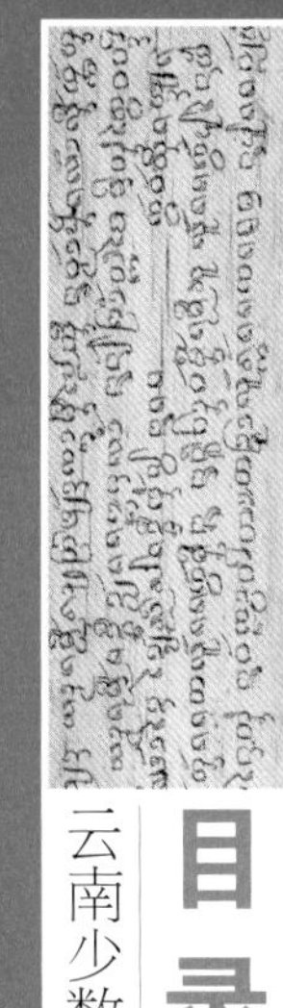

目录

贝叶经简介

贝叶是贝多罗树——一种主要生长在热带、亚热带地区，形状很像棕榈树的棕榈类木本植物的叶子。贝叶经，顾名思义即刻写在贝叶上的经文。在纸张尚未发明之前，印度人已经开始用贝叶作为书写材料记载佛教经典及宫廷资料。贝叶作为早期文献的载体之一，主要用来记录佛教经典。后来，贝叶作为书写文字、记录历史的载体与金石铭刻、兽皮（骨）书等一样，成为一种形制特殊的文献载体。东汉以来，数以千计的梵文贝叶经源源不断地传入我国，部分还被翻译为汉文流传。现在我国很多地方保存有一定数量的梵文贝叶经，如杭州灵隐寺文物馆、浙江天台山国清寺佛教文物陈列室、河南南阳菩提寺、成都宝光寺以及四川峨眉山万年寺等地。清末民初，也有不少用巴利文、泰文、僧伽罗文等刻写的贝叶经从泰国、斯里兰卡等国传入我国，但数量不多。贝叶经的传入，对佛教文化的交流、研究和发展发挥了重要作用，为中华传统文化注入了新的活力，也让贝叶文化在中华大地落地生根。

我国历史上流传的贝叶经文种多样，除梵文、巴利文、缅甸文以及僧伽罗文外，还有傣文、藏文、于阗文、回鹘文、吐火罗文、维吾尔文等文种。贝叶经最先多为随着佛教的“东方之旅”传入我国的佛经教义，随着不同历史时期佛教文化与中华各民族文化的融合与发展，国内流传的贝叶经典籍的内容逐渐丰富。可以说，贝叶经不仅是一种形制特殊的少数民族非纸质典籍，也是中华各族人民在千百年历史发展中留下的珍贵文化遗产，是中华传统文化的重要组成部分。

将植物叶片用作文献载体，需要经过一系列加工、处理。因自然条件、地域文化、生活经验等的不同，不同民族的贝叶经制作工艺各有特点。西双版纳傣族自治州傣族地区的贝叶经制作，首先要将成批的新鲜贝多罗叶砍下，用开水加酸角或柠檬一起煮，待叶片变色后取出，用细沙子搓洗干净，压平晒干，然后按照所需形制规格裁制（一般每叶长约60厘米，宽约10厘米）。随后在叶片靠边的地方钻一个孔，将50叶或100叶叶片串成一册，置放整齐，再用平板覆盖，平板上再压以重石。十天半月之后将其取出，用搓好的线穿成可活动的册子，便可以刻写文字了。贝叶刻本刻写一开始用小刀尖，后来改用铁簪子（铁制针形笔）。刻写好的贝叶，用植物果油掺锅底的黑烟涂于其上，再用湿布擦拭，贝叶上的字迹便清晰可见，擦不掉、抹不去。贝叶制作过程中经过开水沸煮，可以防虫、防水、防变形，经久耐用。部分贝叶经还在经本四边涂上彩漆，抹上金粉，给人一种古朴大方、庄重美观之感。

贝叶经根据书写方式可分为贝叶写本和贝叶刻本两种。写本是用笔墨在贝叶上书写抄录；刻本则用铁制针形笔把文字刻写在贝叶上。

西藏自治区是目前可知的全球保存贝叶经最多、最丰富的地方，保存有众多梵文、藏文和巴利文等贝叶经古本，其中有不少孤本、善本、珍本。藏区贝叶经多是贝叶写本，多用梵文写成，少量用藏文字母转写梵文，甚或直接用藏文书写。其中有部分写本有藏梵文题跋或藏梵文夹注。我国藏区的贝叶经规格无定制，大小不一，或 50 厘米 ×6 厘米、或 47 厘米 ×5 厘米，或 33 厘米 ×4 厘米，等等。经书叶数多者为 120 ~ 180 叶，少的则是 10 ~ 100 叶。贝叶经按字体可分为正楷本、朱匝体本、黑体本等。装帧形式由单孔本过渡到双孔本。2007 年，在中央有关部门和西藏自治区党委、政府的关心指导下，成立了西藏贝叶经保护领导小组，全面开展西藏自治区内珍贵贝叶经写本的抢救保护、收集整理等工作。在相关部门和专业人员的努力下，西藏贝叶经写本抢救保护工作取得了显著成绩，基本摸清了西藏贝叶经写本现状，制定了保护章程，并编写了西藏自治区所藏贝叶经写本总目录。调查结果显示，布达拉宫、罗布林卡、哲蚌寺三处所藏贝叶经数量相当可观。布达拉宫有 200 多函 500 多部；罗布林卡有 60 多函 200 多部；哲蚌寺仅有 1 函 213 页，是 13 种经论的合集本。这三处梵文贝叶经涵盖佛教经典、印度文学、法典、语法、戏曲、医学和天文等内容。此外，西藏博物馆收藏有梵文贝叶经 259 函，约 800 部，包括梵文语法、诗歌、历算、词典等内容。其中有 8 函是藏文手写本，除 1 件或为 7 世纪写本外，其余大多是 10 ~ 13 世纪的写本。夏鲁寺、俄尔寺、萨迦寺等寺院中，还发现了大约 400 种梵文贝叶经写本。由此，可大致估算出在我国藏族地区现存的贝叶经有 1000 多函。

云南贝叶经在傣族地区分布较广、较常见，主要是巴利文本和傣文本。在傣族文化中，“迈兰”（贝叶）是他们钟爱的“五树六花”之一，“戈兰”（贝叶树）被视为承载傣族历史文化走向光明的神舟，所以，贝叶经也被奉为神圣的经典。云南傣族地区从佛寺到民间的贝叶文化是傣族文化的代表和象征，不仅佛寺收存贝叶文献成为传统，民间“赕佛”献经献书也蔚然成风。

傣族地区的各类经书、文献中称在贝叶上刻写文字的时代为“绿叶信时代”，同时记载了一些关于贝叶经起源、使用和传播的美好传说传世。通过这些记载，我们知道傣族贝叶经是傣族地区出现较早的一种经书，是傣族先民留下的宝贵文化遗产。云南傣文因使用地区和文字形式的不同，分为傣泐文（西双版纳傣文）、傣那文（德宏傣文）、傣绷文（也称“傣德文”）和金平傣文。因各地傣文使用、翻译、研究等程度参差不齐，加之本书收录的傣文贝叶经主要流传于西双版纳傣族自治州，下文以傣泐文贝叶经为例作介绍。

傣文贝叶经，傣语称“坦兰”，规格主要有每页四行式、五行式、六行式和八行式四种，傣语分别称“兰戏”“兰哈”“兰贺”“兰别”，以前三种规格的贝叶经最为常见。历史上用傣泐文书写并保存下来的贝叶经文献极为丰富，其中包括不少的佛教经典，这即是我们平常惯称的“贝叶经”。历史上，基于西双版纳傣族社会发展的特点和要求，遍布村寨的佛寺肩负着学校教育的功能。那些七八岁就被送入佛寺当小和尚的孩子，不仅学习佛经，也学习文化科学知识，比如天文、地理、历史、医学、农耕、文学、乡规民约等。渐渐地，世俗典籍进入了寺庙并刻写在贝叶上。这些世俗典籍的前言、后记和正文中往往插入了佛经语录或佛教教义，以此来约束和规范人们的言行。世俗典籍同样受到傣族群众的尊重，并在一定程度上享有“经”的地位和作用。故此，我们所说的傣文贝叶经应该包括两个大类：一类是佛教经典，即为佛经总称作经、律、论的“三藏”，傣语称为“坦”。据传，傣文南传上座部佛教贝叶经有“八万四千部”之多，其间经藏五大类 21000 部，律藏五大类 21000 部，论藏七大类 42000 部，这一数目是否确数无以考证。另一类是一般的傣文书籍，即傣文世俗文献，傣语称为“簿”。根据 1949 年以前的一项调查显示，西双版纳的 500 多座佛寺里保存的“贝叶经”共达 5 万册。有学者认为，这其中有相当数量是被称为“簿”的世俗文献。世俗典籍是傣文贝叶经的重要组成部分，极大地丰富了贝叶经的内涵与外延。佛教经典和世俗典籍在概念上有明确区别，但在民间赕佛活动中，对二者的性质和功能往往不做区分。可以说，傣文贝叶经是傣族社会各种文化知识和思想观念的荟萃之苑。

傣文贝叶经的数量，从现有书目上看多达 2000 多种 5000 多部。按内容和形式大体可分为十九大类：哲学历史类、政治经济类、生产生活类、民情民俗类、语言文字类、文学艺术类、宗教信仰类、佛教经典类、天文历法类、法律类、医理医学类、体育武术类、书画艺术类、制品工艺类、建筑设计类等，范围广泛，内容丰富，涉及傣族社会文化生活的方方面面。明代傣族诗学家祜巴勐在其《论傣族诗歌》一书中说到："自从有了文字和经书，原来的零星歌谣就变得更加系统起来，被人们用文字刻在竹简和贝叶上……"可见，贝叶文化的兴起和繁荣，对傣族文学的发展起到了积极的促进作用。极具地方特色的"傣族社会百科全书"——傣文贝叶典籍，是"七彩云南"民族文化不可或缺的组成部分，也是中华民族文化大观园中独具特色的靓丽奇葩。

谈到云南傣族地区流传的贝叶形制非纸质载体文献，我们还得提到德宏傣族景颇族自治州（以下简称"德宏州"）盈江县文物管理所收藏的一部原由干崖刀氏土司家藏的贝叶式象牙片经书。该典籍以象牙为材质，切片后仿贝叶形制制作，传世者十分罕见。傣语称此类经书为"来过"（音）。经文用巴利文写成，内容有待考证，制作年代尚无定论。仅从实物来看，象牙片经过了精心磨制抛光，用生漆、紫胶、烟垢等混合物书写，材质特殊，制作精细，工艺复杂，花纹精美，富丽堂皇。此外，德宏州境内还有贝叶形制的象骨片古籍留存。

总的说来，云南境内的贝叶经分布地域广泛、数量众多、内容丰富。虽然具体数量尚待考证，但可以肯定的是，经过各级有关部门多年来对傣文贝叶经的抢救保护，一大批珍贵的傣文贝叶经已得到各级部门的收藏保护。更为可喜的是，随着国家对民族文化抢救保护力度的加大，越来越多的机构、部门和科研人员加入到傣文贝叶经的翻译整理工作中。云南省少数民族古籍整理出版规划办公室自1984年成立至今，一直秉承组织、协调、联络、指导全省少数民族古籍抢救、保护、翻译、整理、出版和研究的工作职责，加强对少数民族古籍文献的保管与抢救保护。目前，单位共收藏彝族、瑶族、傣族、壮族、纳西族、傈僳族等民族古籍3000余册，其中傣文古籍1200余册（卷），包括绵纸经700余册、贝叶经500余册，主要是傣泐文、傣那文古籍。对傣文贝叶经的翻译整理工作首屈一指的当属西双版纳傣族自治州2001年启动的《中国贝叶经全集》100卷。经过西双版纳州民族研究所及60多名专业技术人员8年的辛勤努力，有贝叶经原文、老傣文、新傣文、国际音标、汉文直译、汉文意译"六对照"的《中国贝叶经全集》在2006～2010年陆续出版，该书共收录贝叶经典籍139部727个章节，达8500多万字。这一倾注了众多专家、学者多年心血的鸿篇巨著的问世，既是傣族人民的一件大事，也为各民族古籍抢救保护和翻译整理工作提供了可供借鉴、参考的有益经验。近年来，鉴于傣文贝叶经在德宏傣族景颇族自治州各民族中发挥的情感纽带作用和积极影响力，该州也将抢救保护和翻译整理德宏傣文贝叶经提上了议事日程。此外，云南省少数民族古籍整理出版规划办公室，近年来也组织了专家团队对库藏傣文古籍进行释读编目，目前已完成500部贝叶经编目，并在此基础上，结合《云南少数民族古籍珍本集成》《云南少数民族非纸质典籍聚珍》等项目，启动了对傣文贝叶经的翻译整理及出版工作。

云南傣族地区的贝叶经，蕴含傣泰民族传统文化的整体内容，是傣族文化的根脉所在。我们相信，在新的历史时期，贝叶经这一重要的、形制特殊的少数民族非纸质文献，会得到更好的抢救保护，进一步彰显其独具特色的历史文化价值。

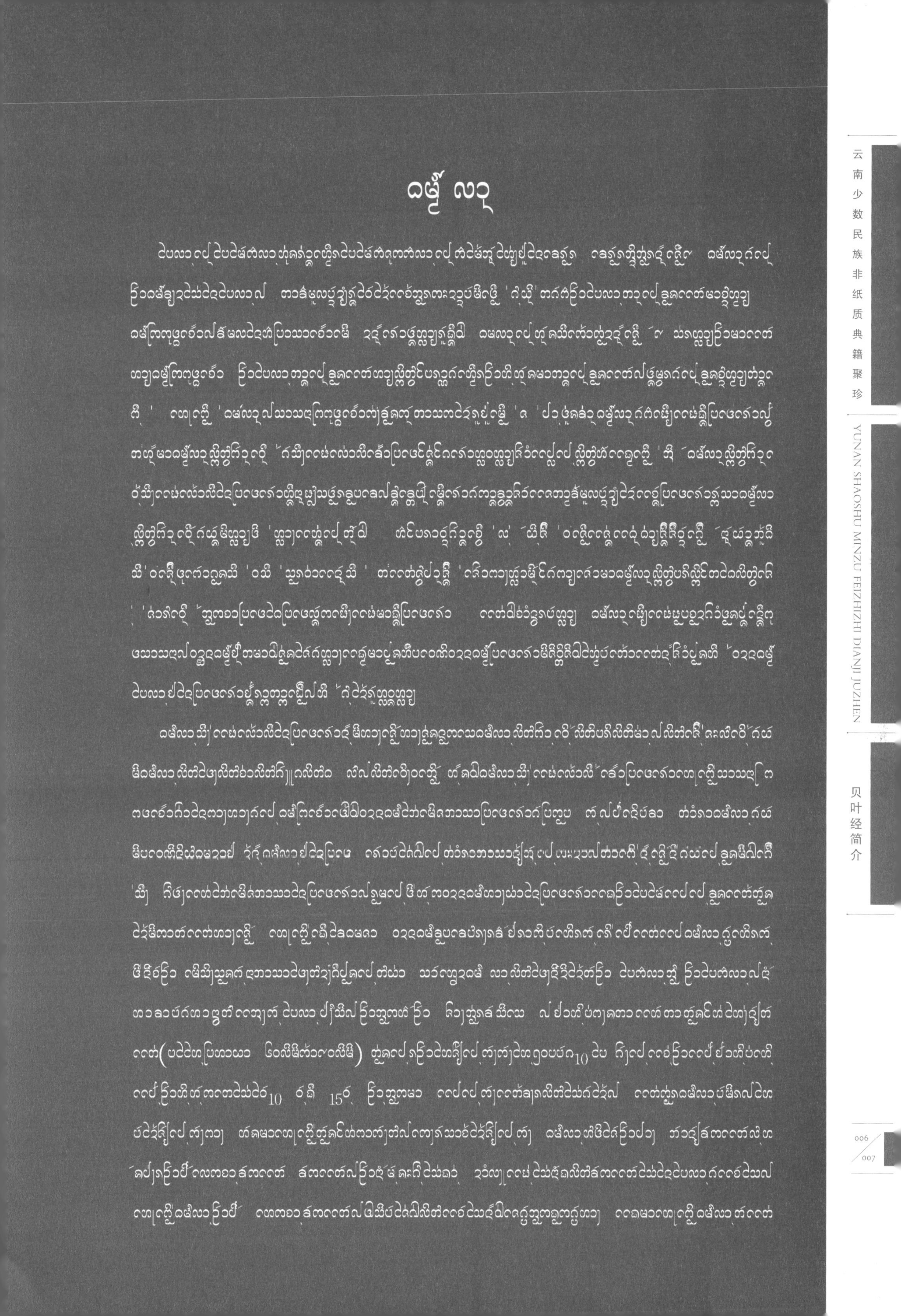

[illegible]

[illegible]

[illegible]

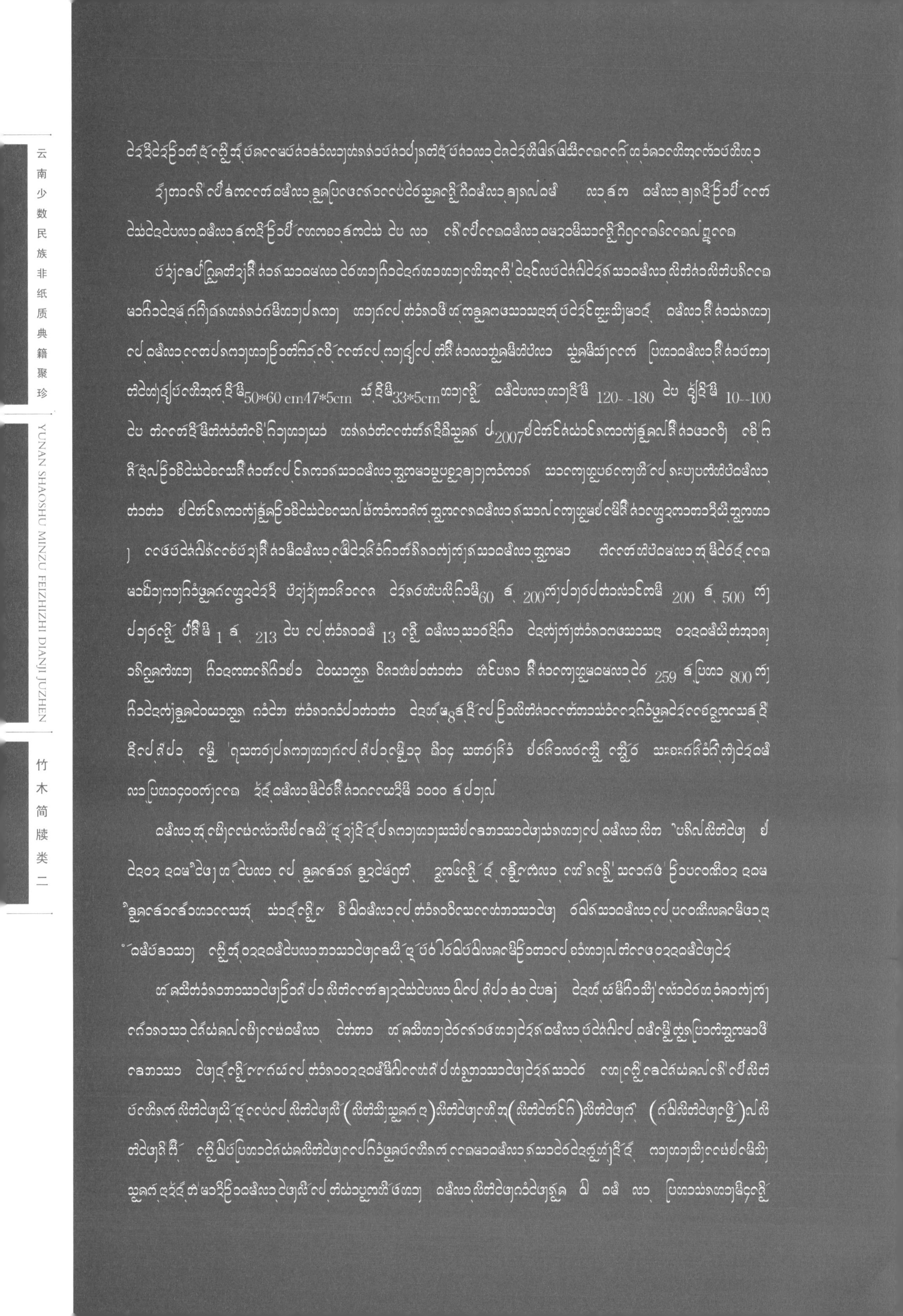

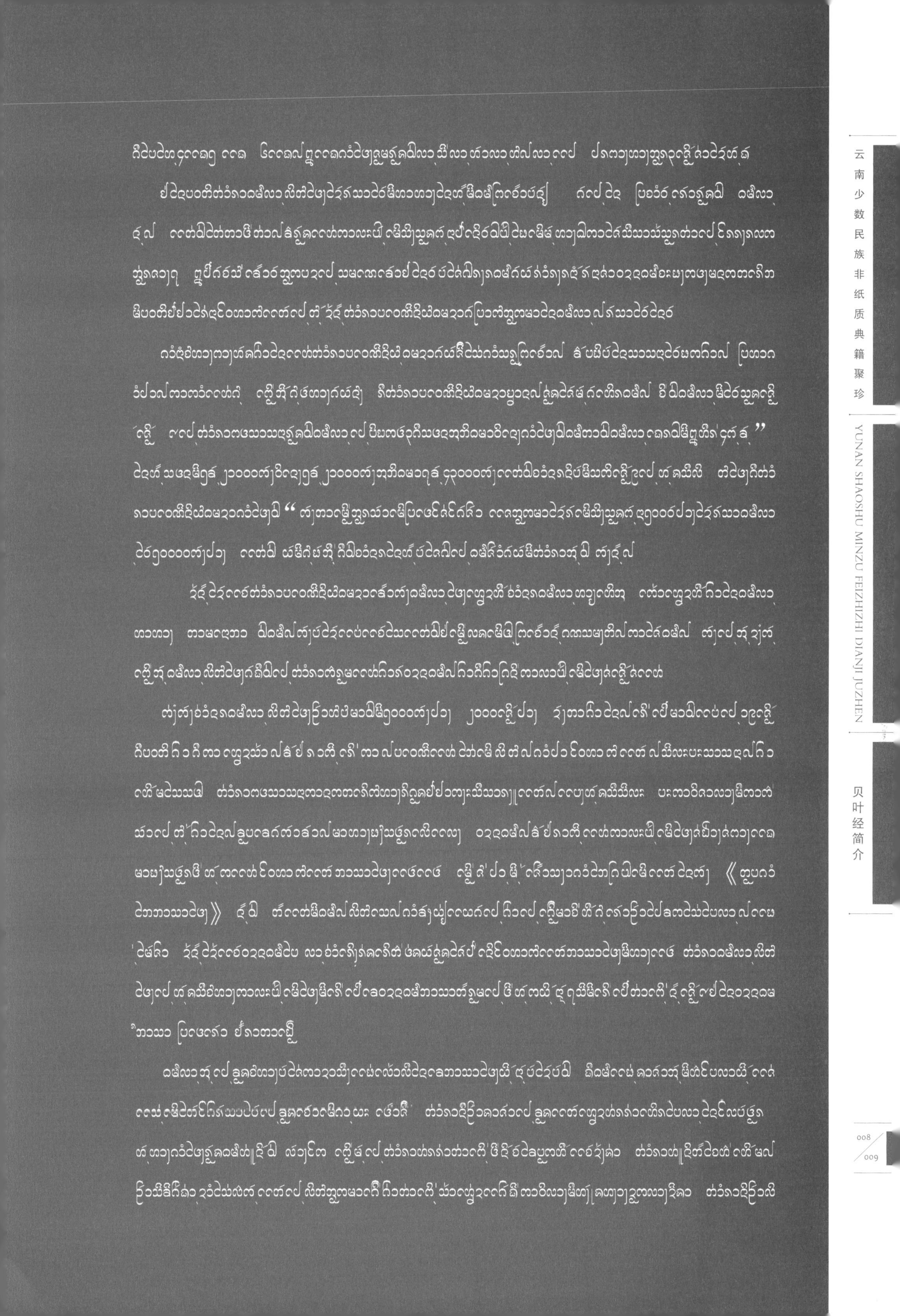

[illegible]

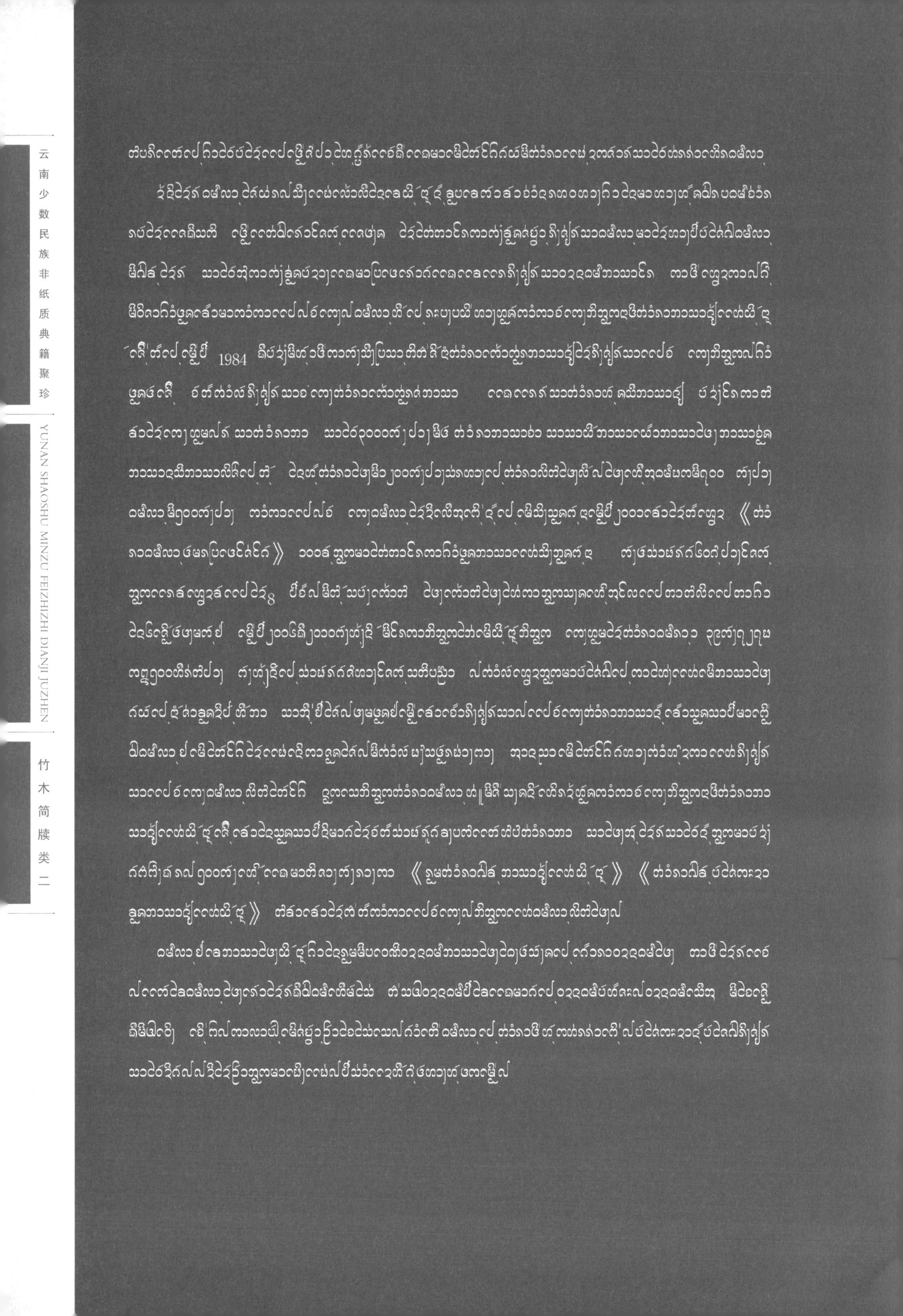

YUNNAN SHAOSHU MINZU FEIZHIZHI DIANJI JUZHEN

云南少数民族非纸质典籍聚珍

章相

《章相》又译作《粘响》，傣族民间叙事长诗，全诗长达10000余行，系傣族“五大诗王”（《吾沙麻罗》《粘巴西顿》《兰嘎西贺》《章相》和《巴塔麻嘎捧尚罗》）之一。主要流传于西双版纳傣族自治州、孟连傣族拉祜族佤族自治县、景谷傣族彝族自治县等地。作者帕拉纳。本书收录版本今藏于云南省少数民族古籍整理出版规划办公室，共12册，182叶。刻本，由都可在1841年誊写。梵夹装。开本高4.5厘米，广46厘米。每叶5行，行54字。内容完整，保存完好，入选第一批《国家珍贵古籍名录》（编号：02372）。

《章相》产生年代久远、声名远扬，在云南傣族地区流传广泛，版本众多，诸如原藏于西双版纳傣族自治州政协文物室的手抄本、收录入《中国贝叶经全集》第7卷的贝叶经版本、藏于云南省少数民族古籍整理出版规划办公室的贝叶经版本及各地歌手收藏的不同手抄本等。《章相》虽版本较多，但故事内容基本一致，具有较强的思想性和艺术性，情节完整，描写生动。我们以收入《中国贝叶经全集》第7卷的《粘响》为蓝本对该书内容做一个概述。故事讲述了苏里亚的母亲未婚先孕，其父——勐章相的国王——将她放逐。苏里亚出生后在母亲和外婆的照料下健康成长，并在帕拉西的教授下，学得了各种武艺与法术。苏里亚和母亲在荷花湖因妖怪作祟分离，后得龙祖母赏识，被带入龙宫迎娶了龙女。而苏里亚的母亲被商队搭救，几经辗转回到勐章相与父亲相见。在苏里亚离开龙宫寻母的过程中，他结识了武艺高强的丢瓦些纳和捧玛些纳，三人结拜兄弟，并一起回到外婆住的英麻板（雪山林）。悔悟的勐章相的帕雅，去英麻板接回了自己的王后和孙子，还将王位传给了孙子苏里亚。苏里亚做了帕雅后，通过宝镜爱上了公主婻尖达琅西。他们以绿鹦鹉表达爱慕之情，传递情书。可苏里亚派去求亲的人却被女方的哥哥桑卡达拒绝。苏里亚只好用抢亲的方法将公主抢走。桑卡达觉得丢了面子，于是调兵遣将去攻打勐章相，战败，自己也成了俘虏。战争结束后，苏里亚又把龙女接到王宫，夫妻二人一起治理着勐章相。

长诗利用傣族人民喜闻乐见的说唱形式，带有浓厚的神话和幻想色彩。诗中关于战争的描写也很有特点，每次战役都写得生动、新颖，层层深入，引人入胜。对战争中使用的兵器、战术、战象、战马以及战前的宗教祭祀、战争中将士的情绪等方面的描述，也具体而生动。故事开头和中间部分还有一些例行的诵经、宣佛或礼佛的敬语。可以说，无论是从诗歌的主题思想，还是所反映的社会生活，乃至诗歌的艺术成就和审美价值等方面看，《章相》都堪称是傣族诗歌发展的巅峰。

以《章相》为代表的“五大诗王”的出现，说明贝叶文化的兴起和繁荣，对傣族文学的发展起到了决定性作用。明代，傣族地区的贝叶叙事文学进入了一个新的阶段，诗歌的篇幅、题材、主题内涵乃至创作方法都呈现出飞跃性的发展。从体裁上看，傣族贝叶文学中的散文类作品包括神话、传说、故事、传记、小说等；韵文类作品包括民歌、情歌、叙事长诗等。从来源上看，傣族贝叶文学大体可分为三部分：一是引入信奉南传上座部佛教诸民族国家的文学作品，如众多的佛经故事和印度民间故事；二是记录、整理和改编傣族民间古老的口传文学作品，例如《巴塔麻嘎捧尚罗》；三是由佛寺培养的傣族知识分子创作的作品，例如《章相》。

几千年来，傣族人民孜孜不倦地用铁笔将文字刻写在贝叶上，通过浪漫主义手法，对古老的创世神话、佛经文学作品进行汇集、加工、改编，甚至转写，成就了创世神话史诗《巴塔麻嘎捧尚罗》，造就了勇士史诗《章相》……给后人留下了宝贵的精神财富。

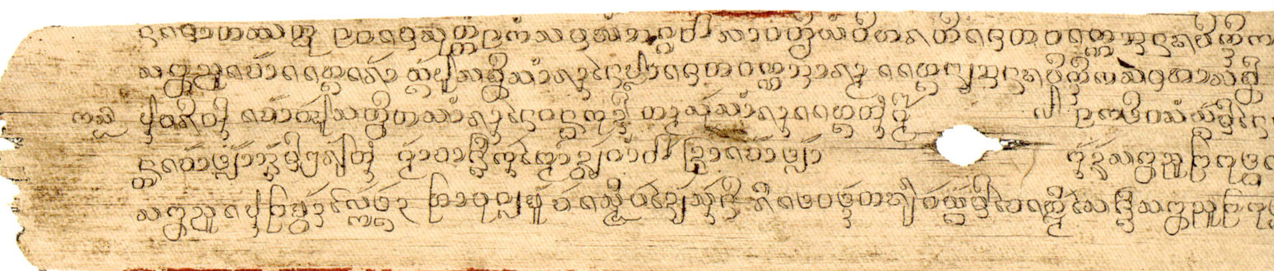

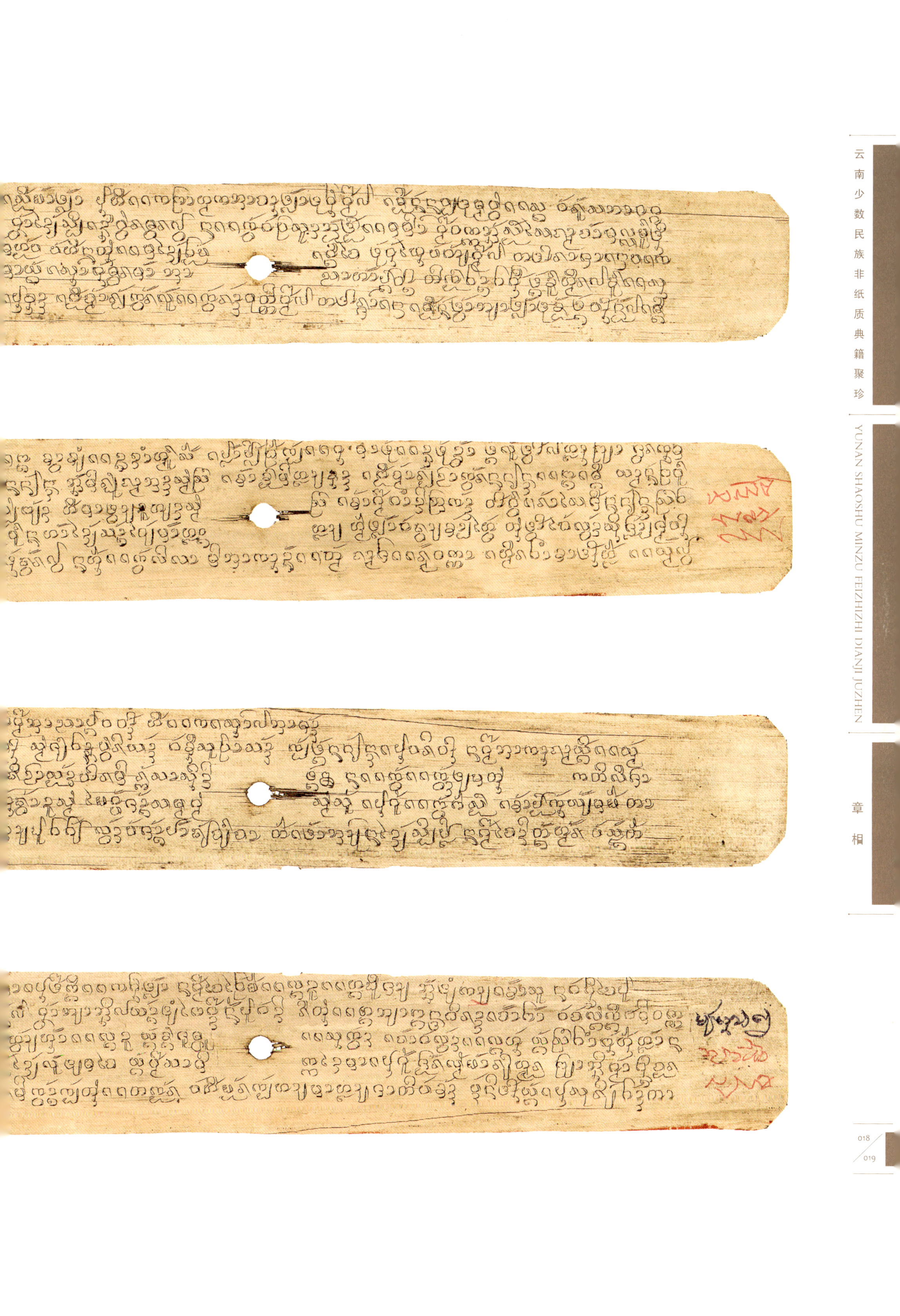

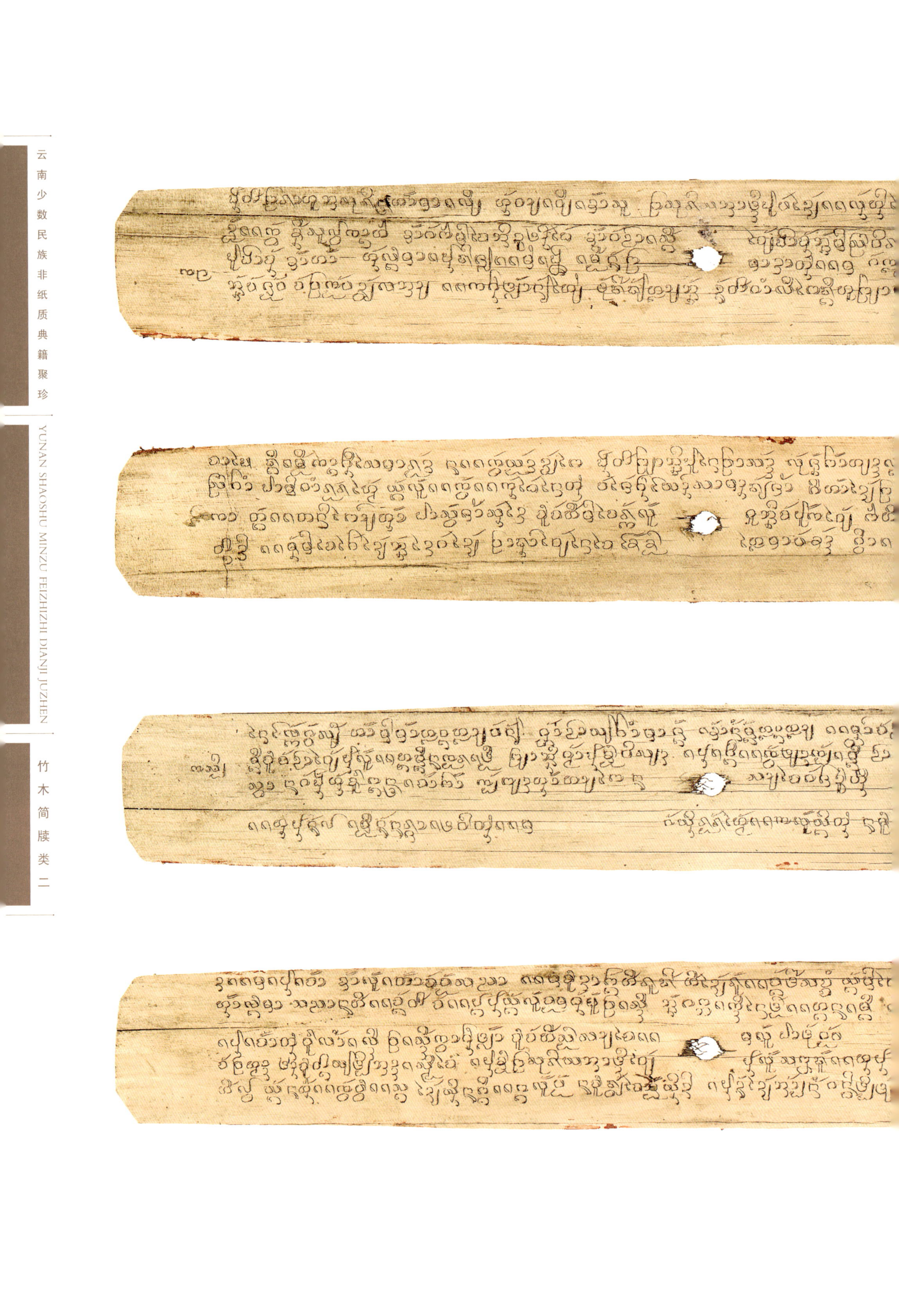

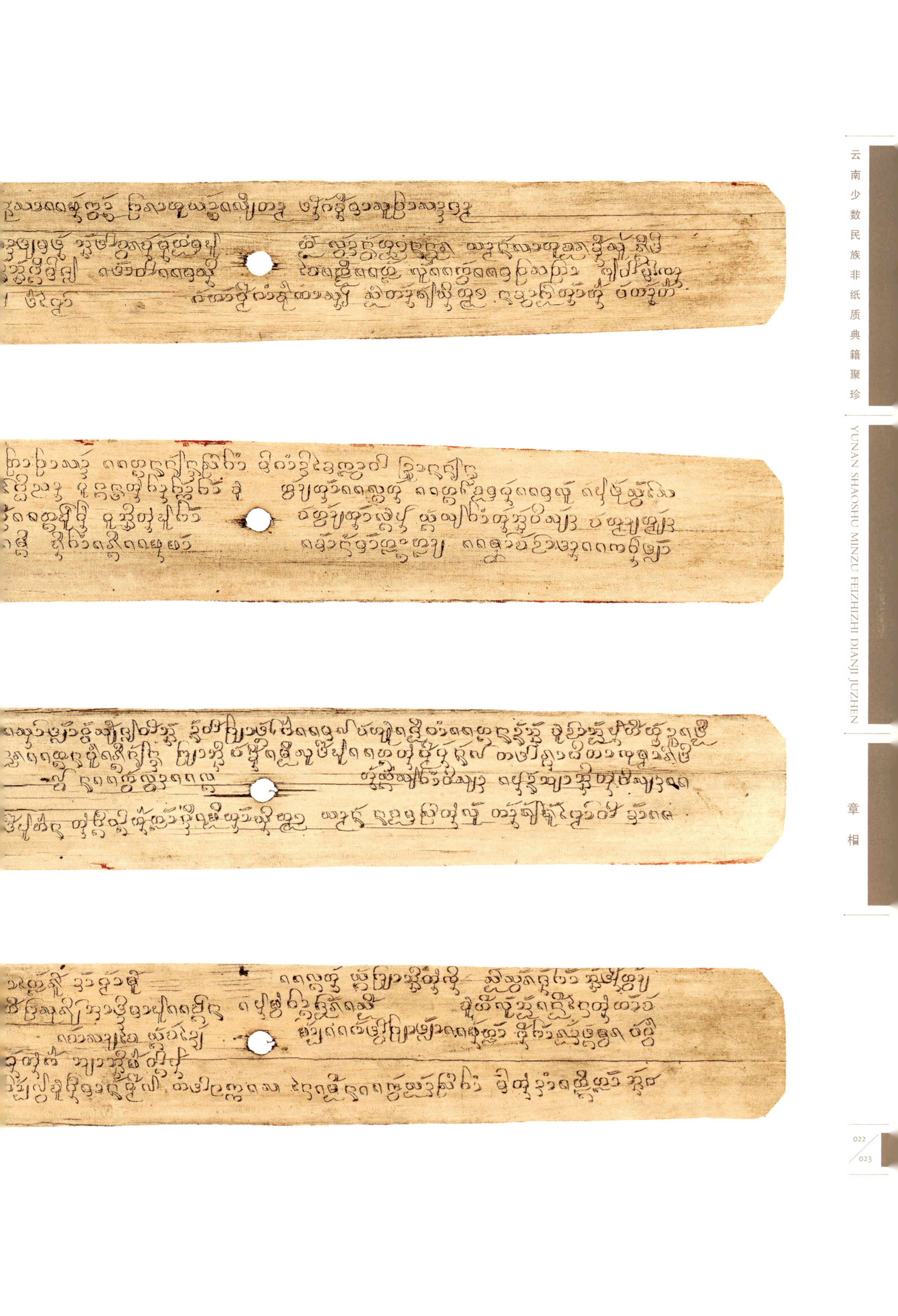

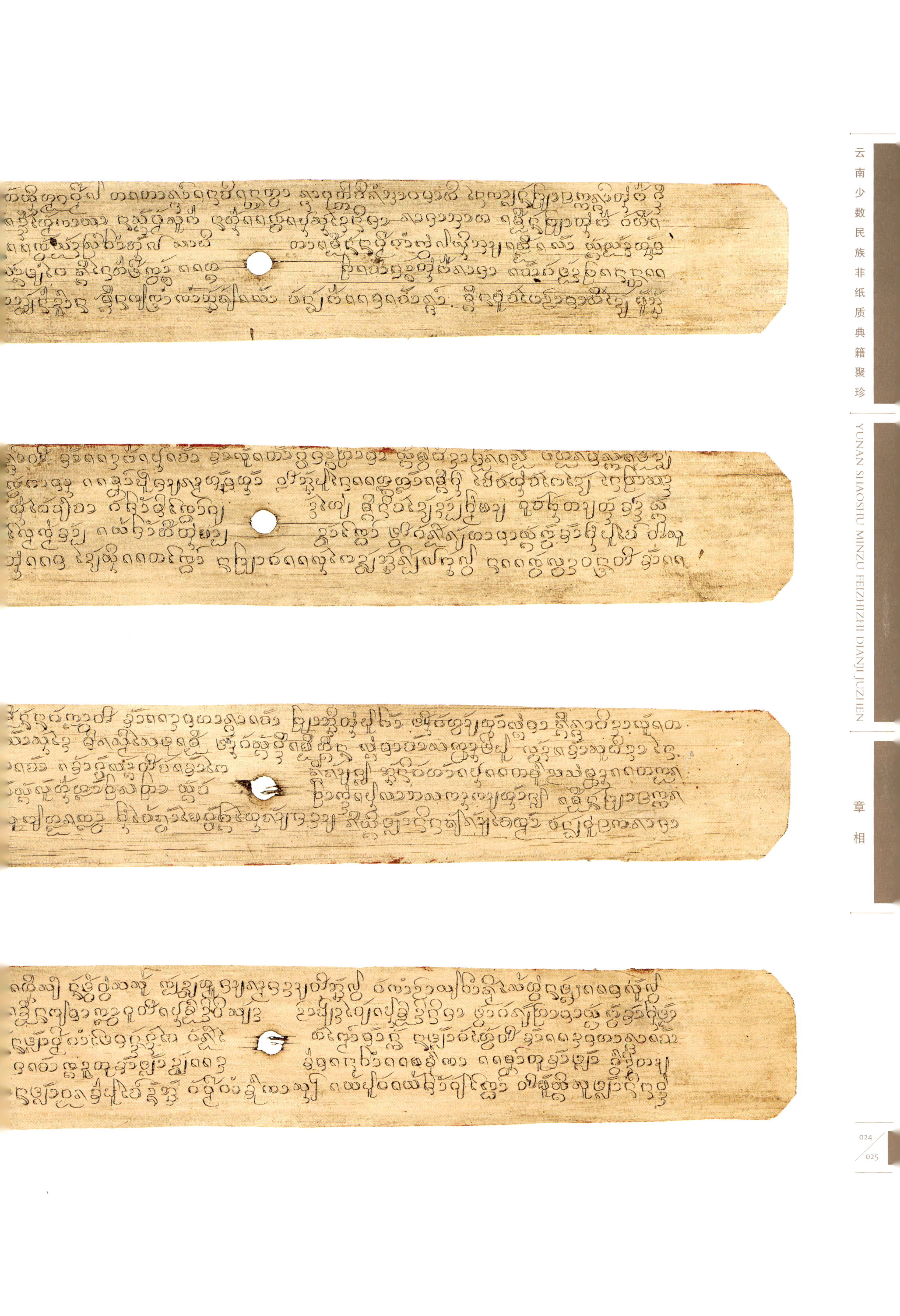

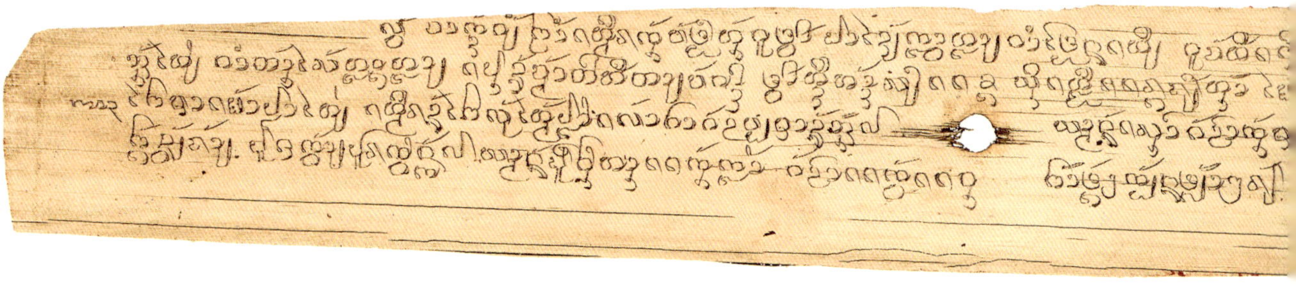

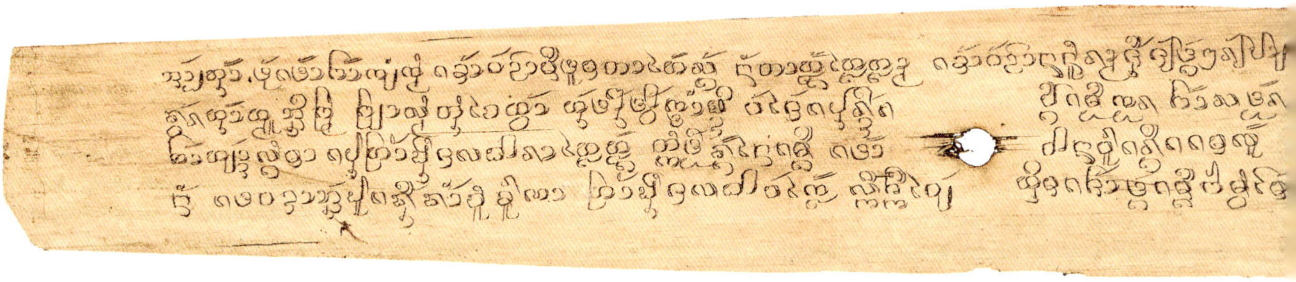

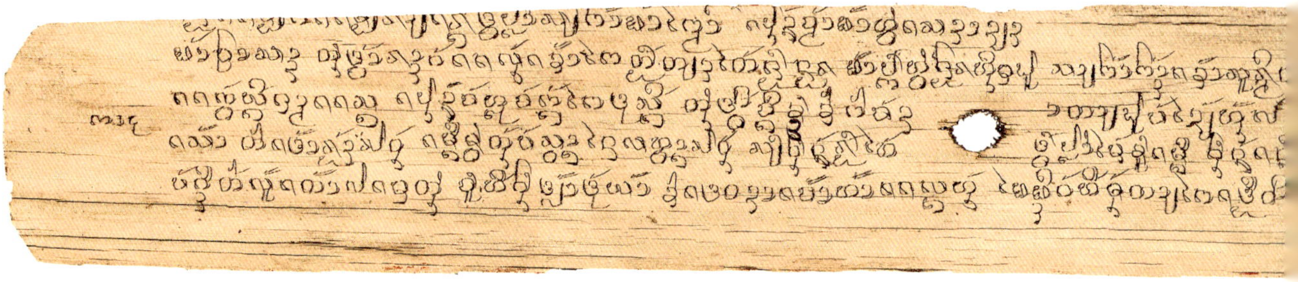

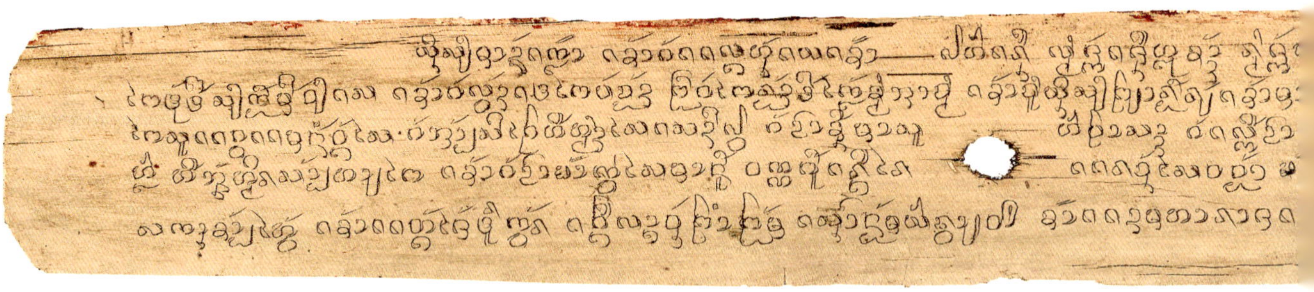

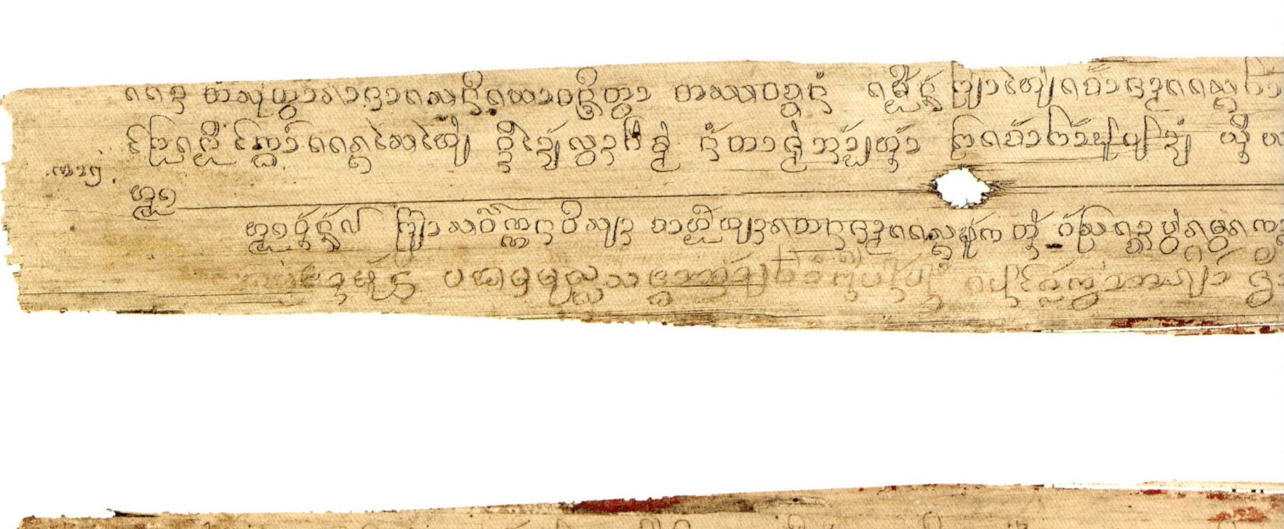

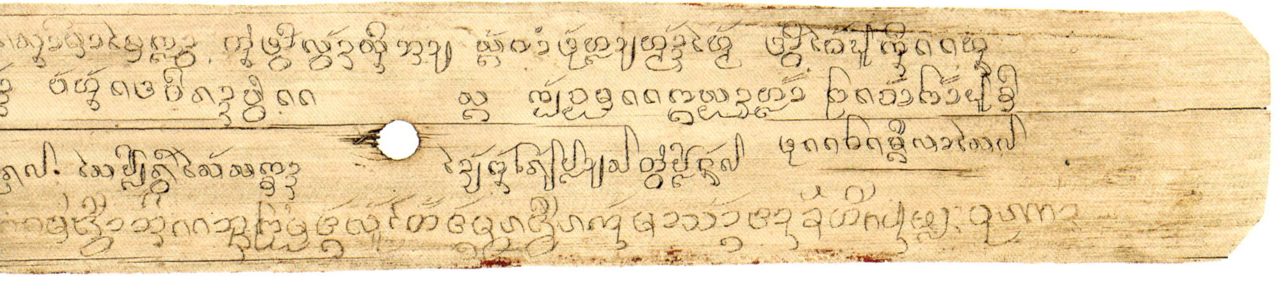

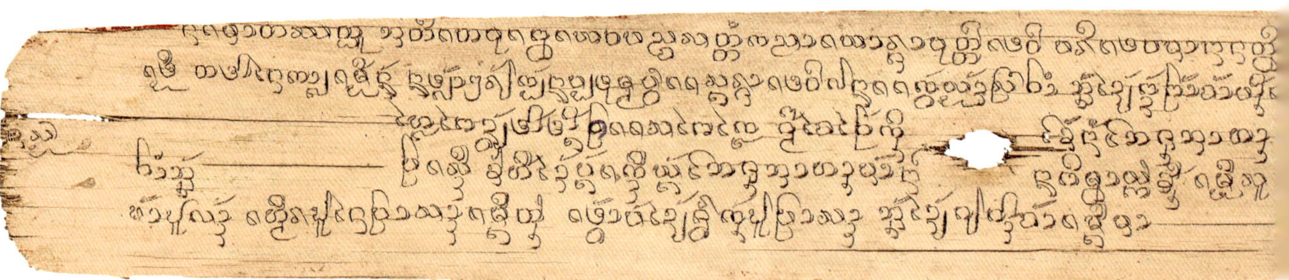

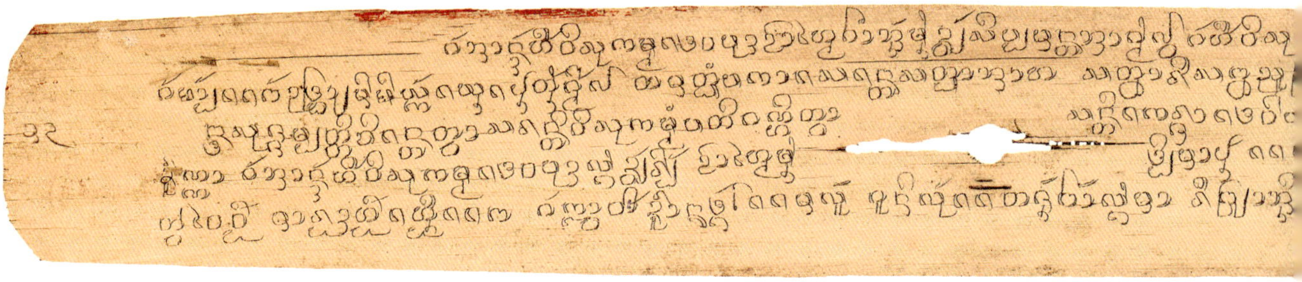

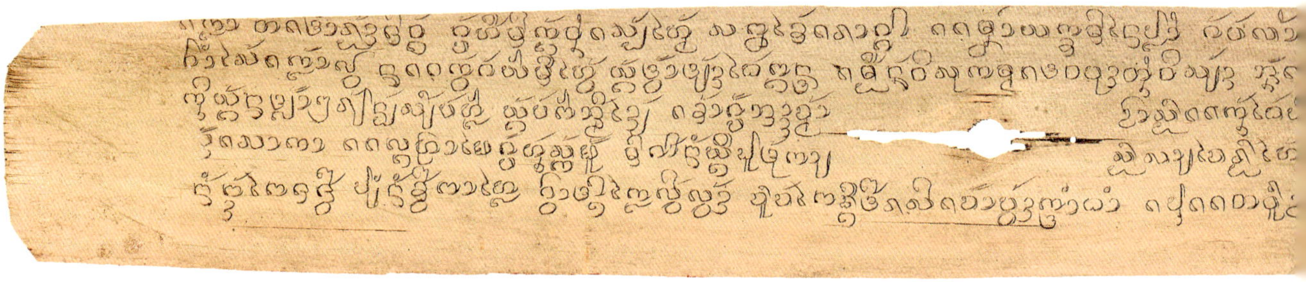

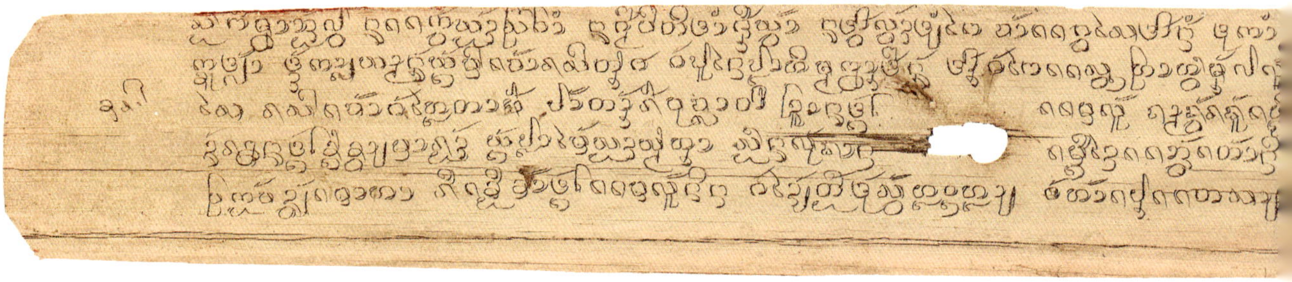

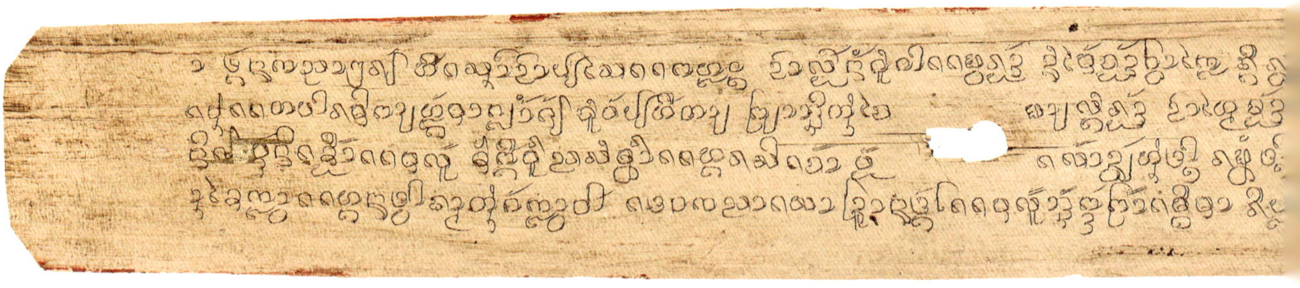

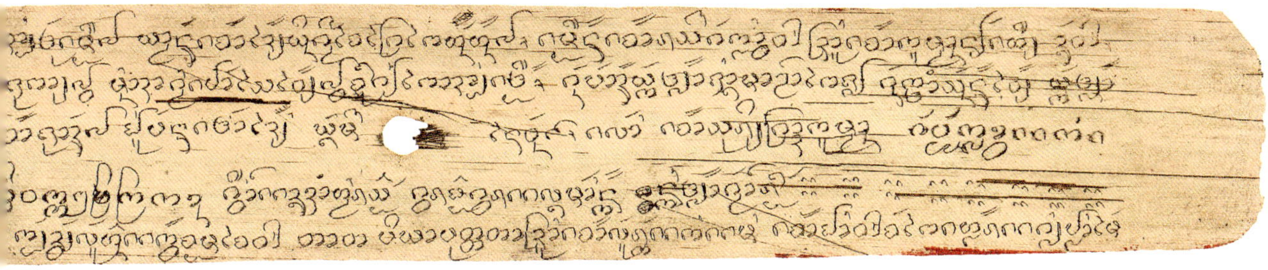

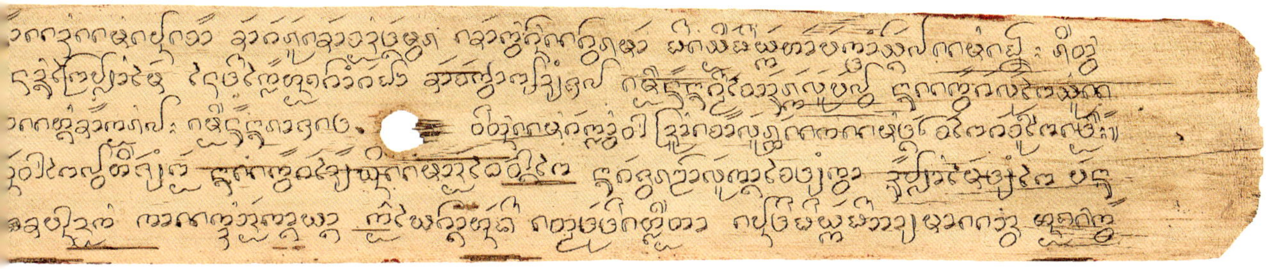

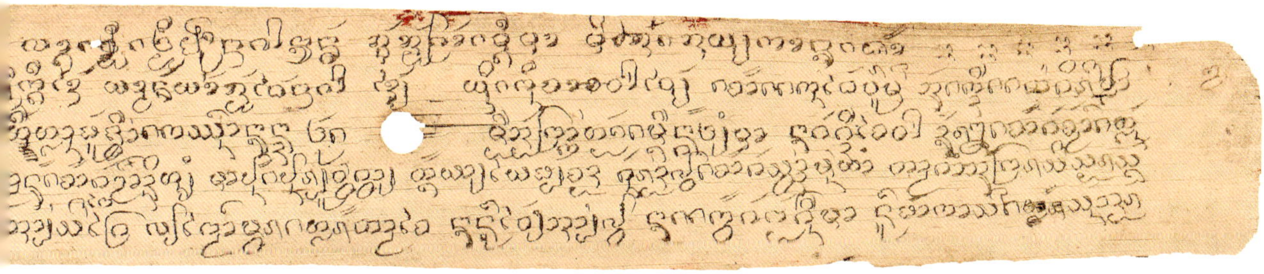

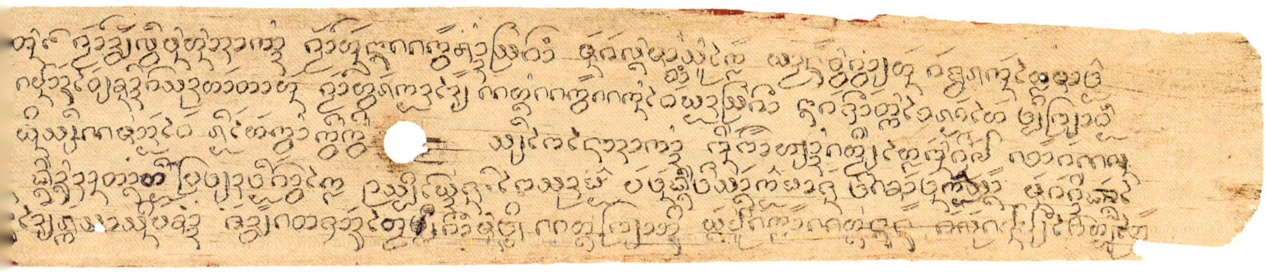

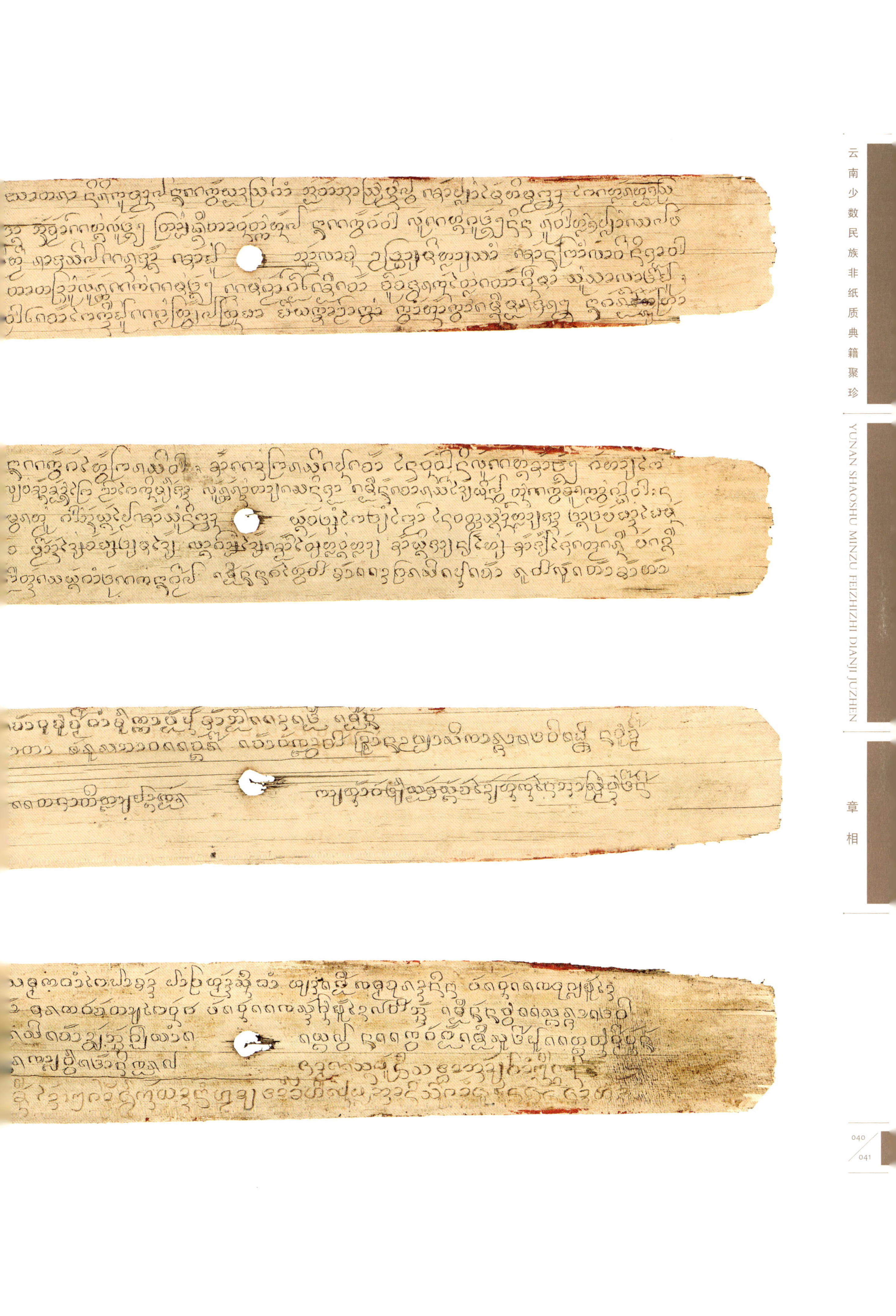

第三册

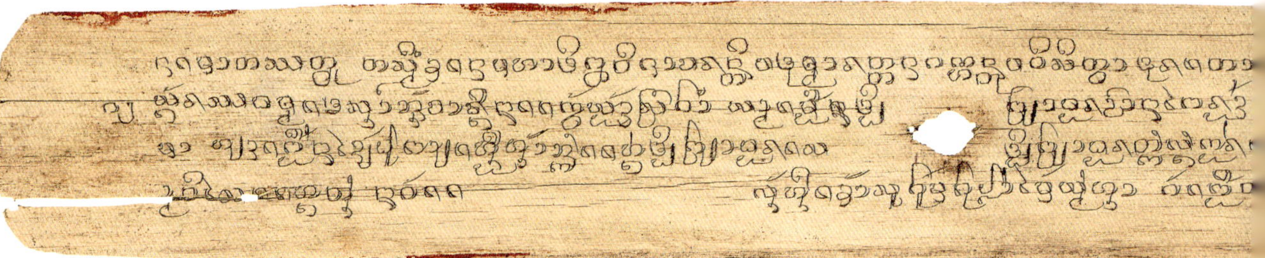

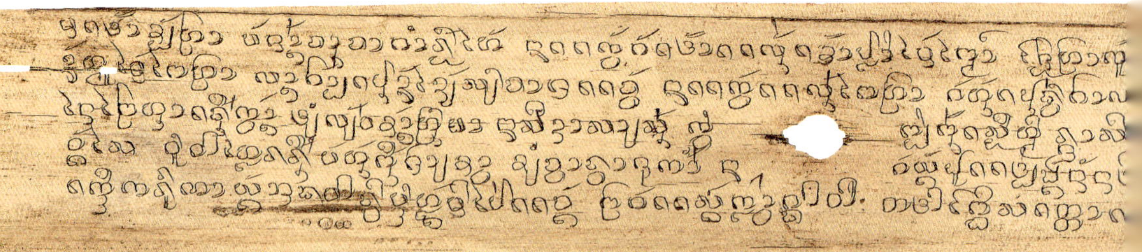

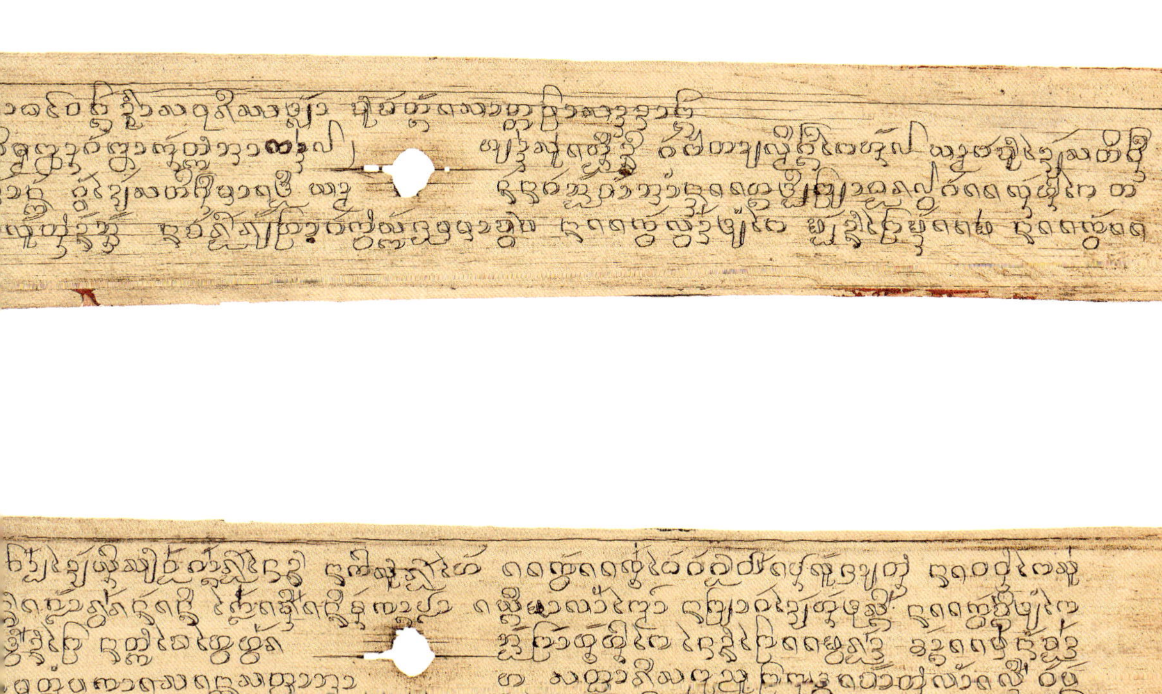

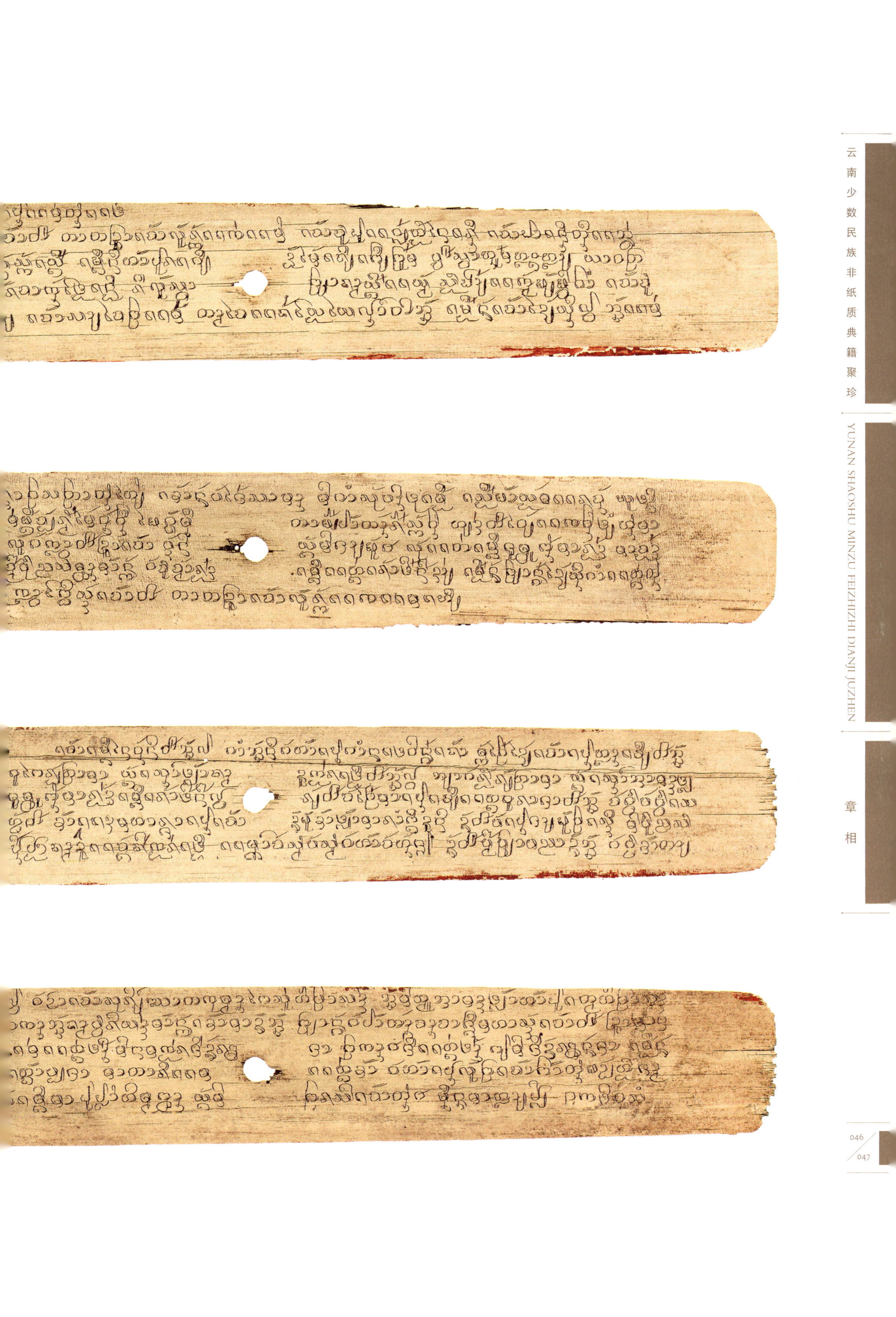

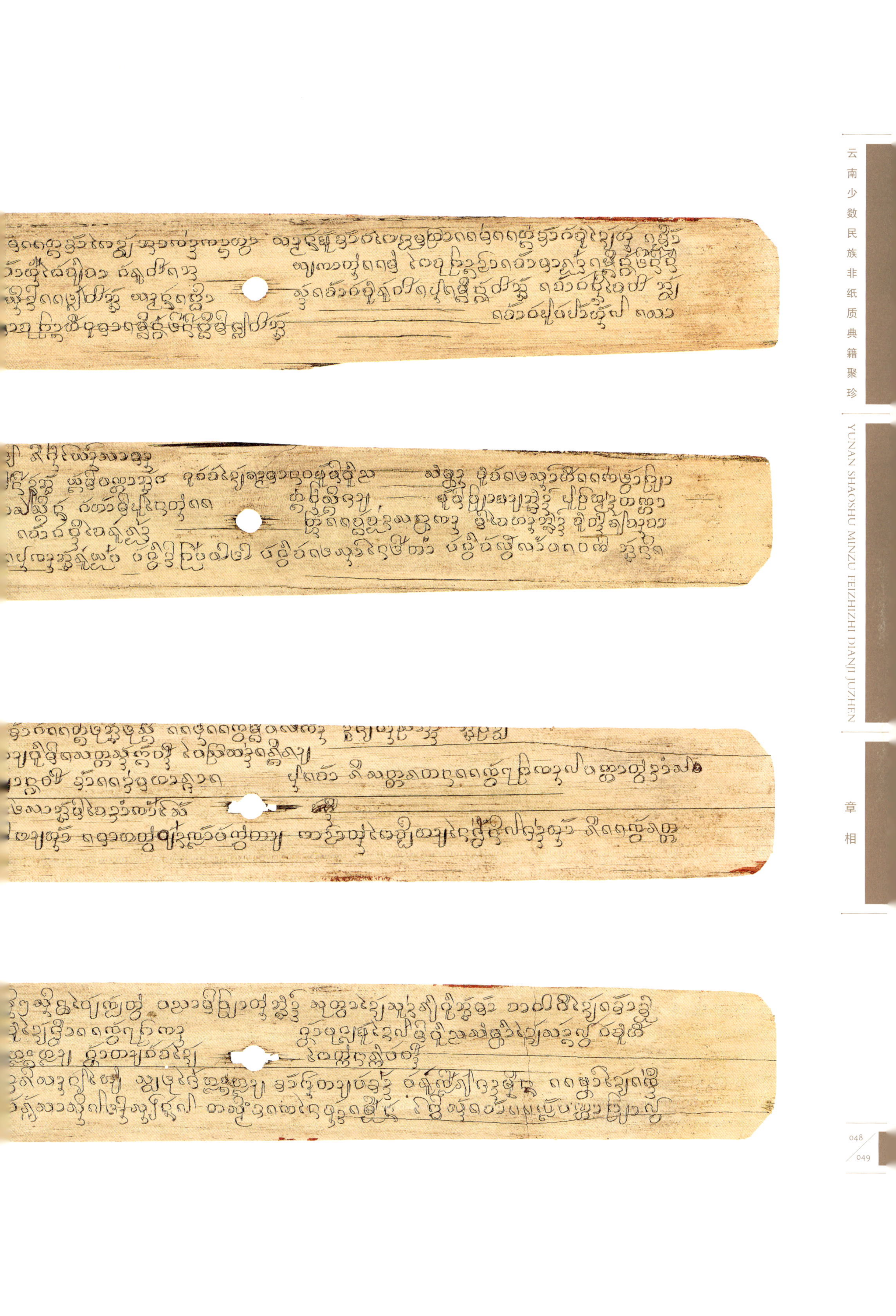

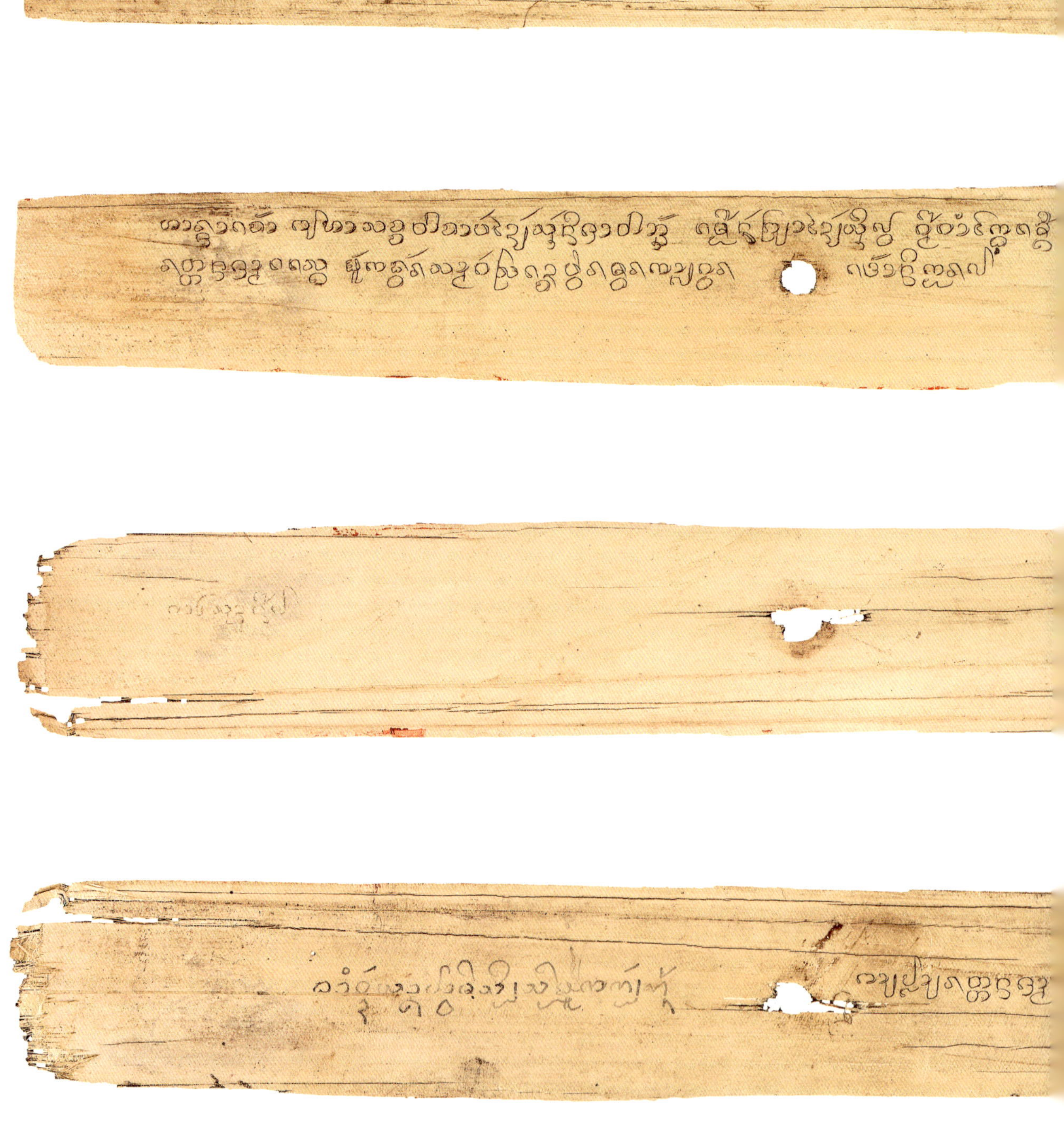

第四册

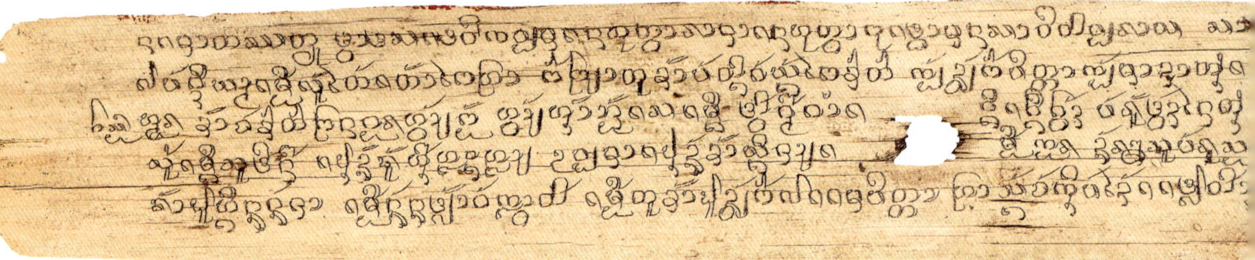

章相

章相

章相

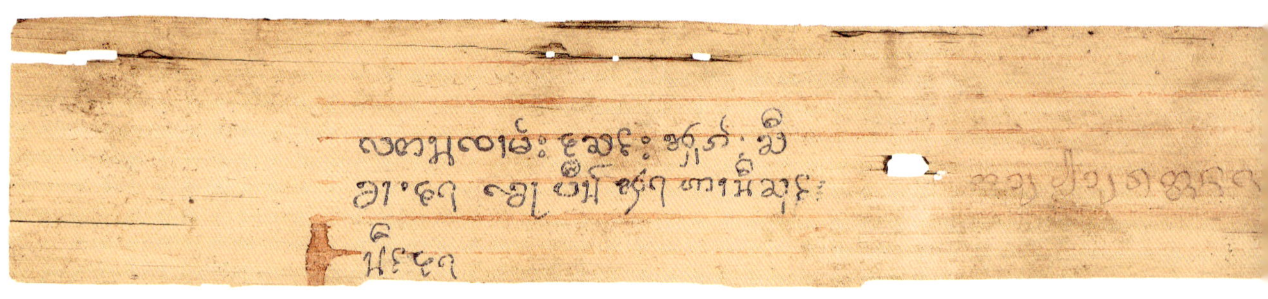

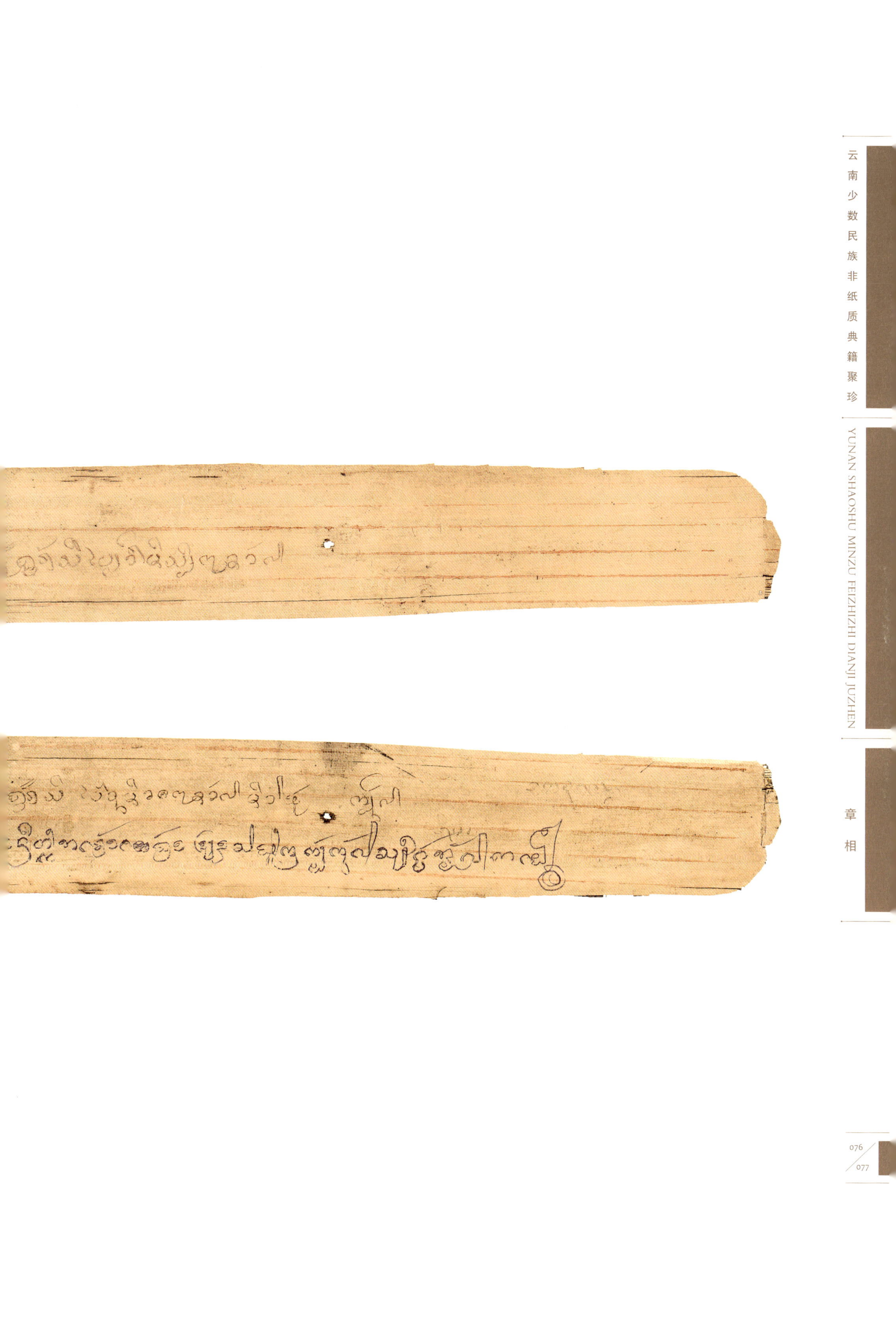

第五册

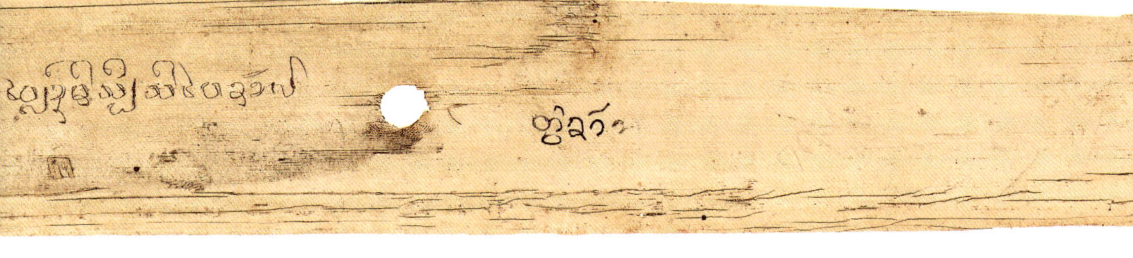

章相

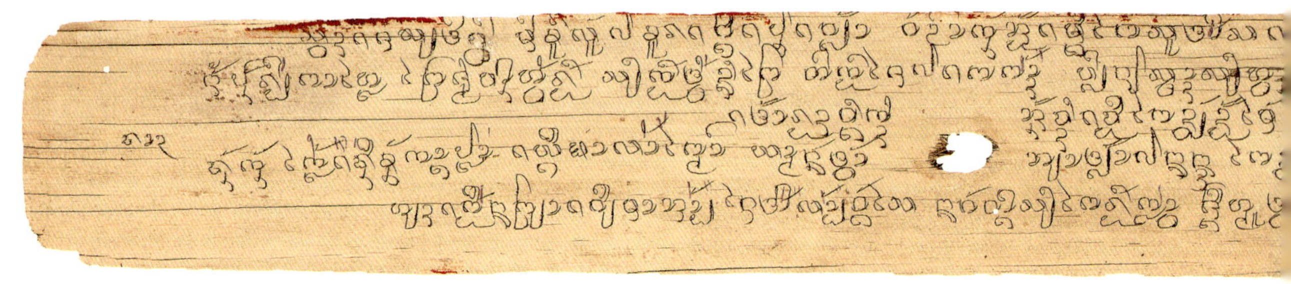

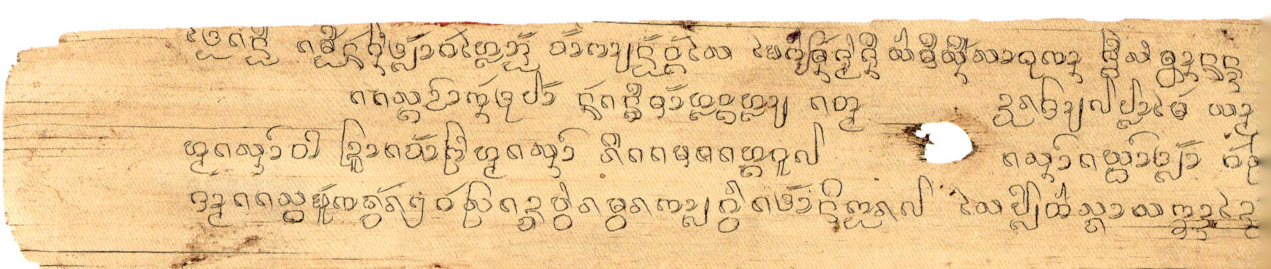

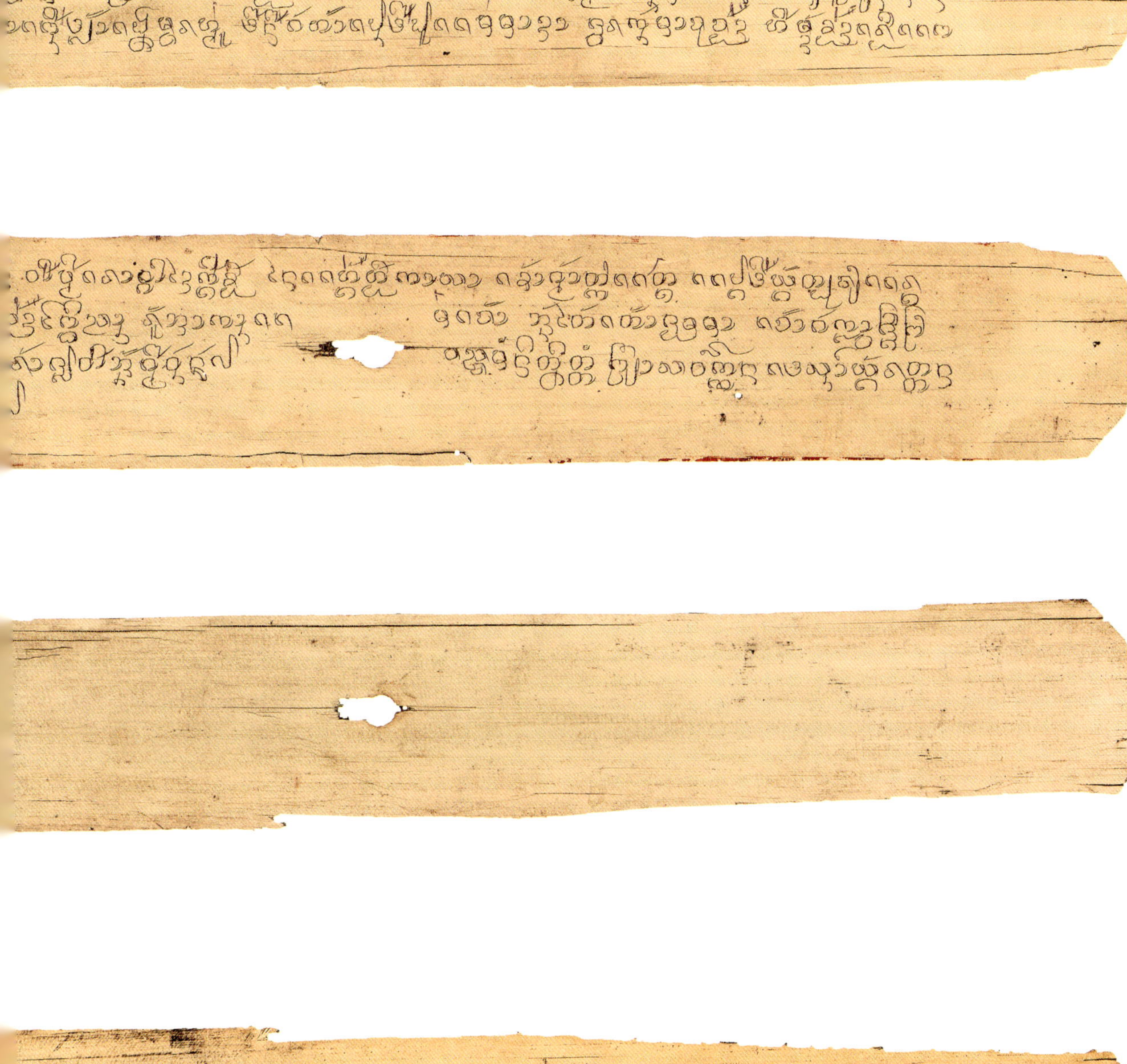

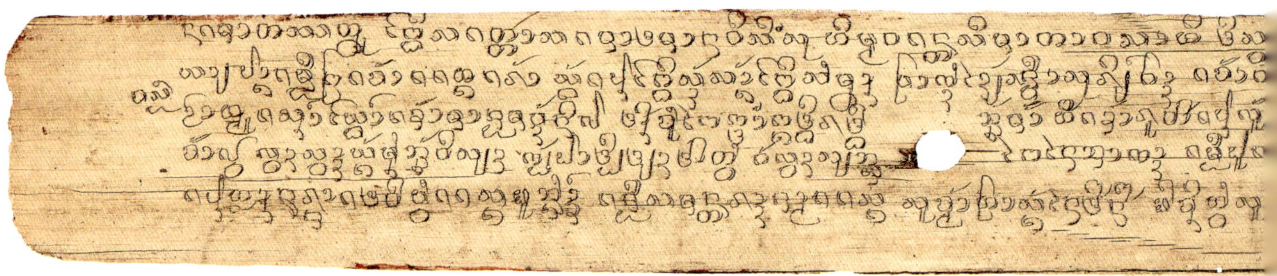

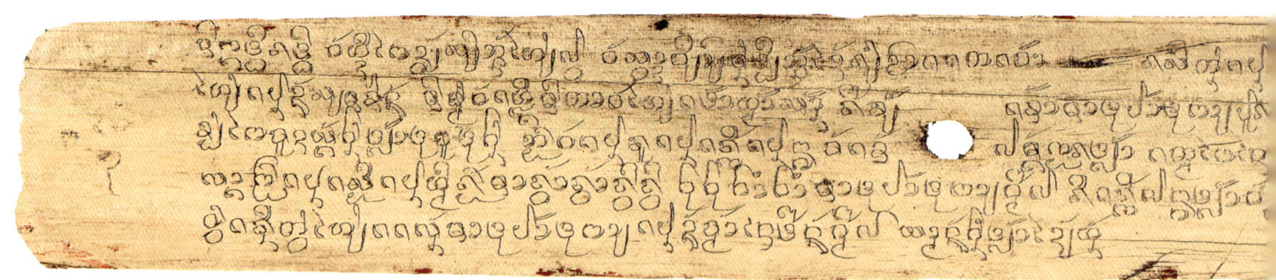

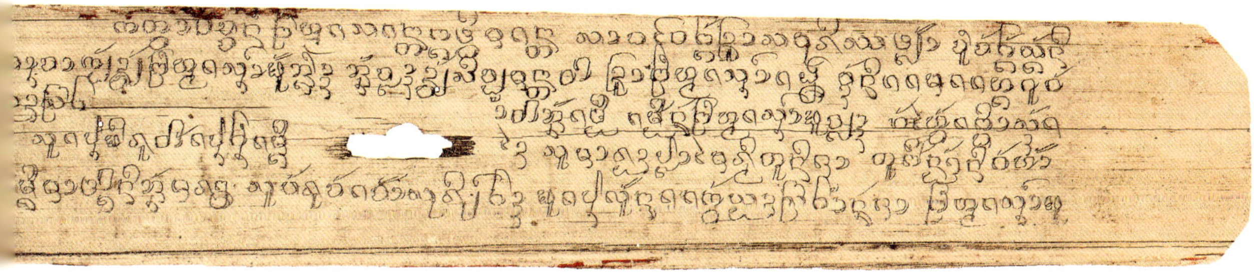

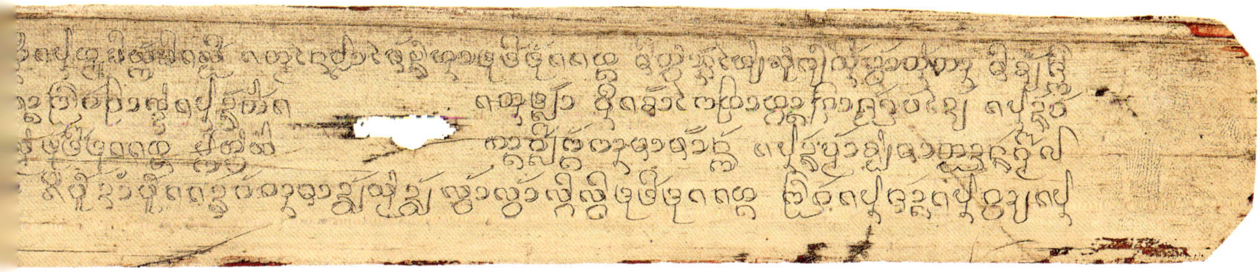

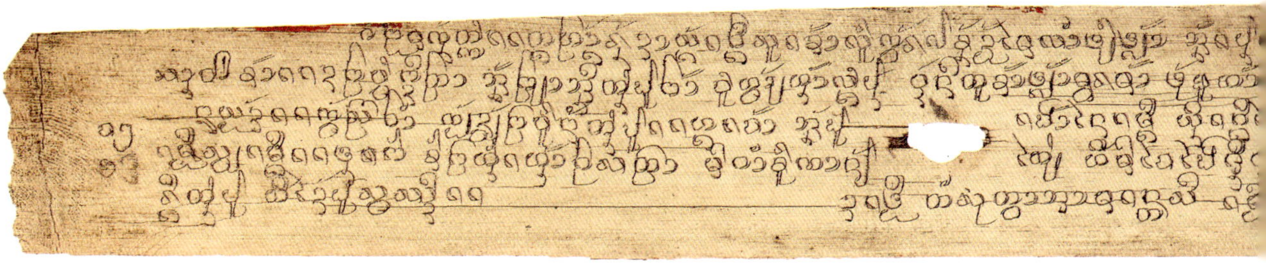

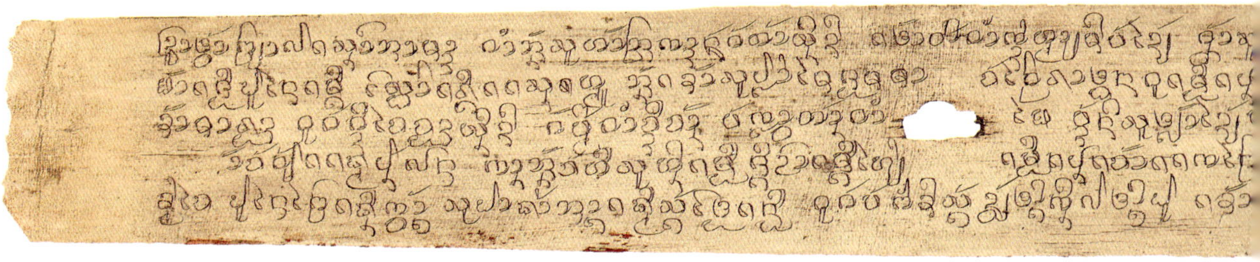

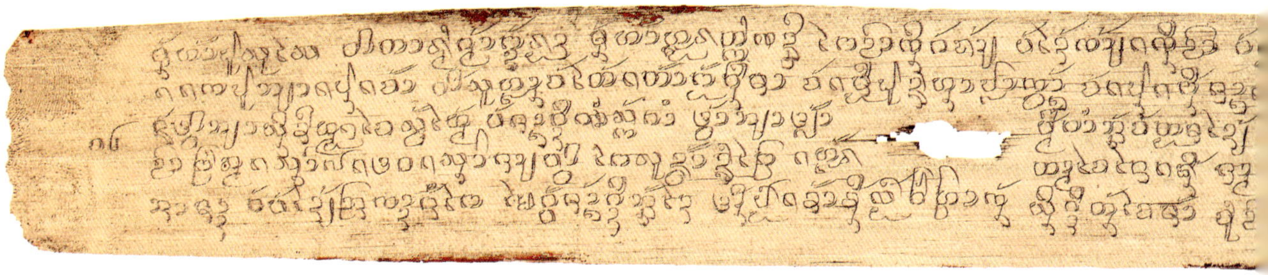

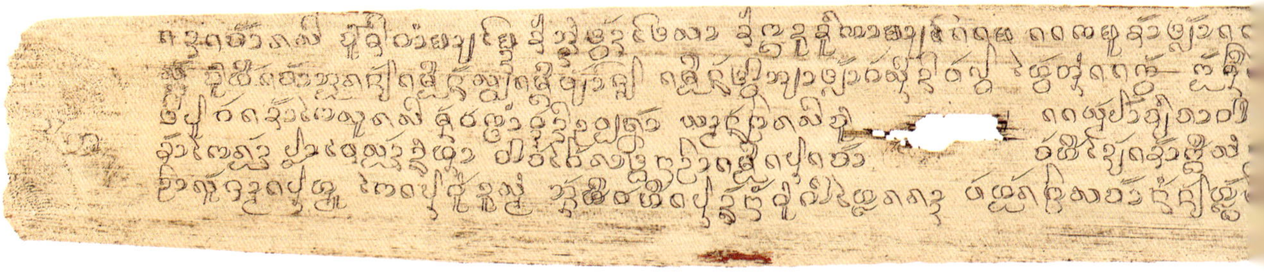

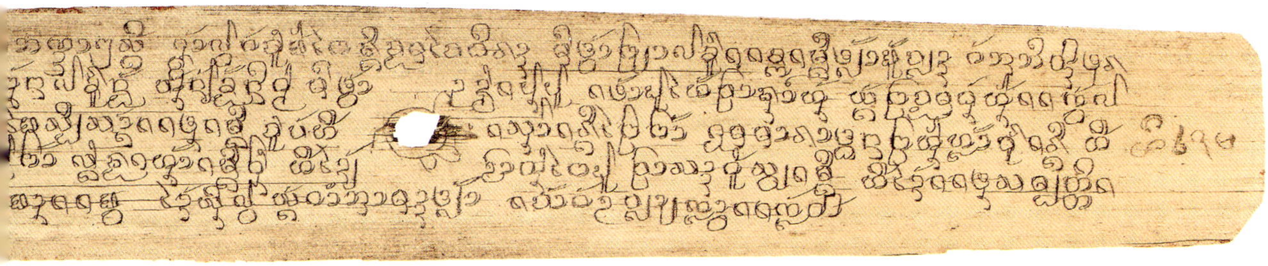

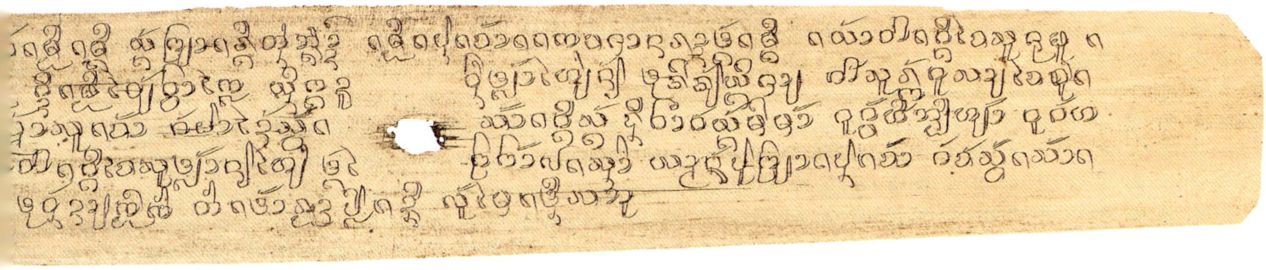

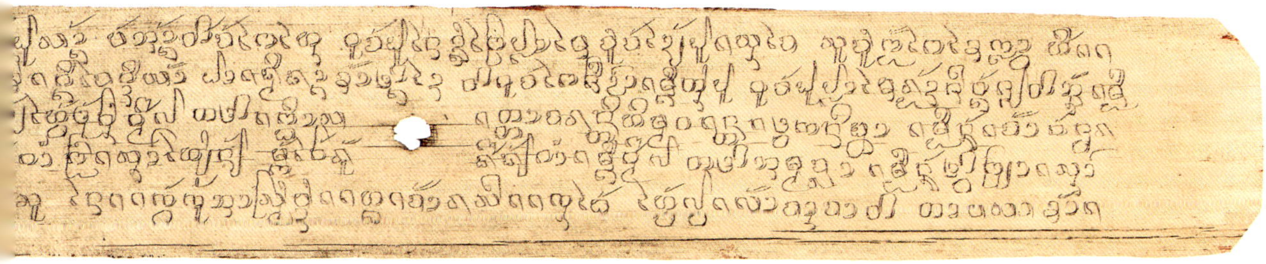

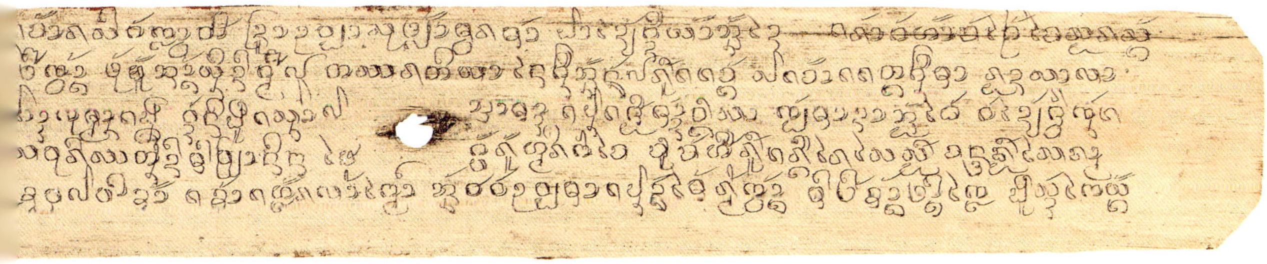

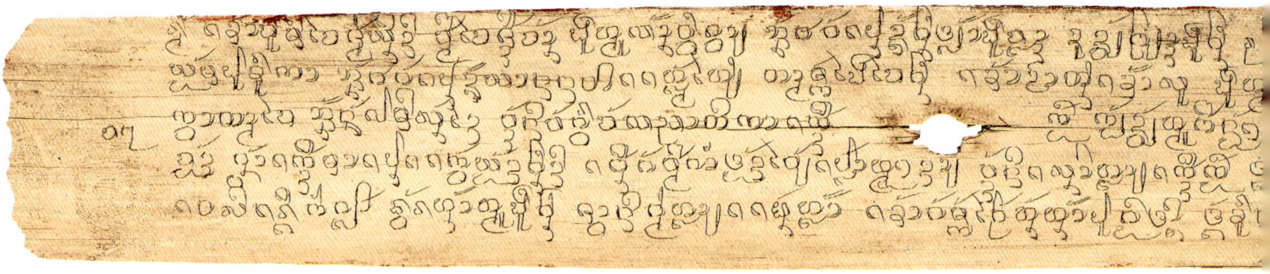

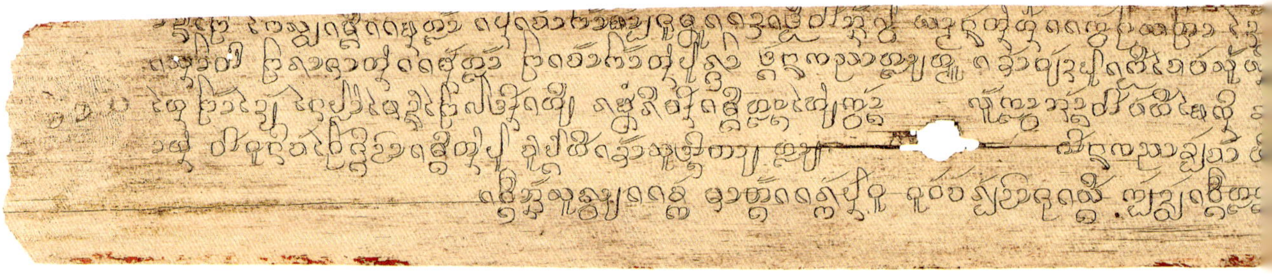

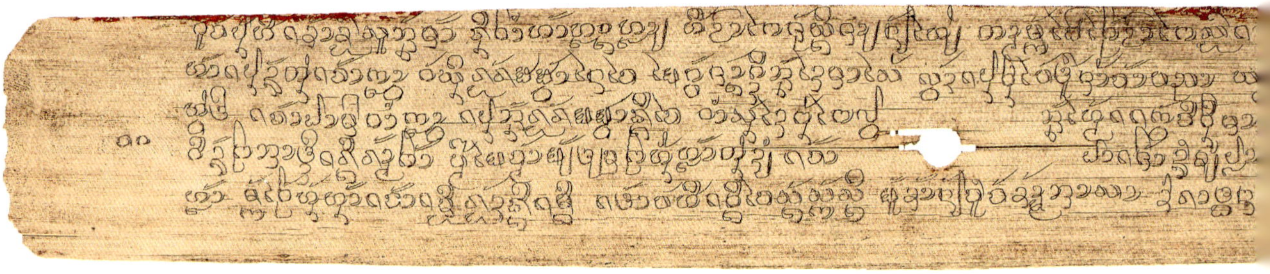

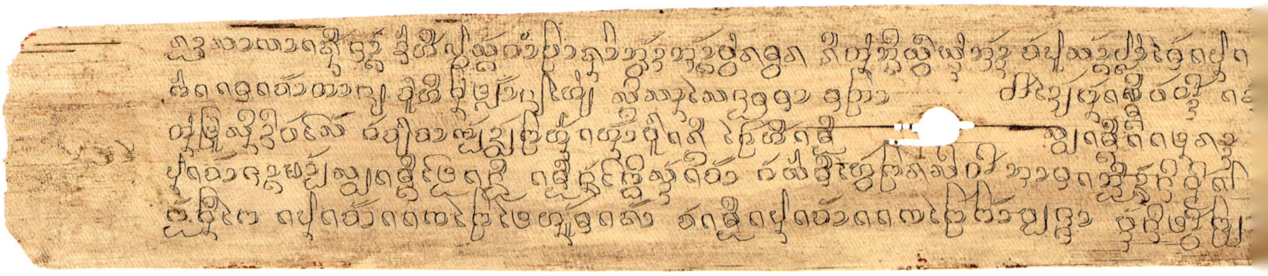

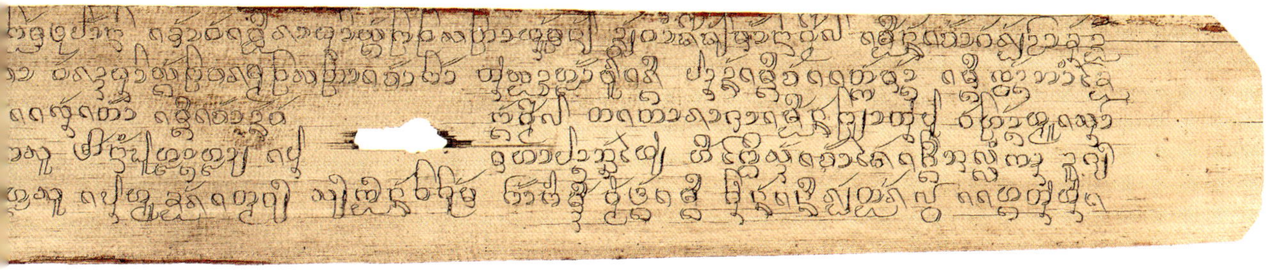

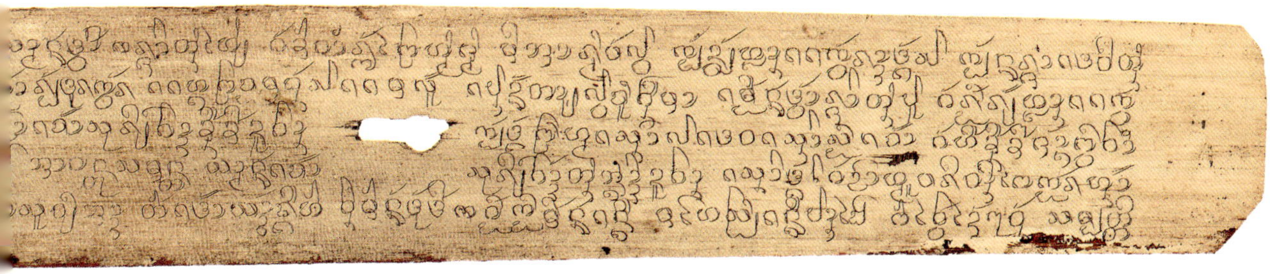

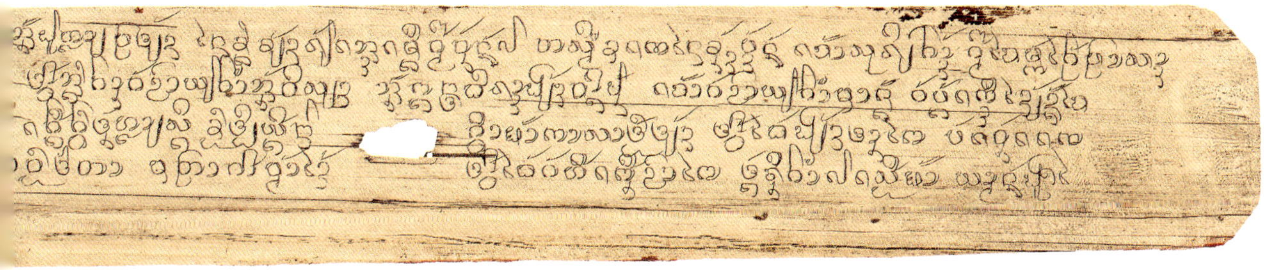

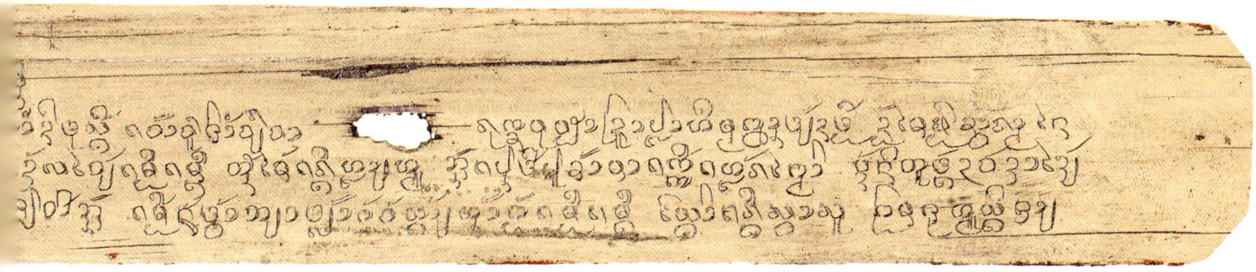

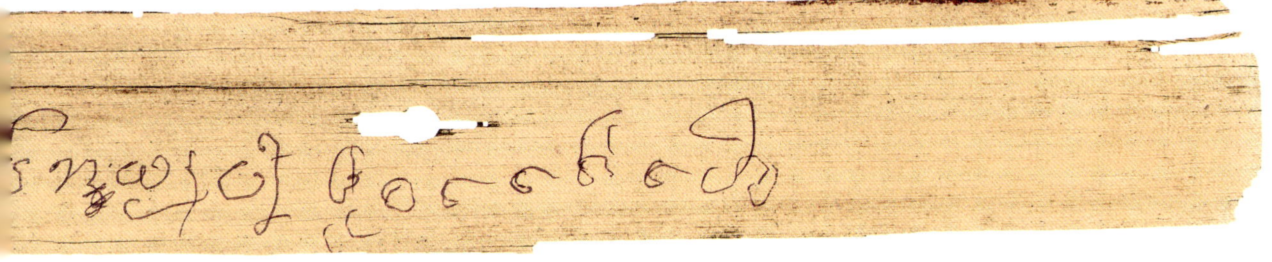

第七册

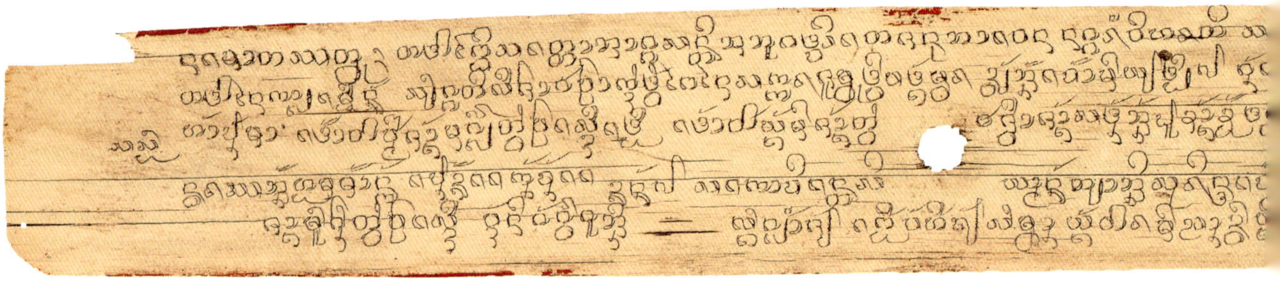

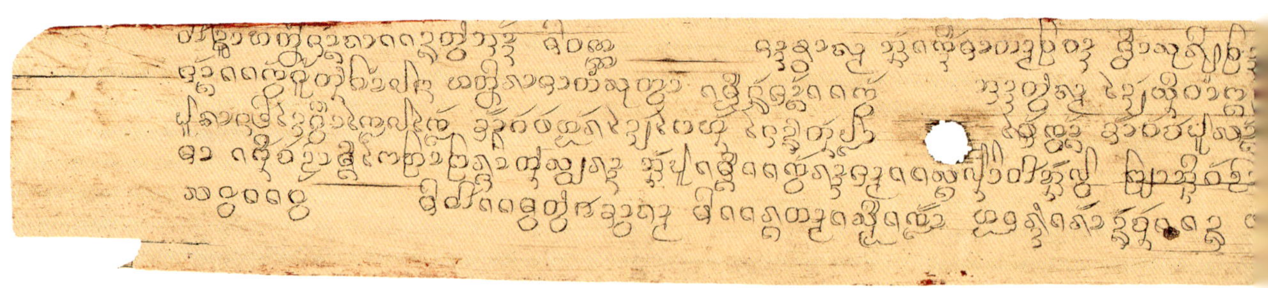

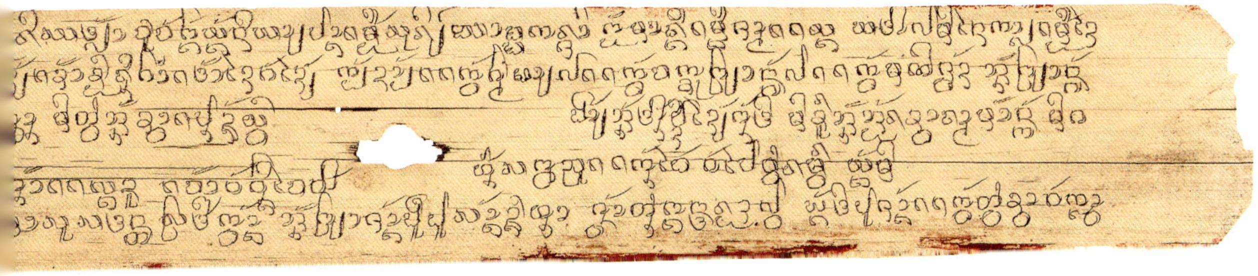

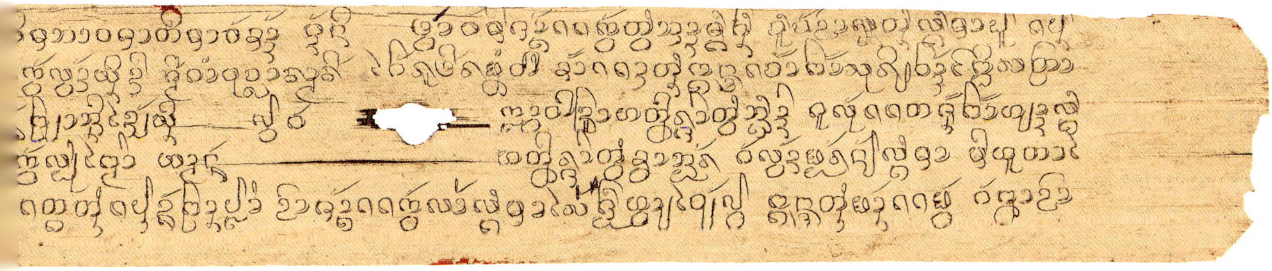

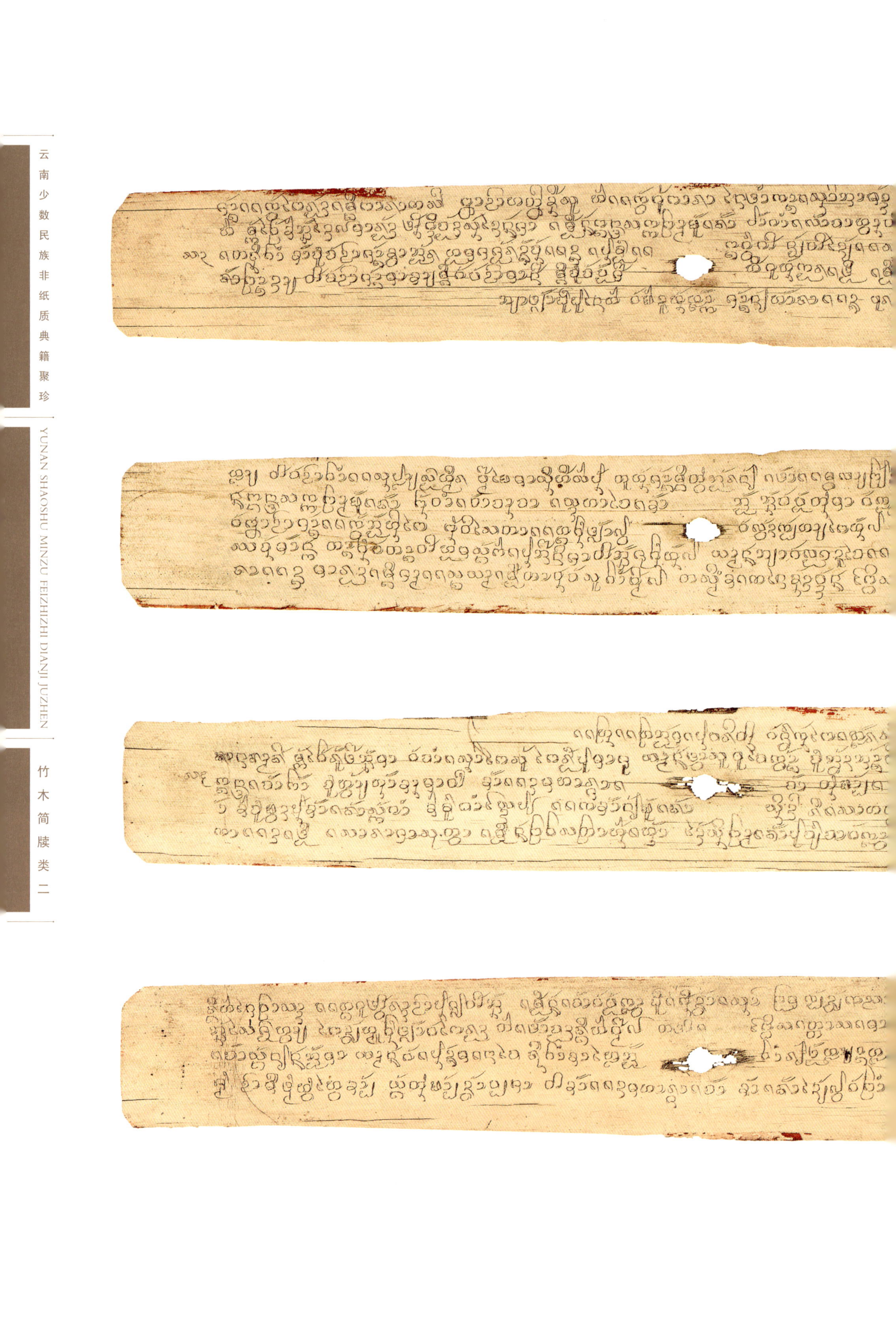

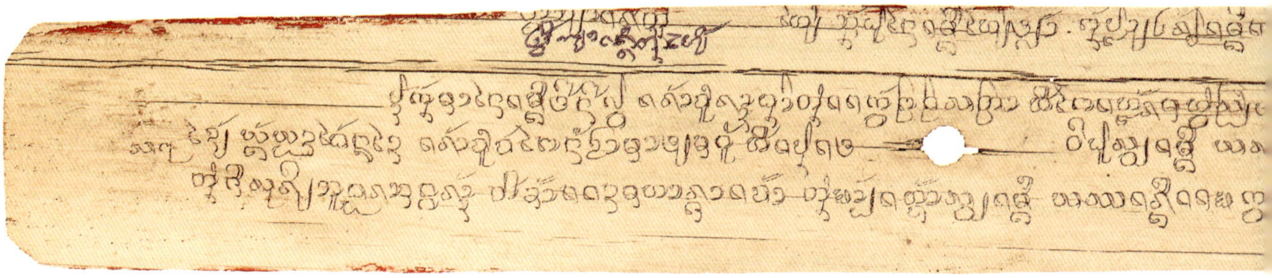

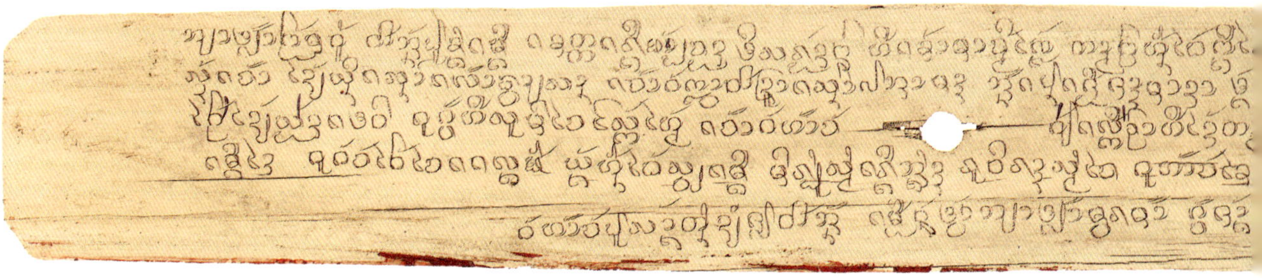

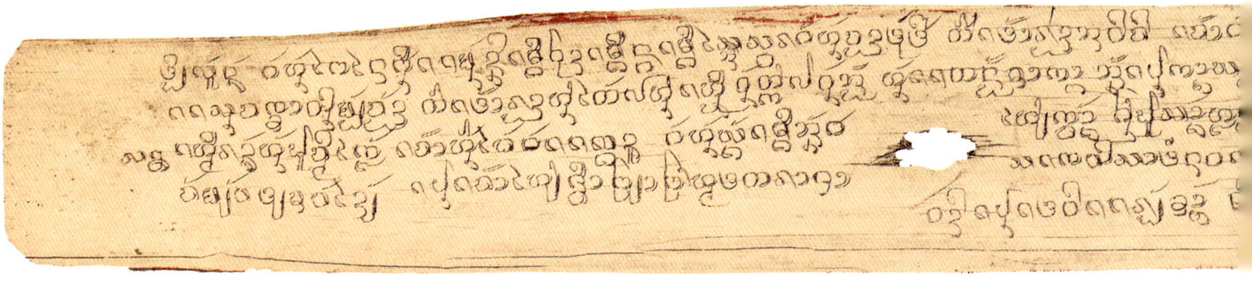

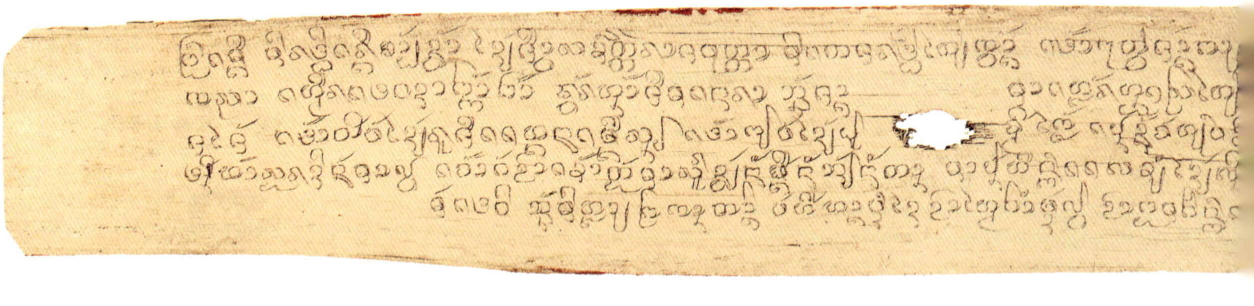

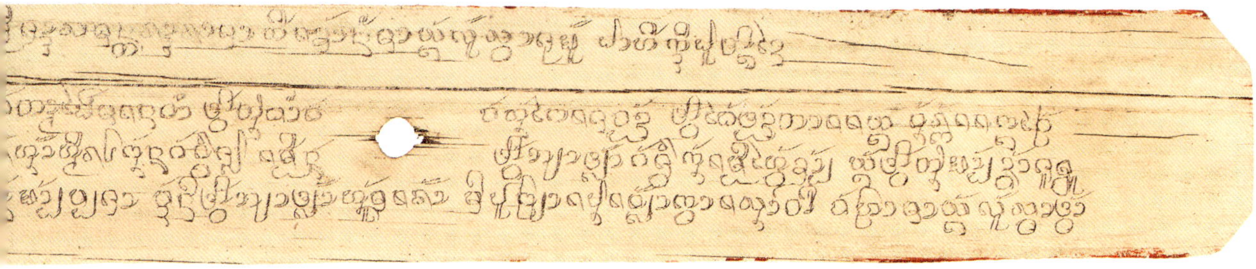

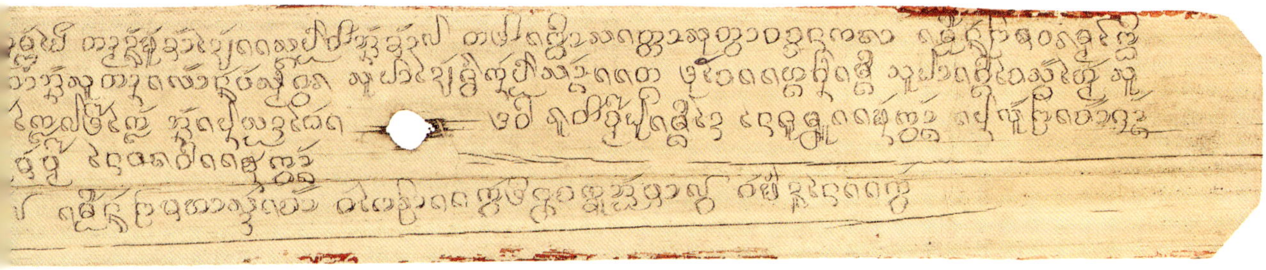

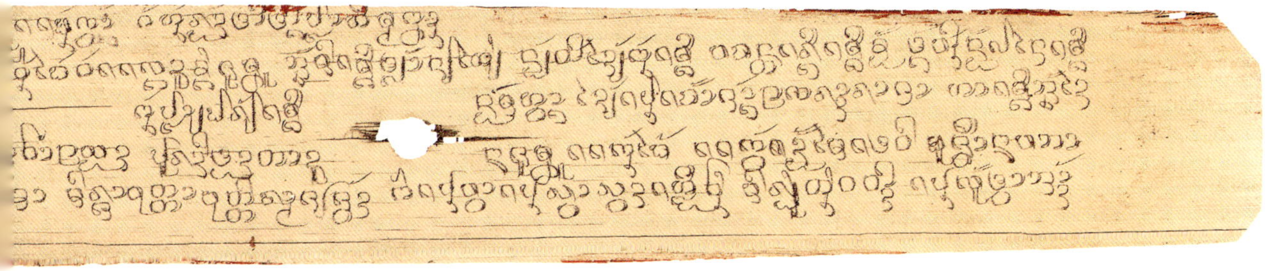

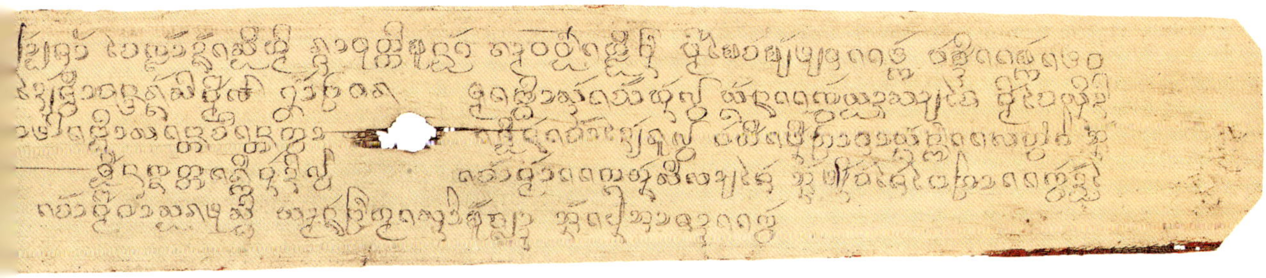

章相

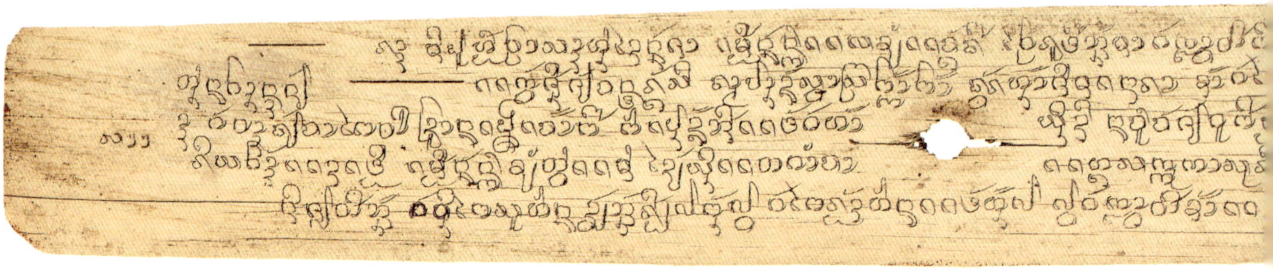

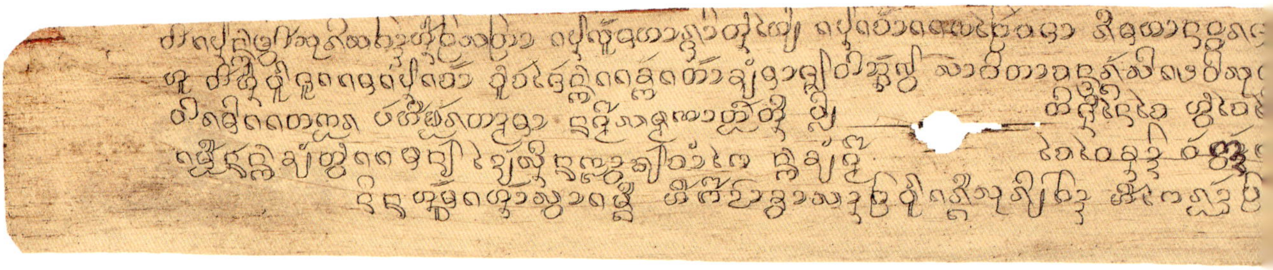

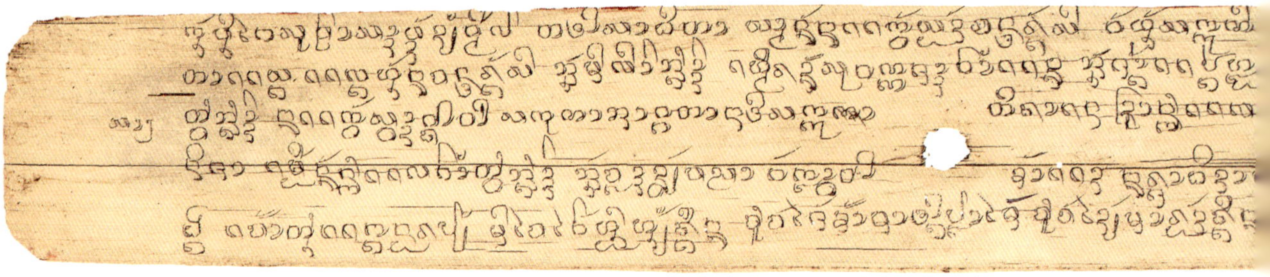

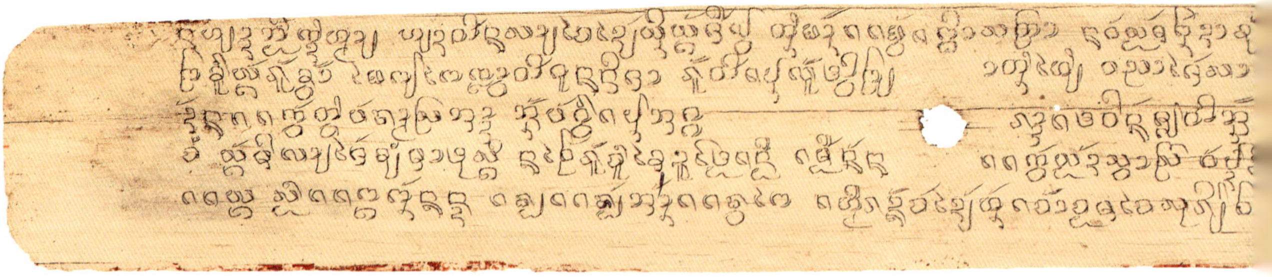

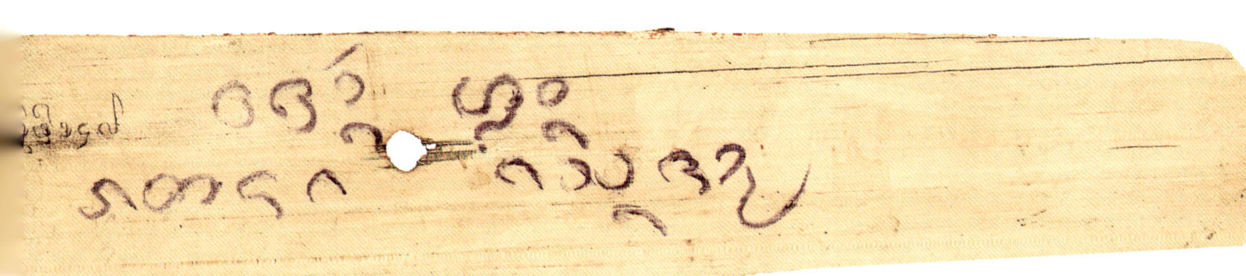

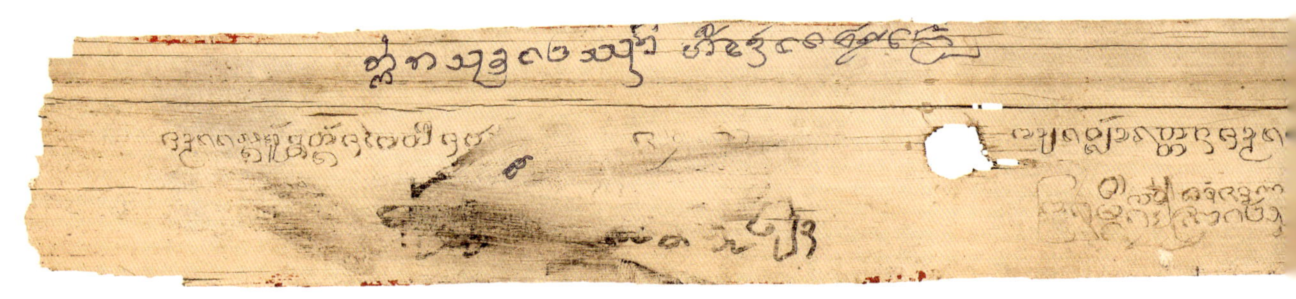

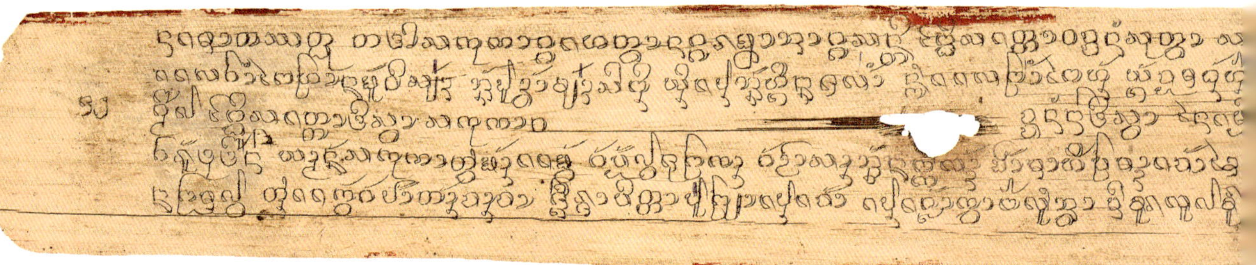

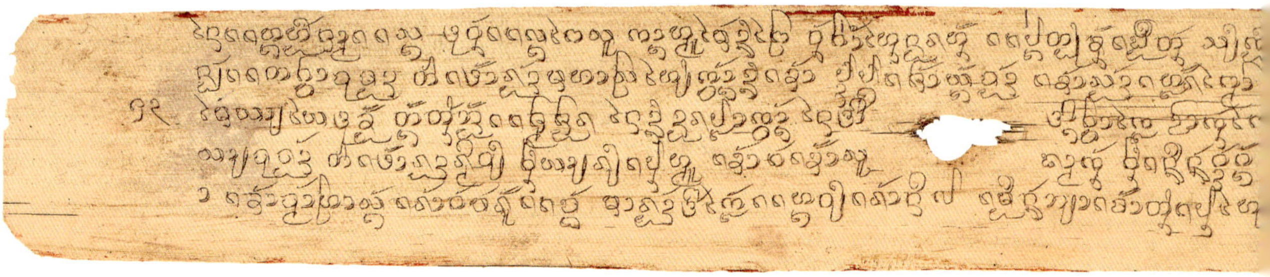

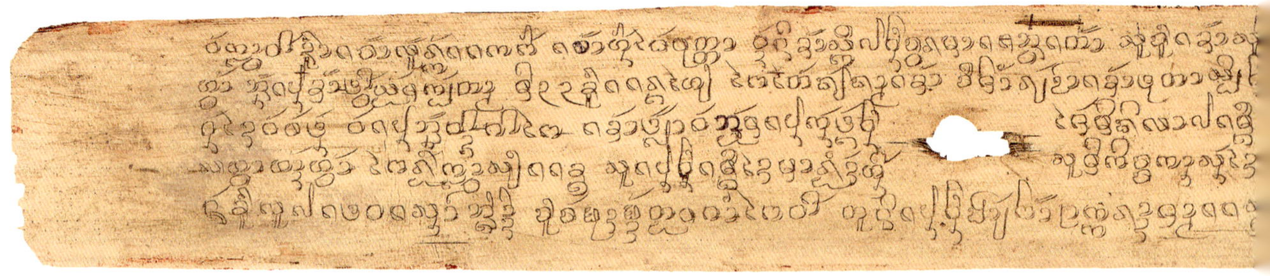

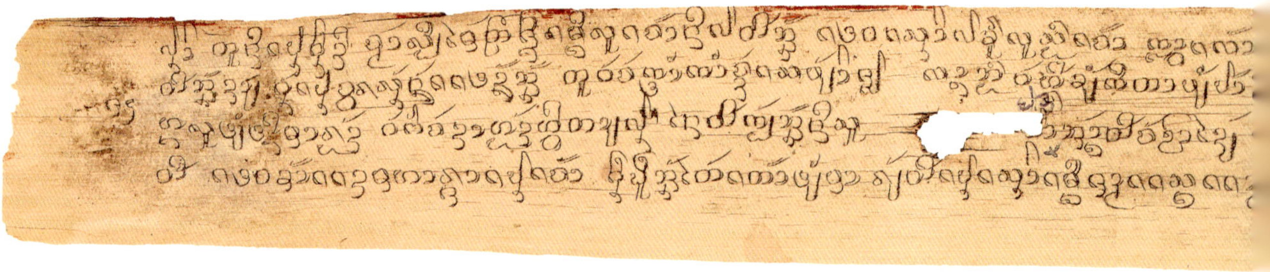

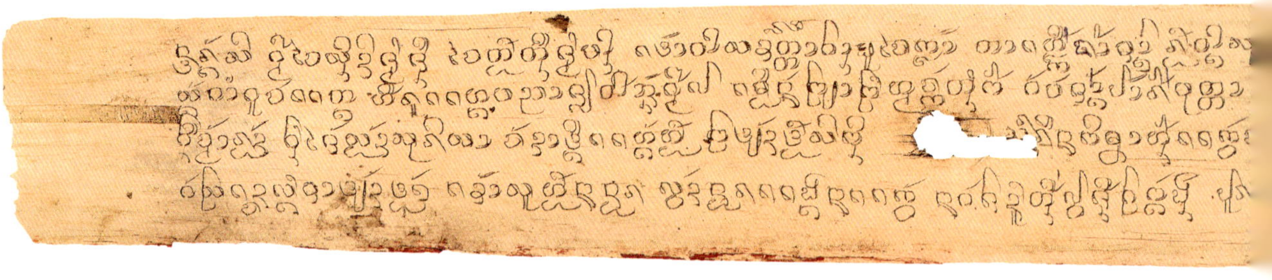

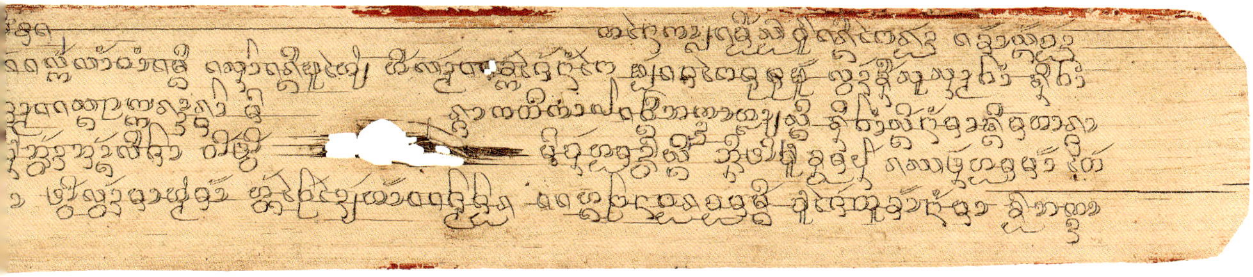

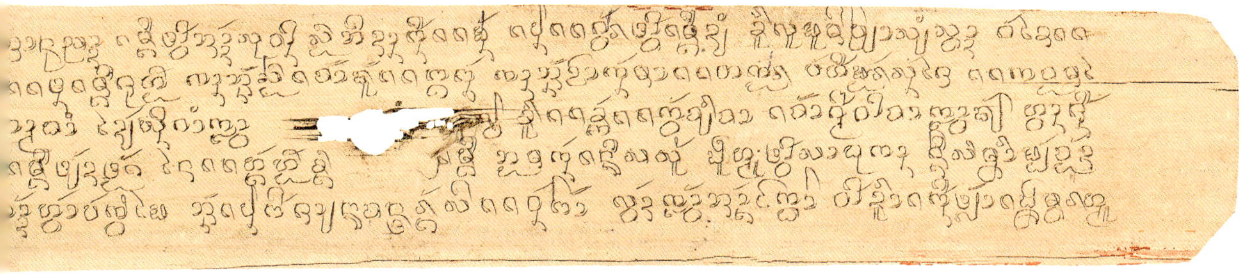

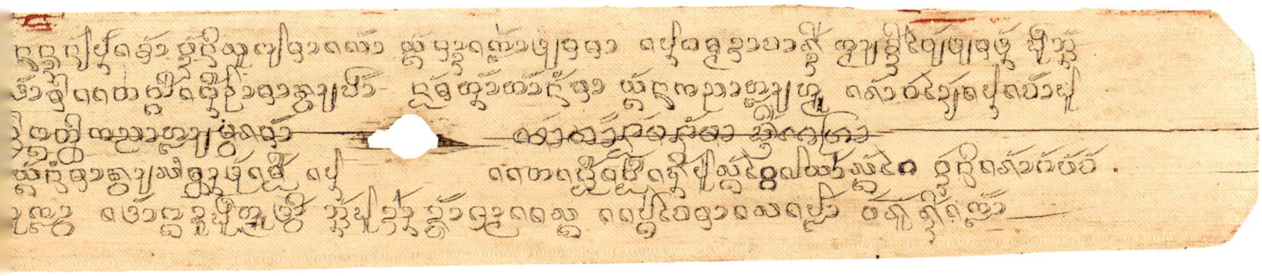

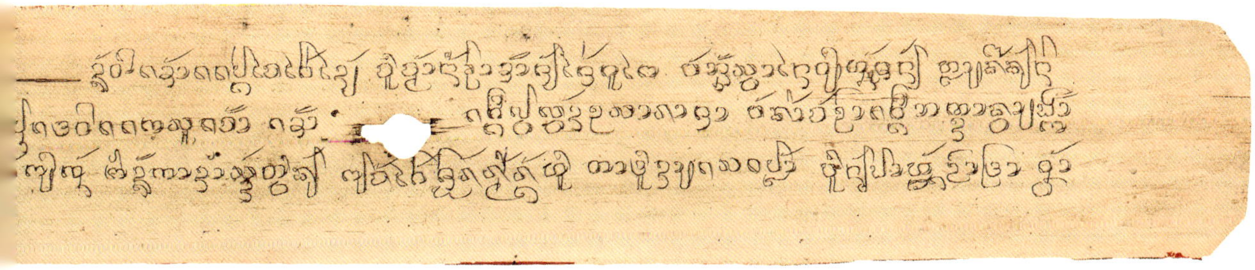

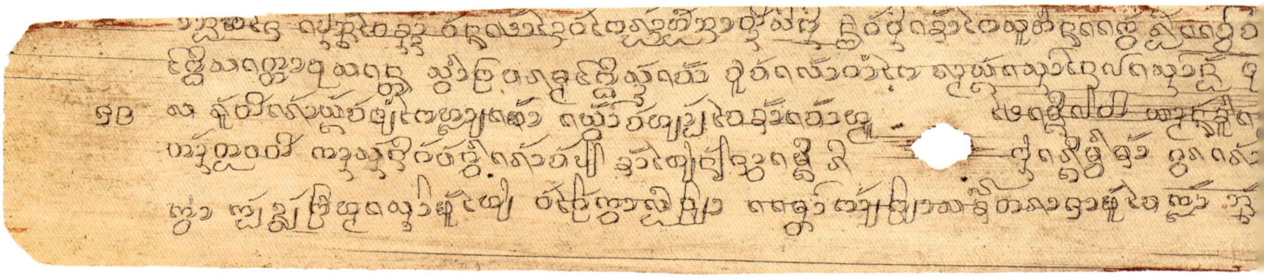

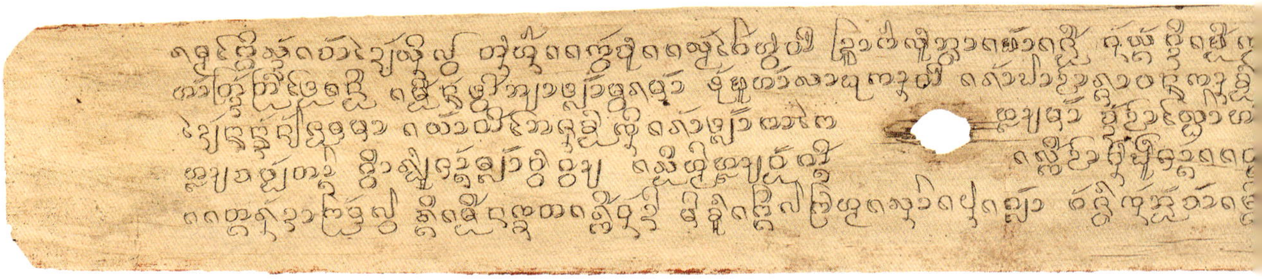

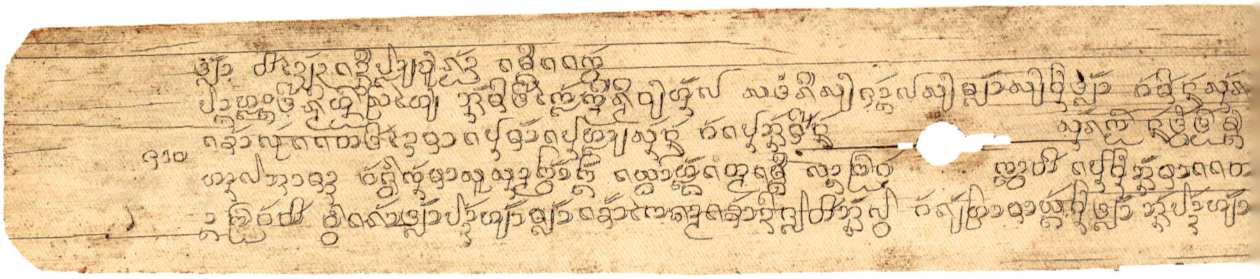

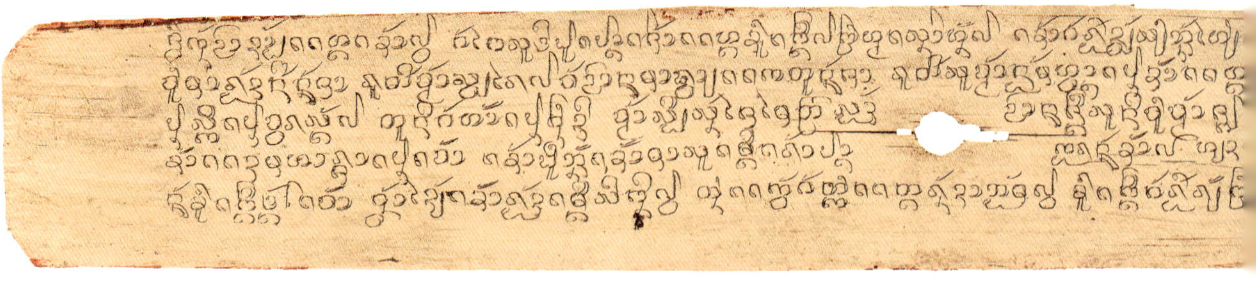

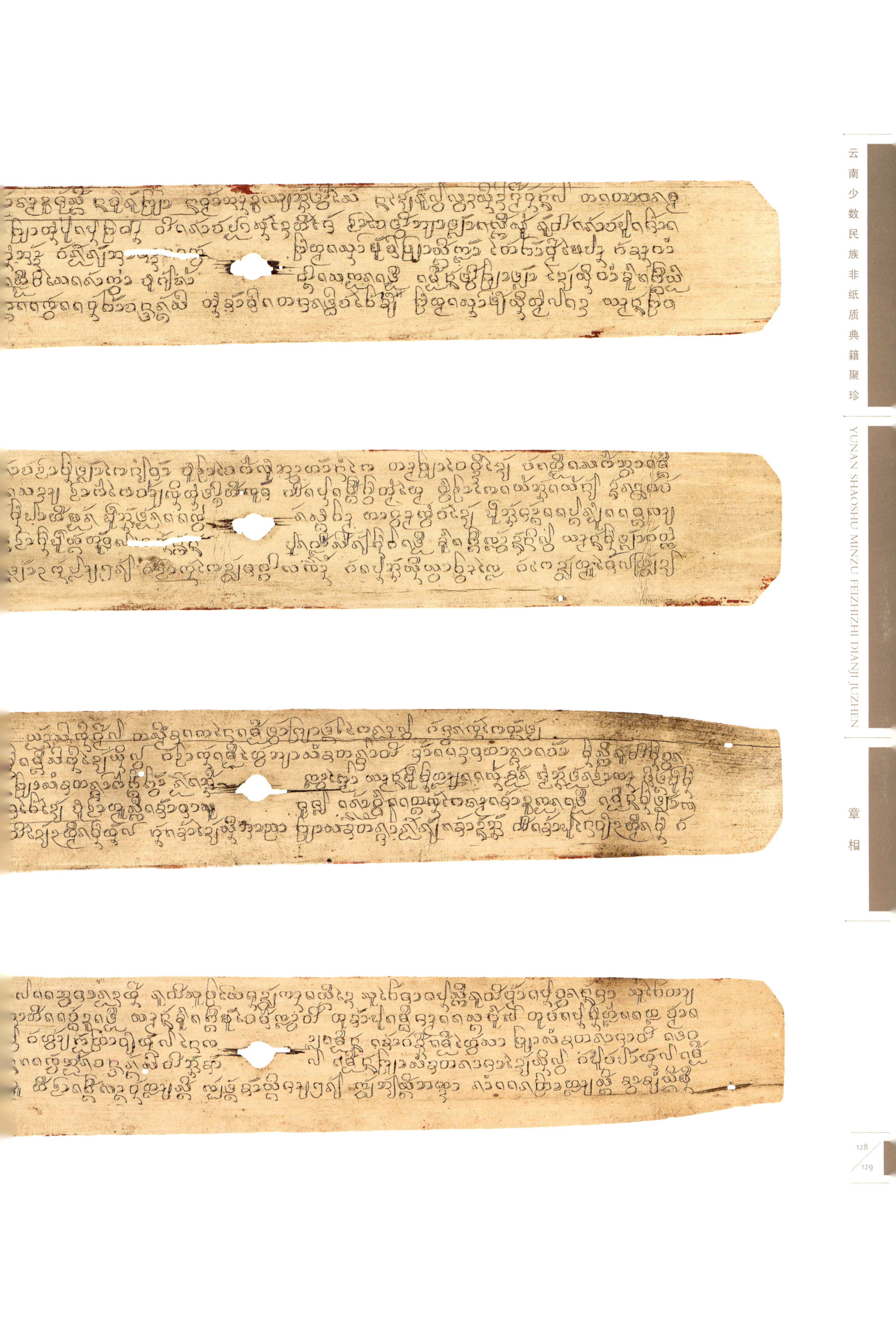

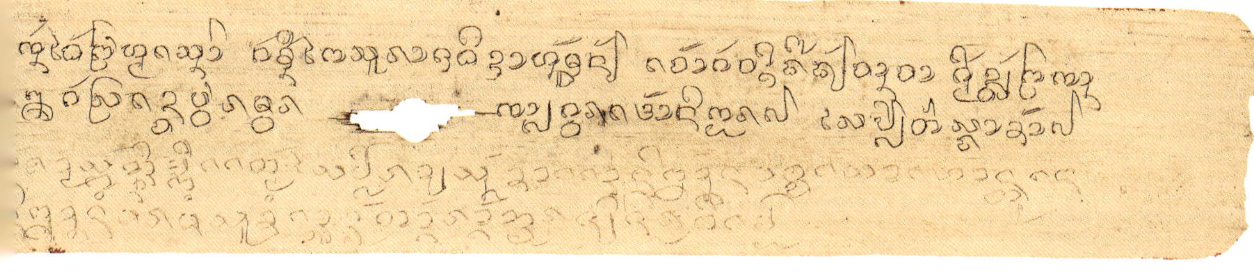

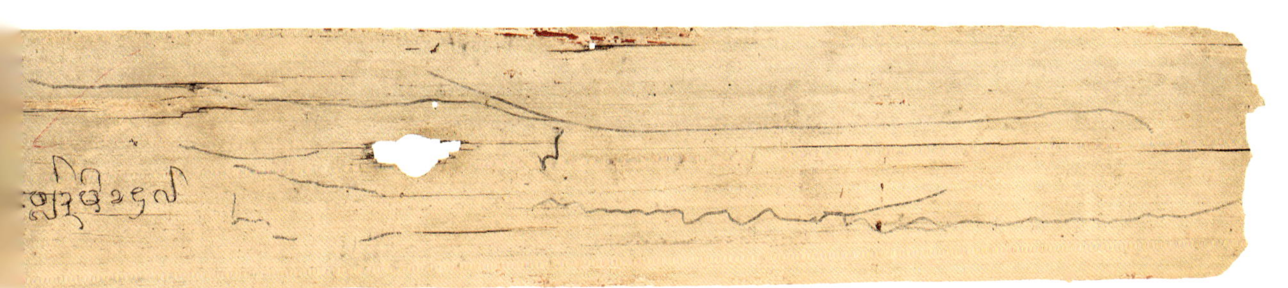

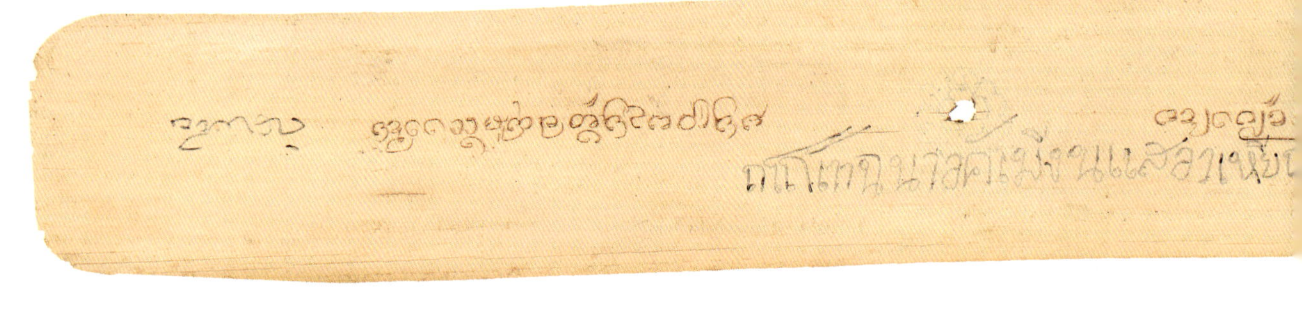

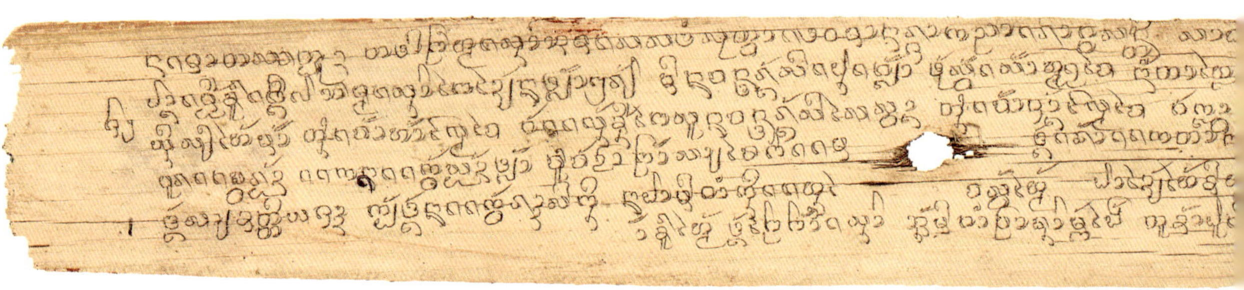

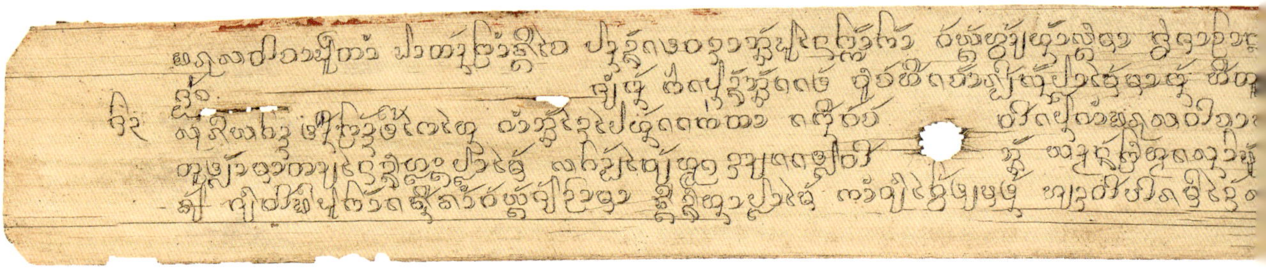

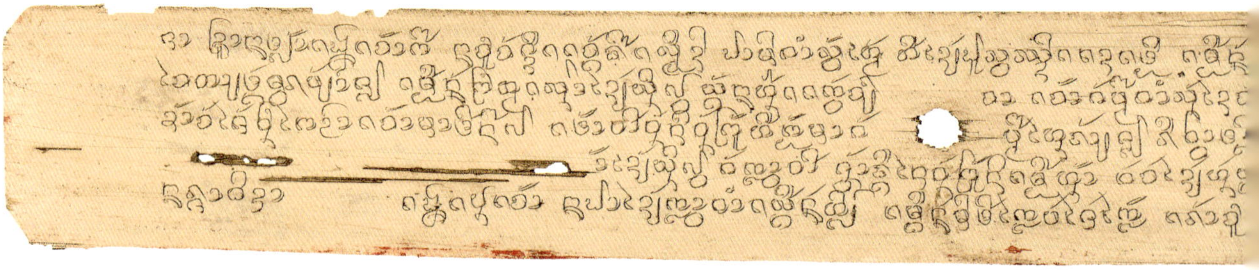

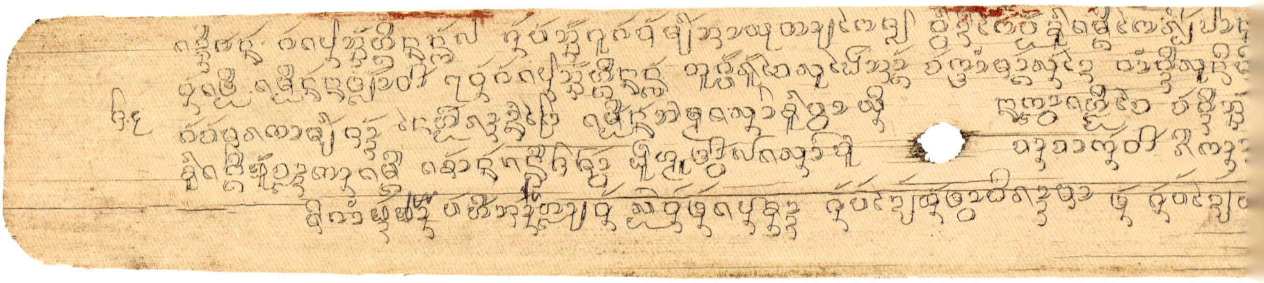

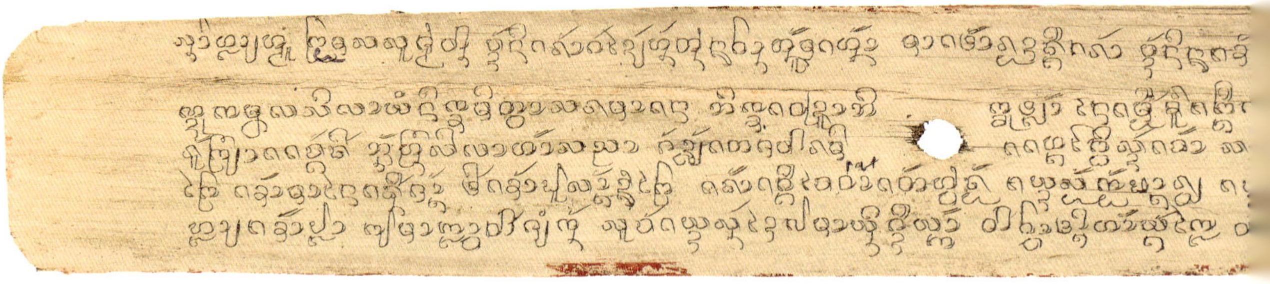

章相

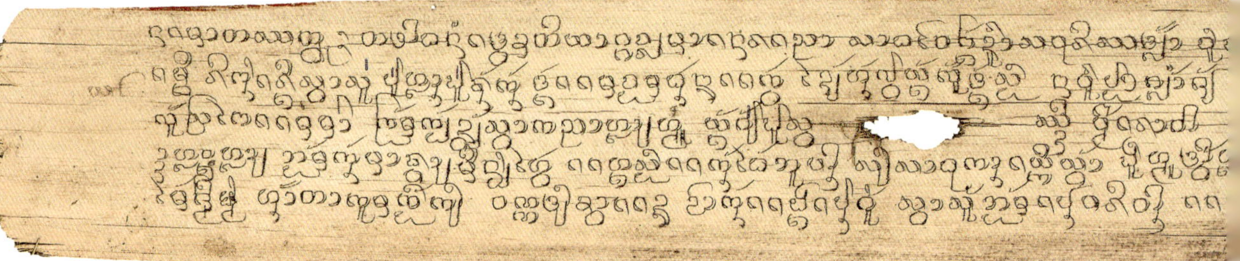

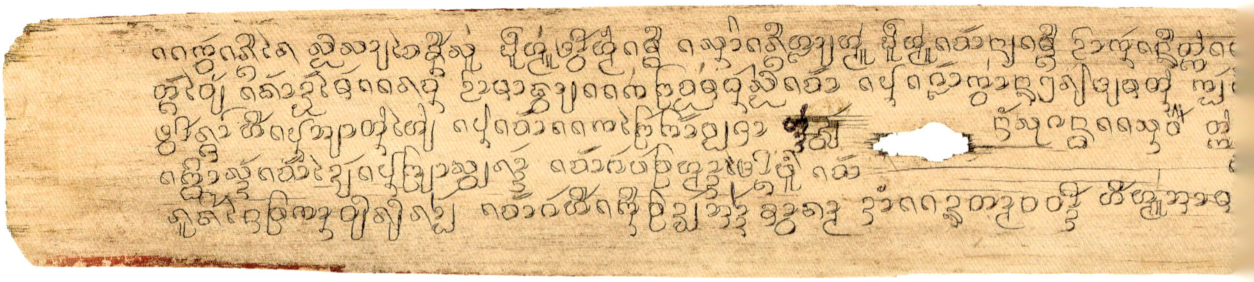

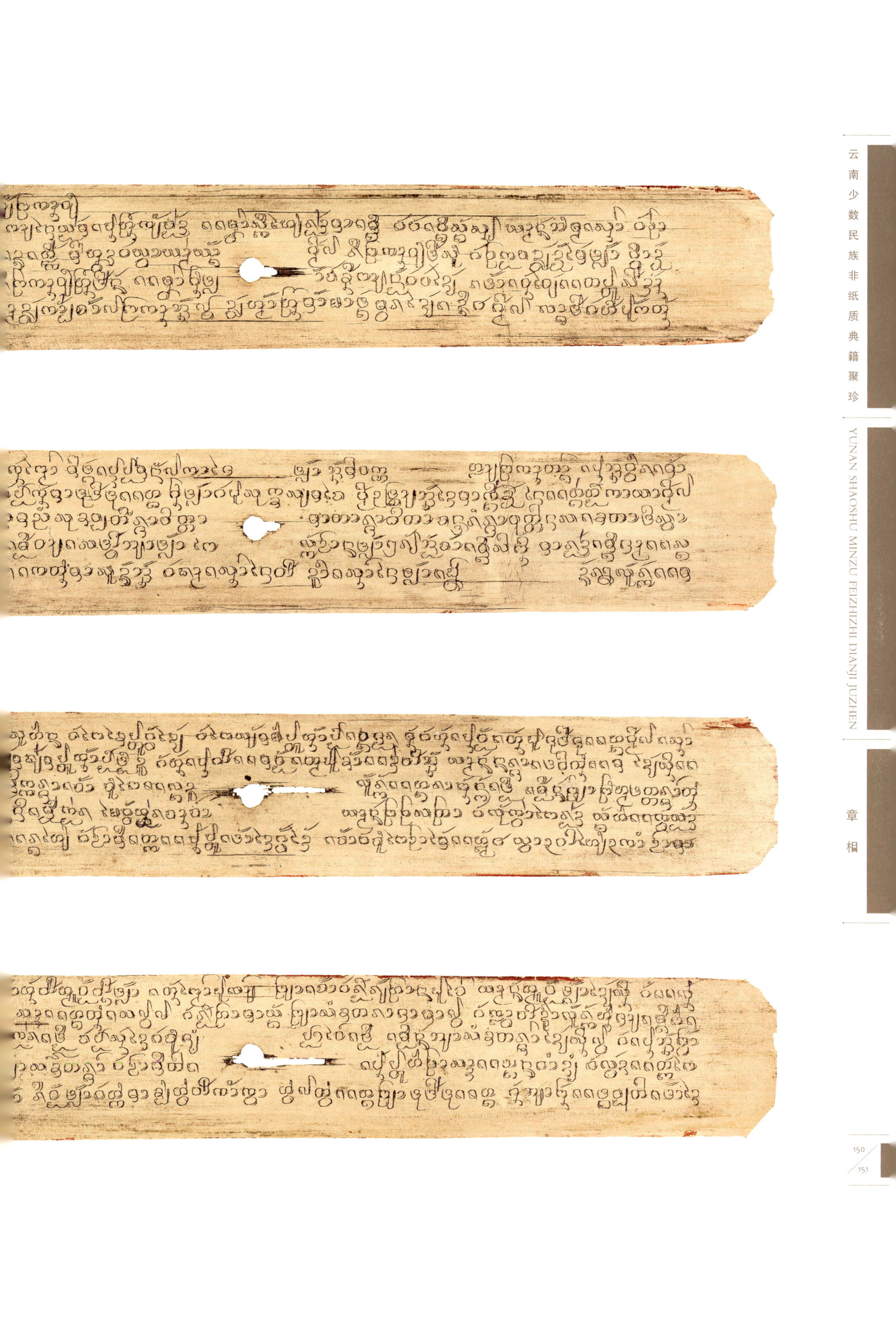

章相

章相

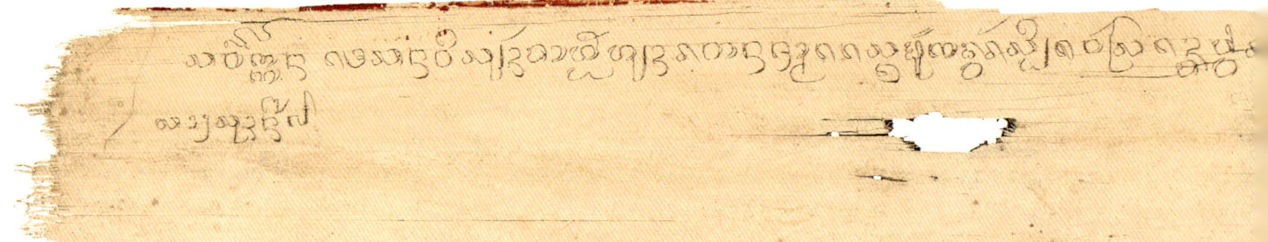

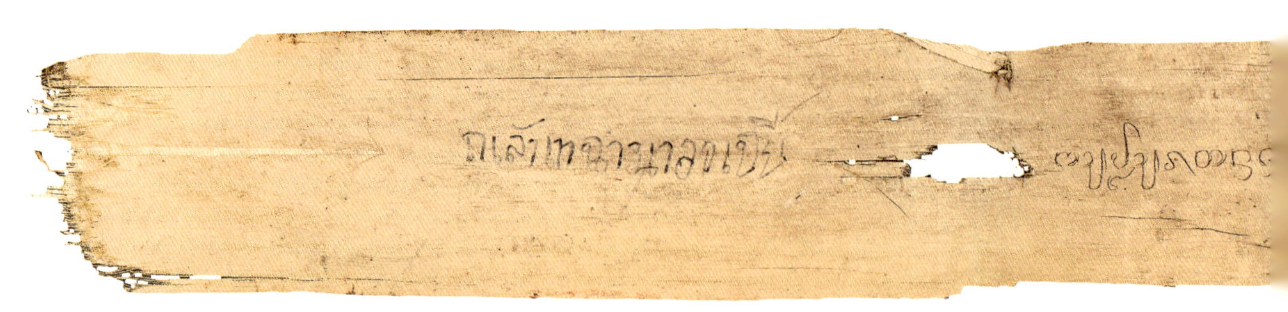

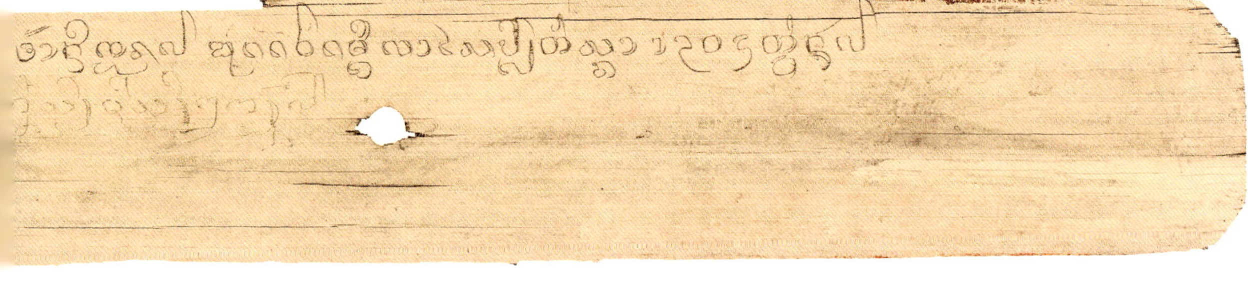

第十一册

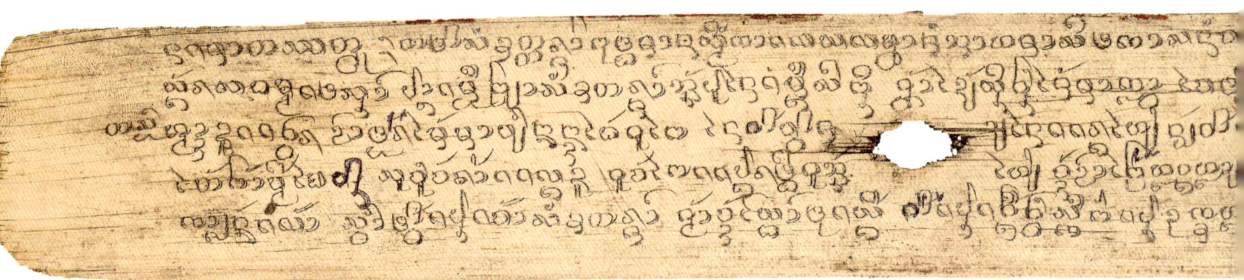

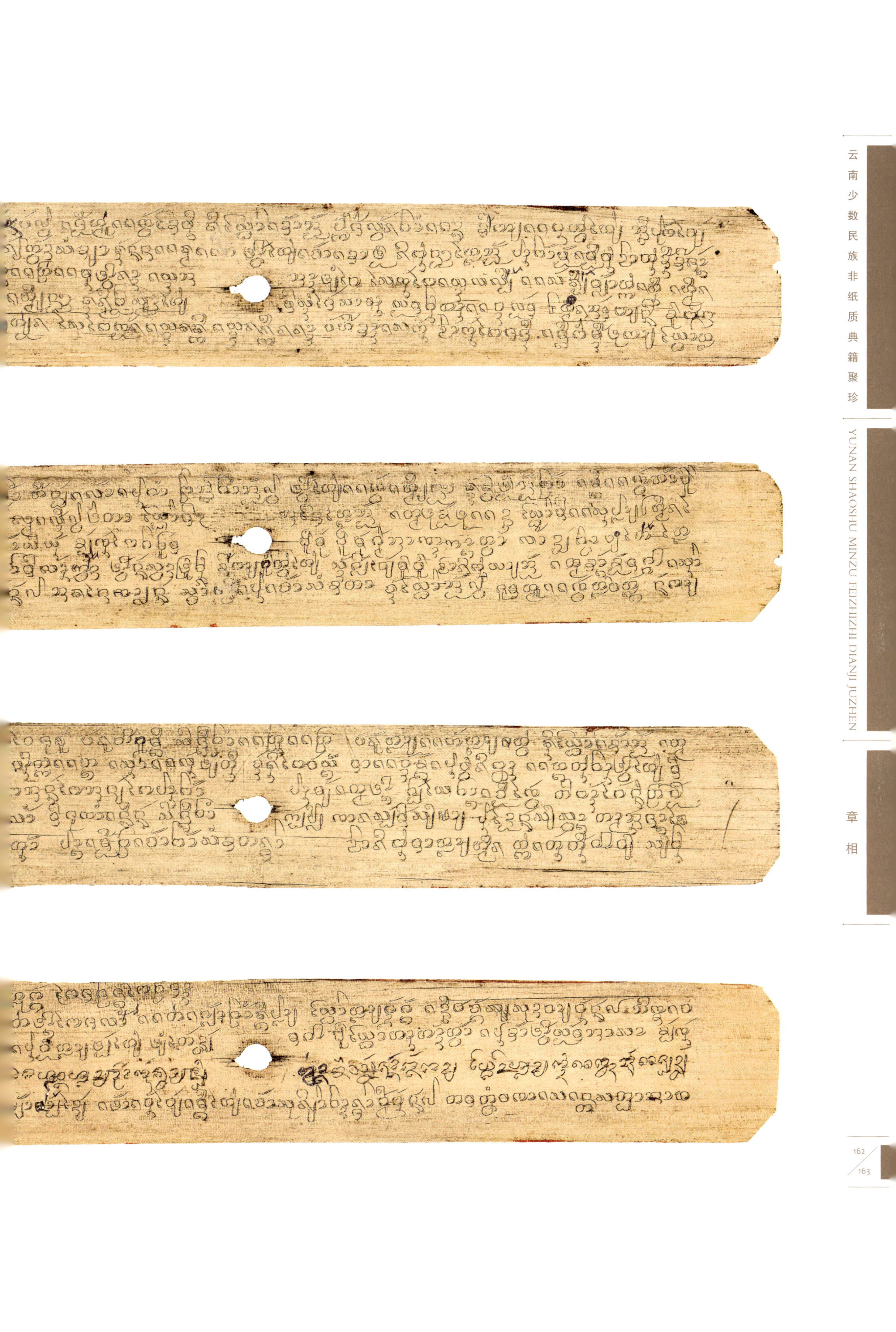

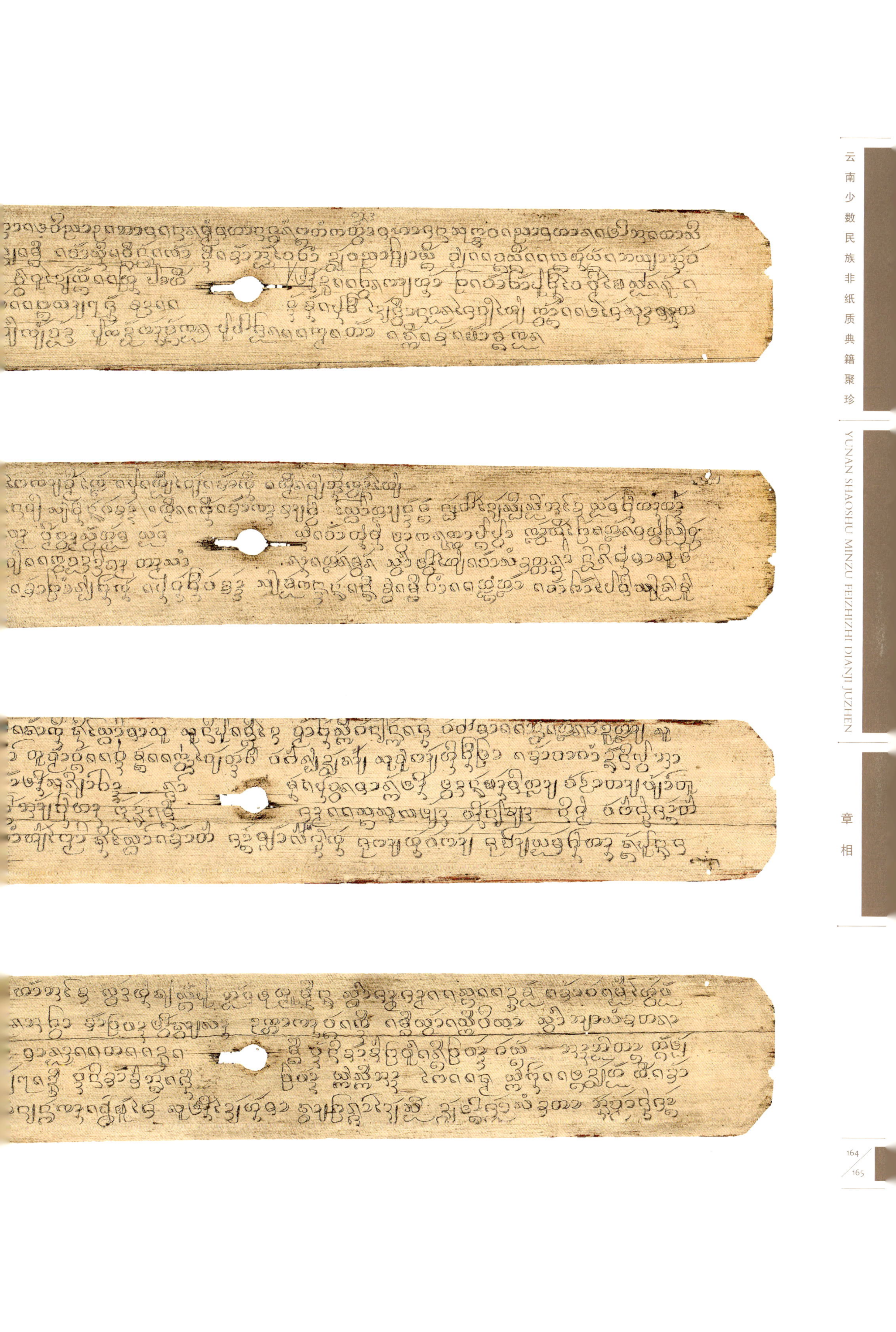

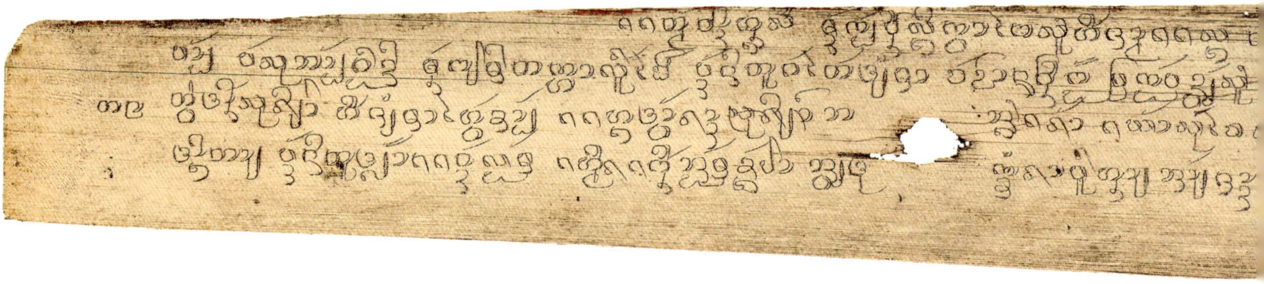

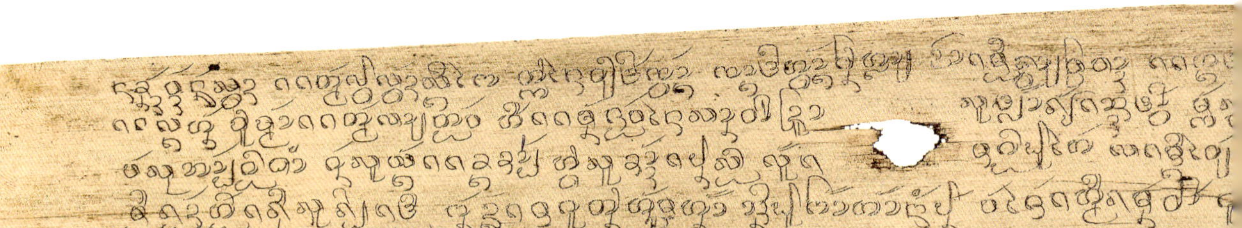

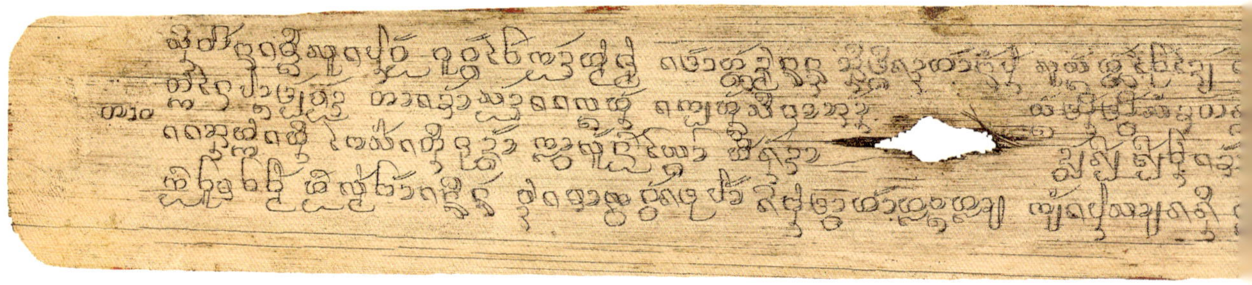

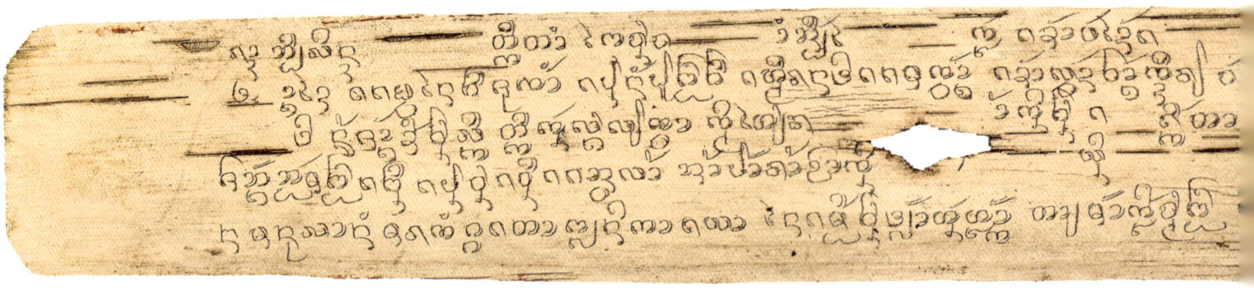

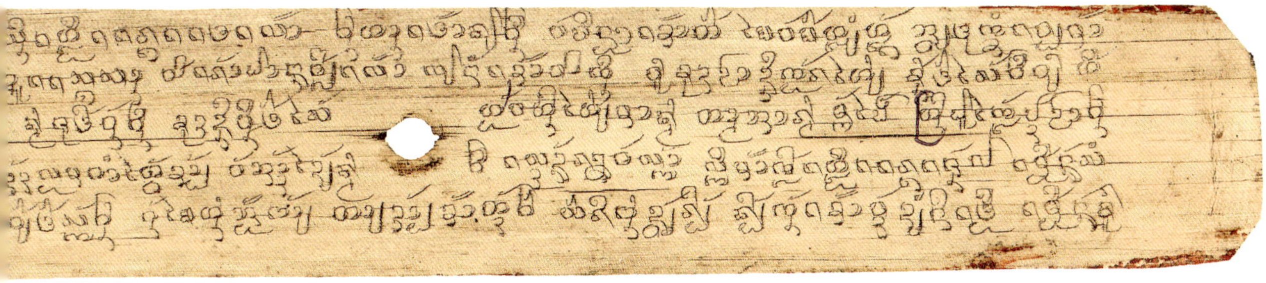

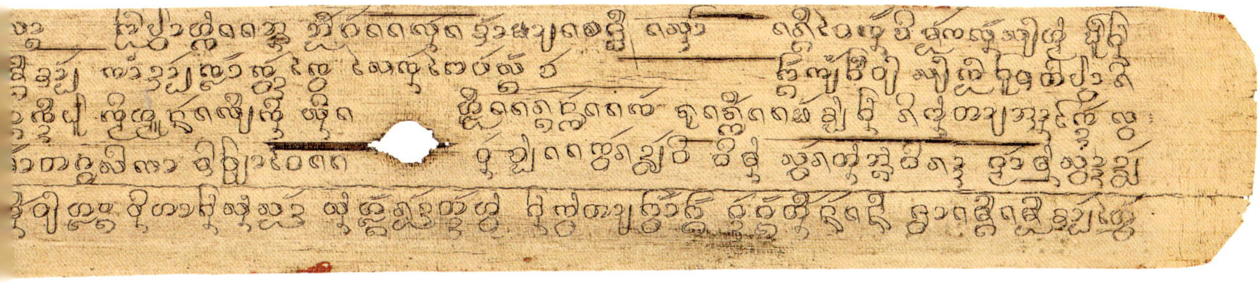

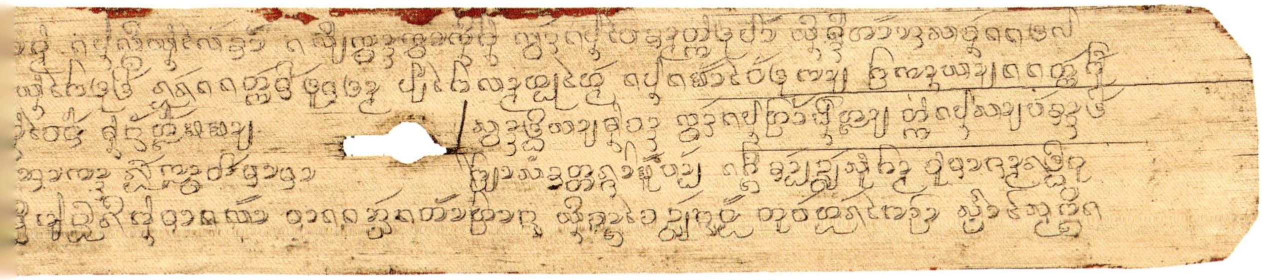

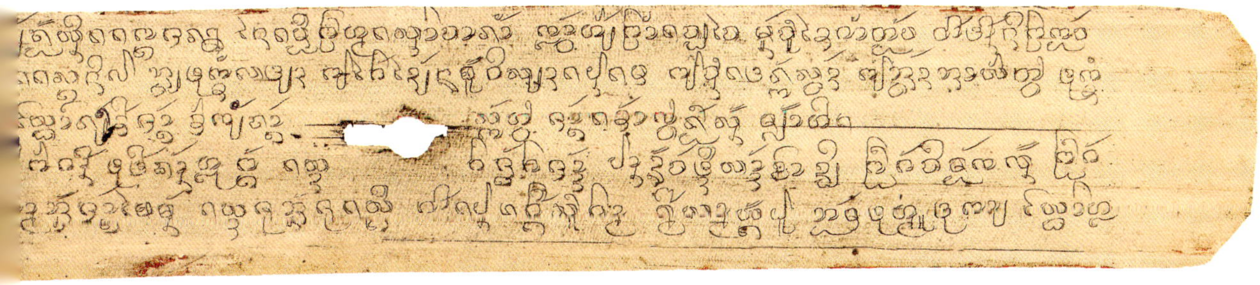

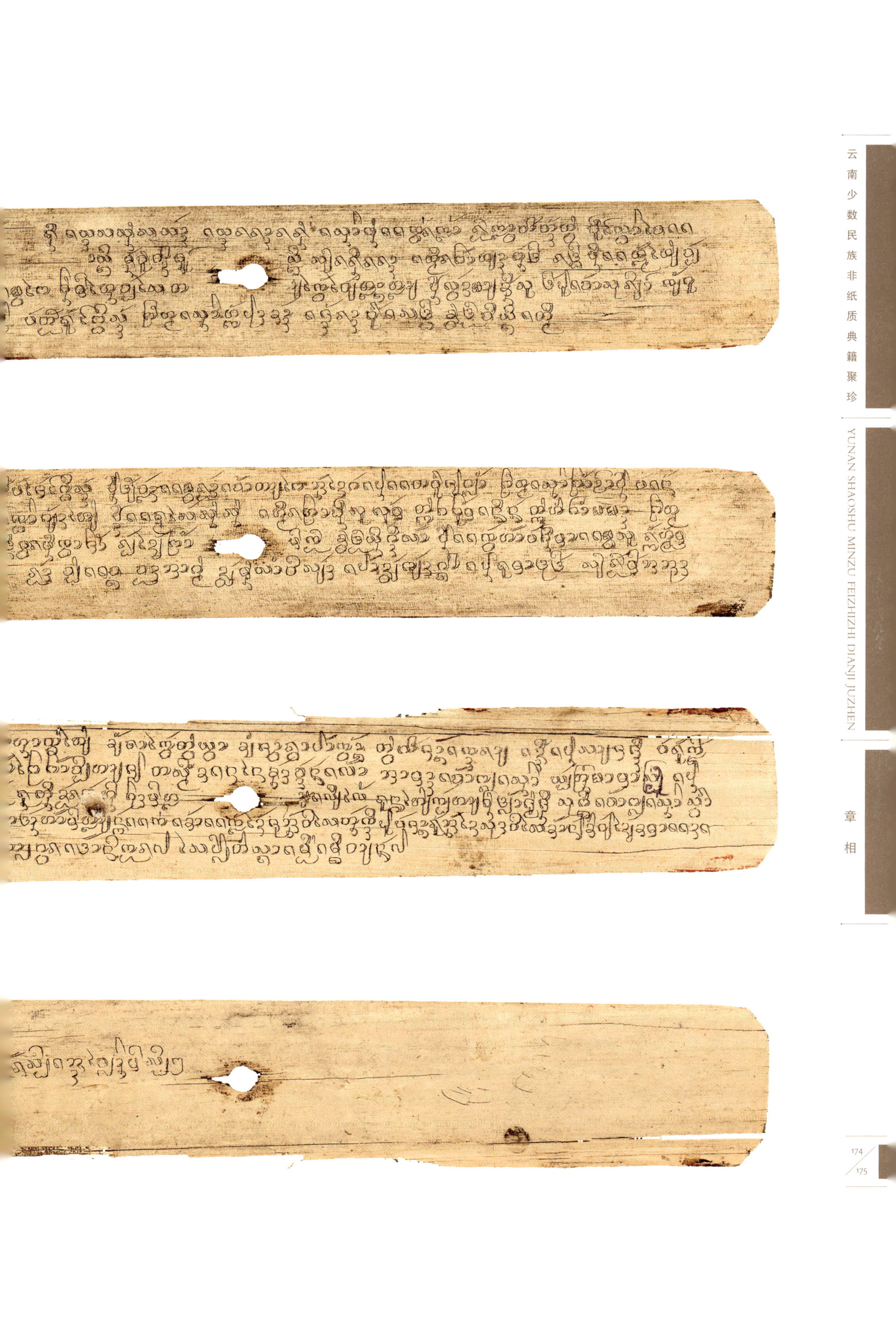

第十二册

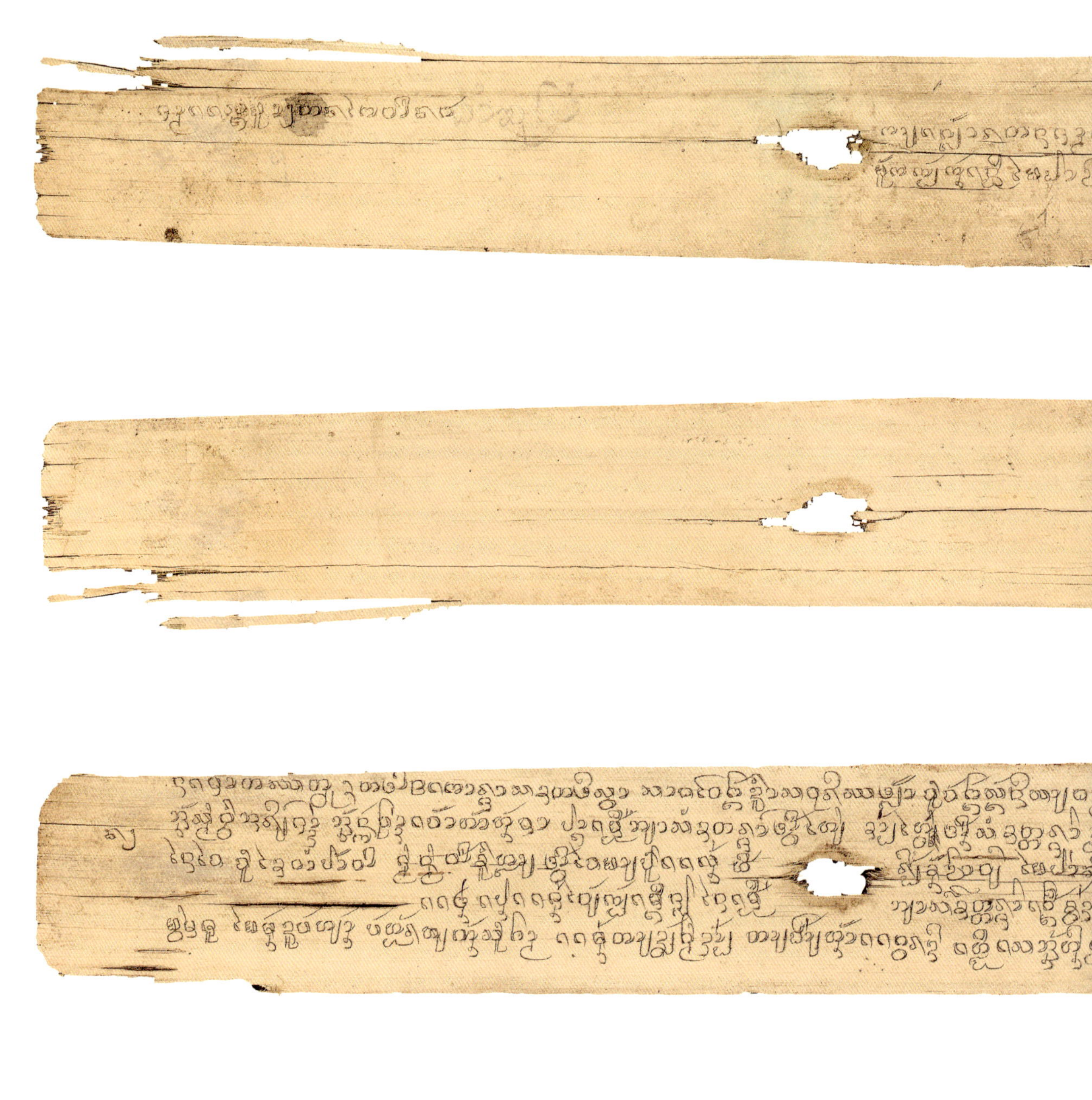

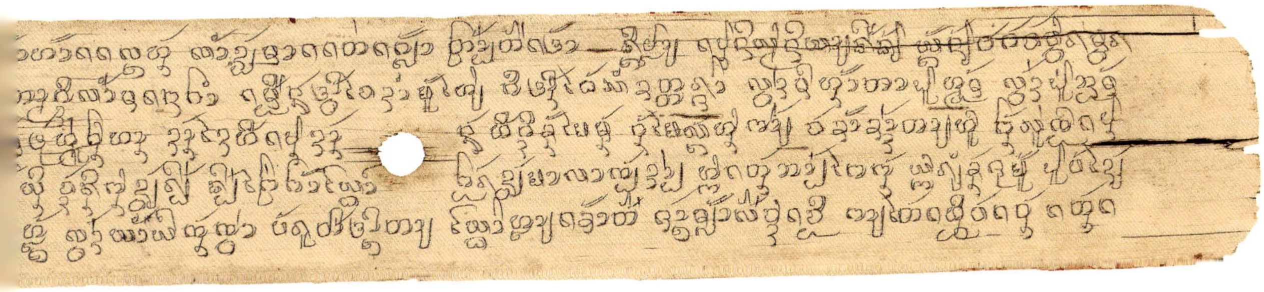

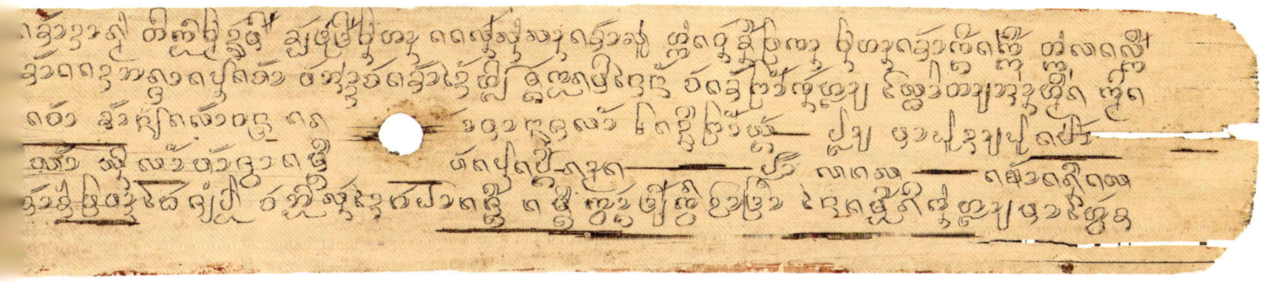

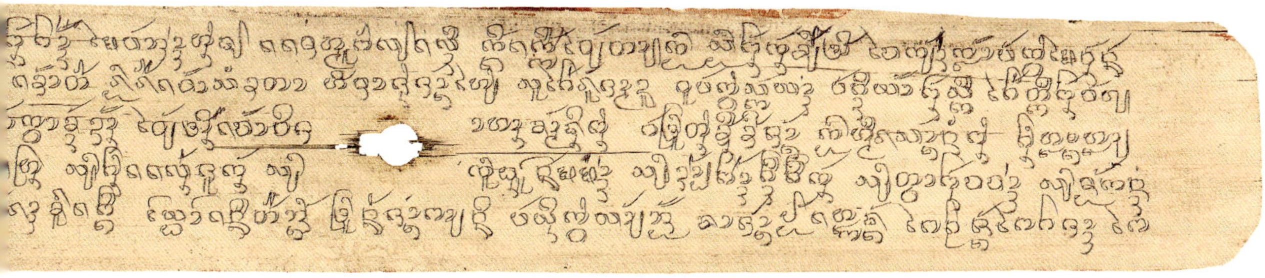

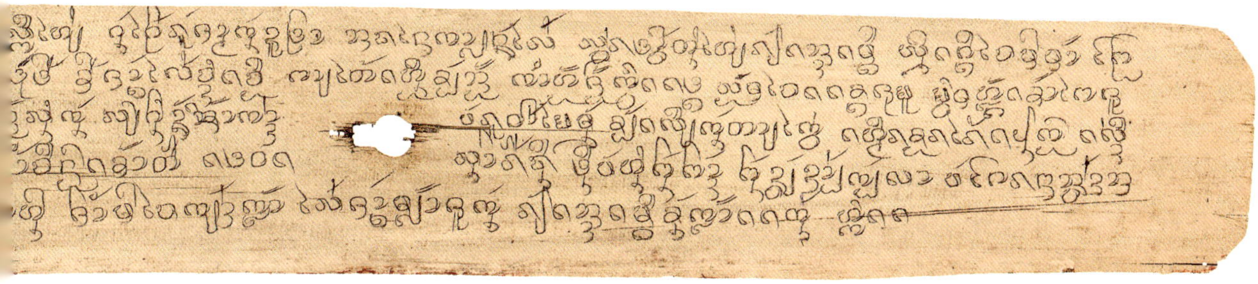

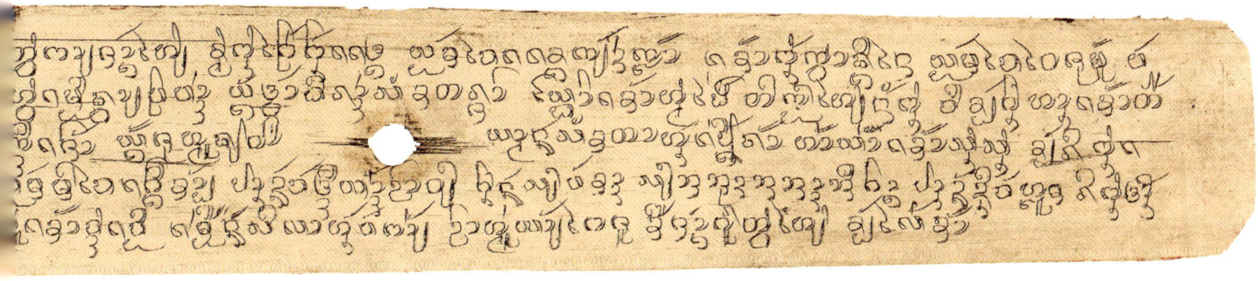

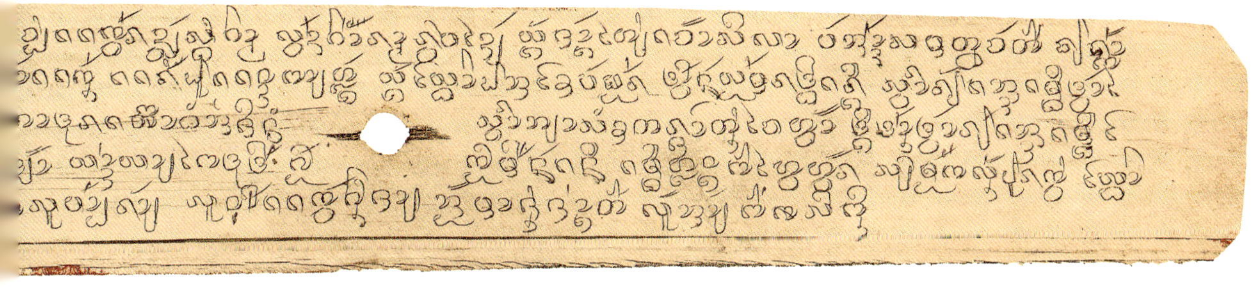

章相

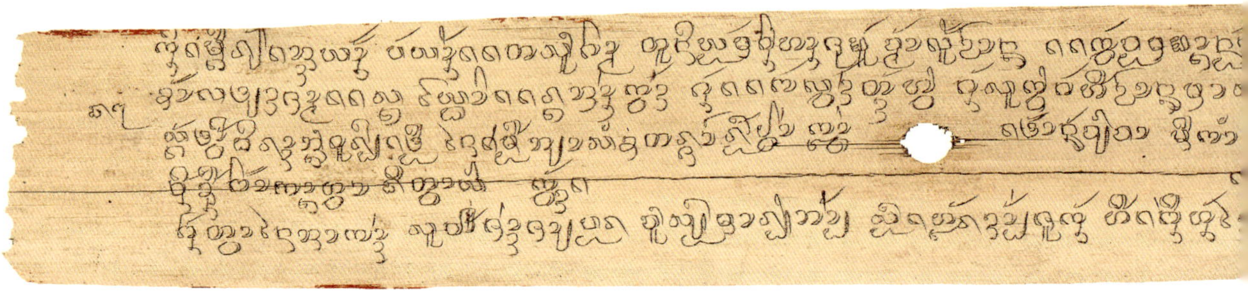

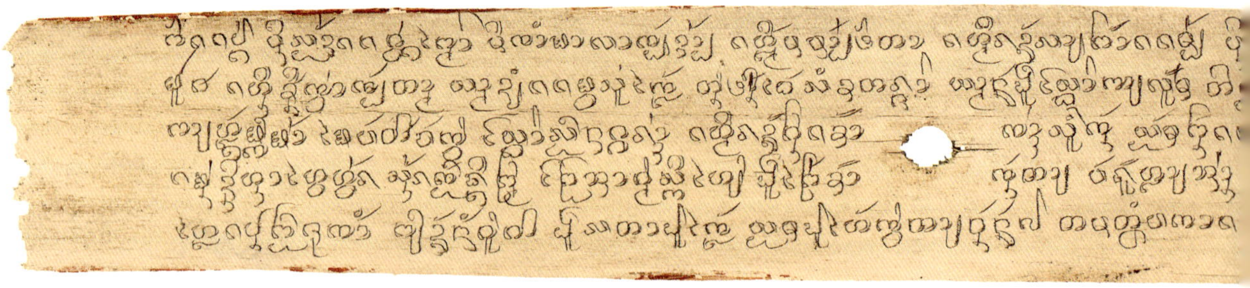

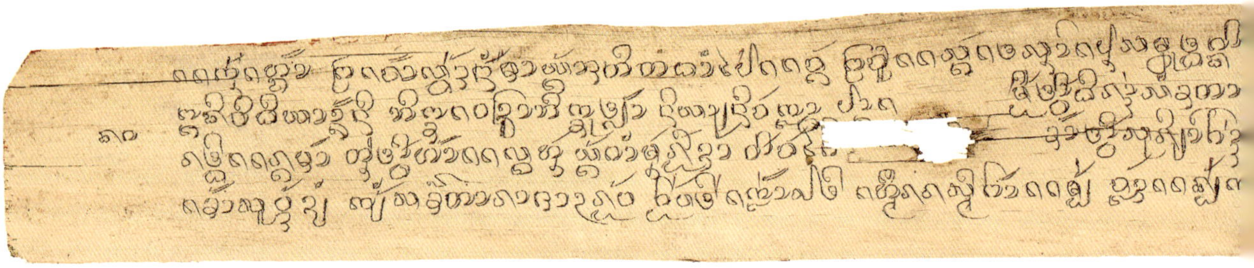

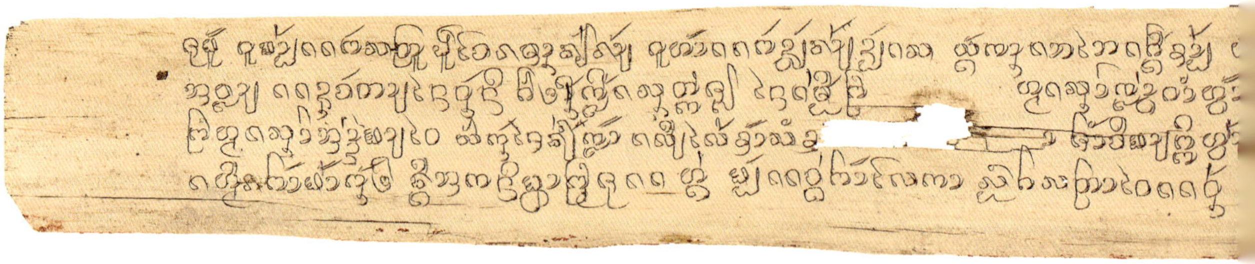

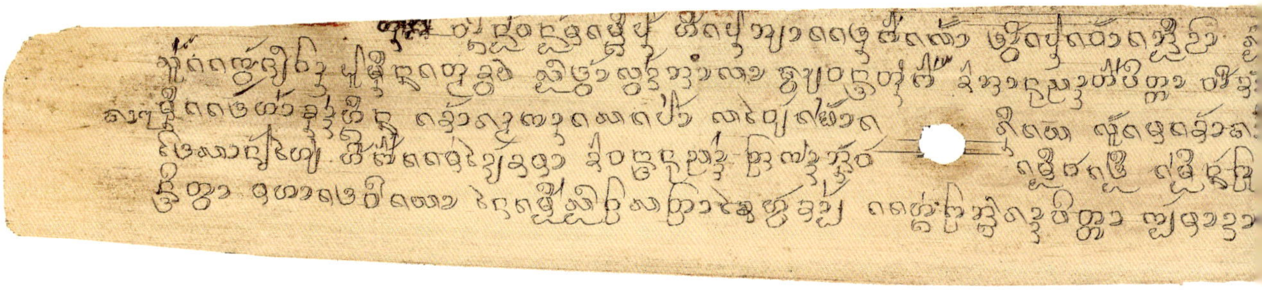

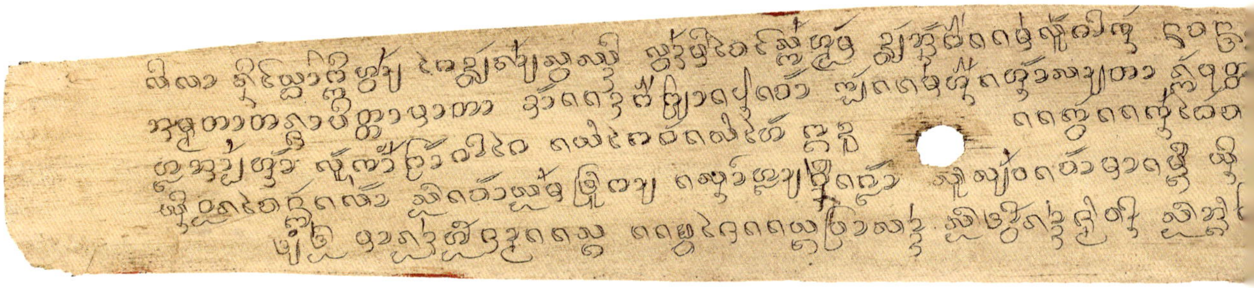

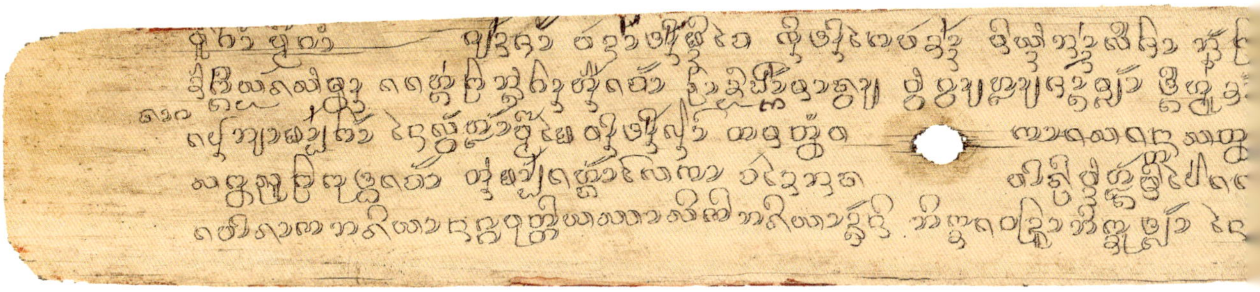

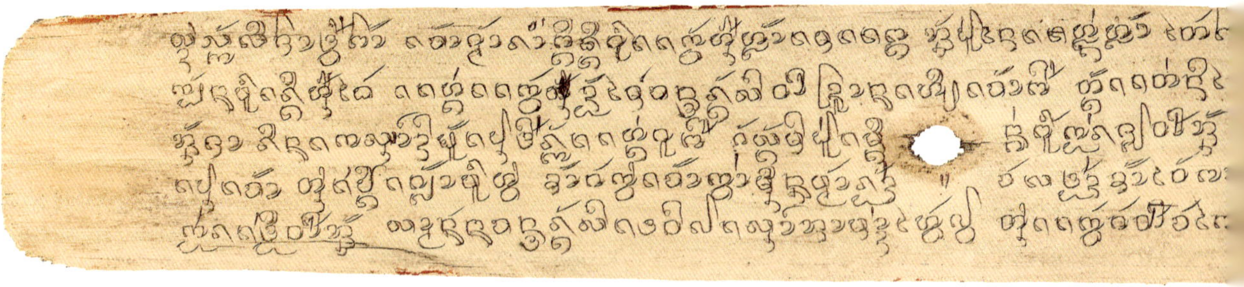

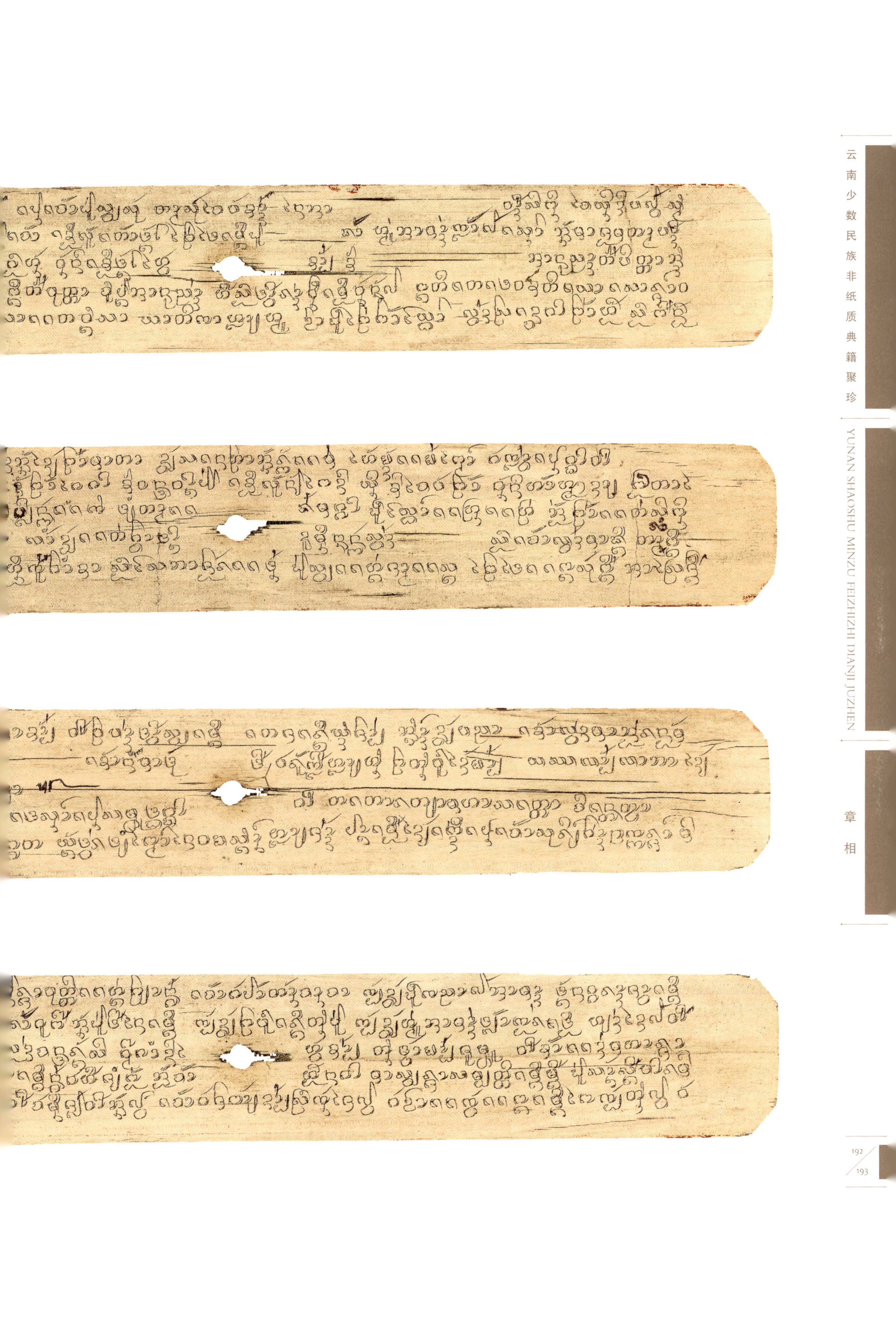

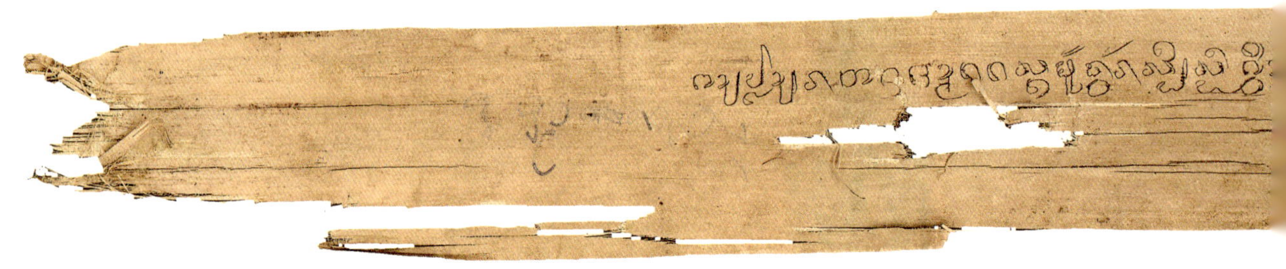

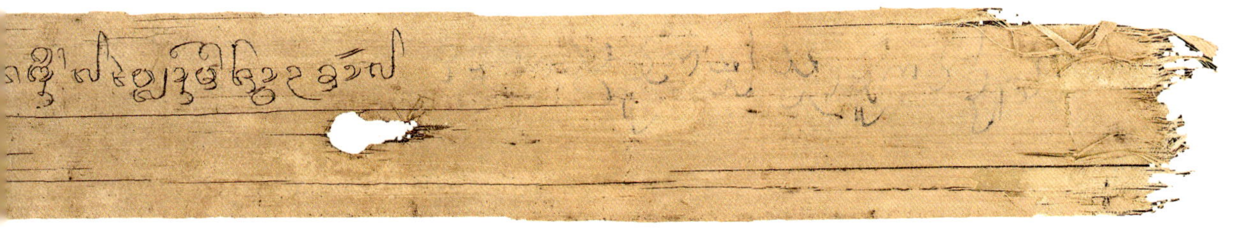

YUNNAN SHAOSHU MINZU
FEIZHIZHI DIANJI JUZHEN

云南少数民族非纸质典籍聚珍

桑玛雅帕拉

《桑玛雅帕拉》，傣族佛经故事，流传于西双版纳傣族地区，9册，206叶。刻本，佚名撰。梵夹装。开本高5.2厘米，广49.5厘米。每叶5行，行74字。保存完好。今藏于云南省少数民族古籍整理出版规划办公室。内容讲述了一位帕雅在孩子出生前请国师给孩子算卦，得知他们将会得到一位王子，但日后这位王子会弑君杀父。然而帕雅不信，坚持让王后生下孩子。孩子出生后，取名阿嘎达先塔鲁，帕雅虽对王子十分疼爱，但还是将他交给一个叫提婆达多的人抚养。长大后的王子经不住提婆达多的蛊惑，杀害了自己的父王，应验了多年前的预言。其父死后不久，王子也有了自己的儿子。一天，他在逗儿子玩耍时，母亲告诉他，“你父亲在世时，也像你疼爱自己的儿子那样疼爱你。”王子听了母亲的话后，为自己犯下的过错悔恨不已。为了赎罪，王子出家当了和尚。待他还俗回来后，成了一代明君。

佛经类故事在西双版纳傣族地区流传的贝叶经中占有一定的比重。傣族文化受南传上座部佛教影响深远，傣族社会的民间习俗也逐渐佛教化，傣族民众从小到大，从生到死几乎都与佛教有关。例如家里一般会设有佛龛或佛坛供奉佛像，每天早晚诵经礼佛；又如小孩一出生，家长便会请高僧长老、出过家的老人、波章等为婴儿取名字，取的名字多数跟佛经佛法有关；再如生日那天，清晨要早起准备好丰盛的食物和鲜花及供品前往寺院，供养僧团，诵经礼佛，受戒祈福，请僧人为其拴线祝福，清扫寺院和佛塔等。有人就连要出远门或到外地工作学习的前几天，都要去佛寺请高僧长老拴线祝福，外出归来也要举行相关仪式。

以佛经故事为代表的贝叶经，除丰富了傣族民间文学的内容和形式之外，更使得佛教思想浸润傣族民众的社会行为、观念意识及伦理道德等方方面面。每逢赕佛或传统节日，高僧或长老会在佛殿里高声诵读佛本生经，在耳濡目染中傣族民众不仅熟记故事情节，佛理也渐渐深入内心。如以《桑玛雅帕拉》为代表的贝叶经，用朴实的经文讲述故事，告诫人们宽容、慈悲等佛教原始教义和精神内涵，倡导民众通过佛事活动实践个人修行、消解自身各种业报。这些蕴含了傣族社会伦理道德、乡规民约、法律法规等内容的佛经故事，将南传上座部佛教文化和傣族传统文化融合、发展，丰富了傣族传统文化的内涵。

以贝叶经为主要传承内容和载体的傣族贝叶文化具有其特殊的自然、社会生境，在不断的发展融合过程中，逐渐成为傣族社会一个完整而独特的文化体系。以贝叶经为核心的傣族贝叶文化不仅是傣民族的优秀传统文化，也是我国多元文化中的一个重要组成部分。贝叶文化不仅存在于我国傣族地区，在东南亚、南亚各国都有，是一条联系各国的文化纽带，可作为东南亚同源民族国际互动交流的桥梁。我们应该从贝叶经所具有的历史、文化、生态、教育、经济及宗教等方面价值出发，推动民族文化的传承保护和创新交融，挖掘弘扬其中蕴含的民族团结进步思想，反映祖国统一、民族团结，体现各族人民共建家园、手足相亲、守望相助的内容。

桑玛雅帕拉

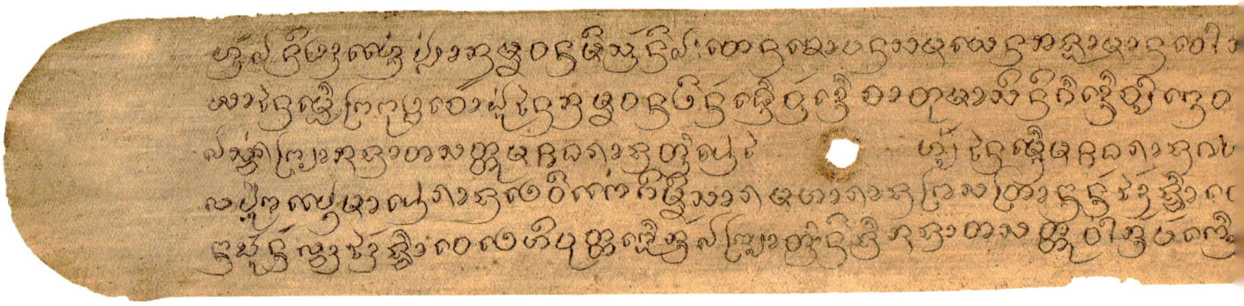

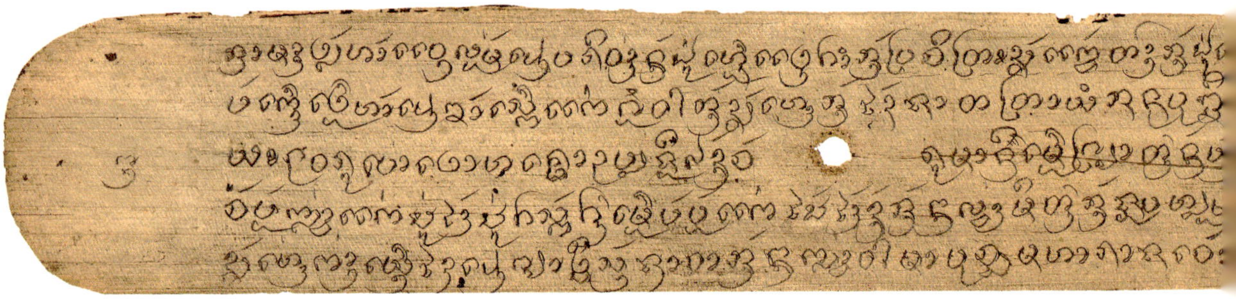

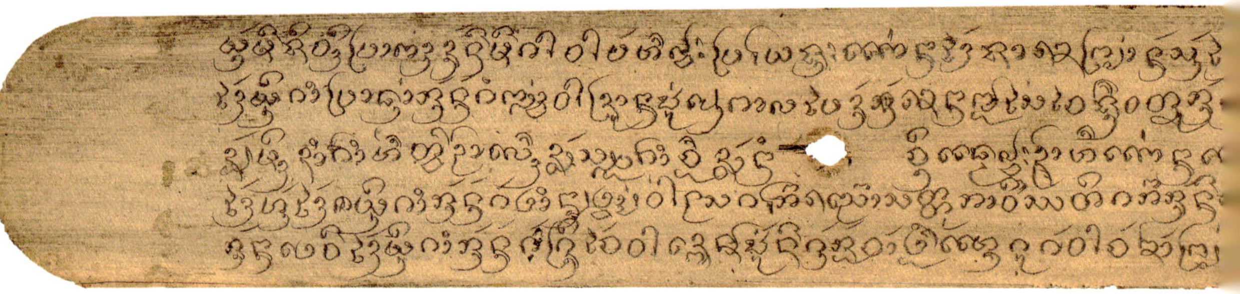

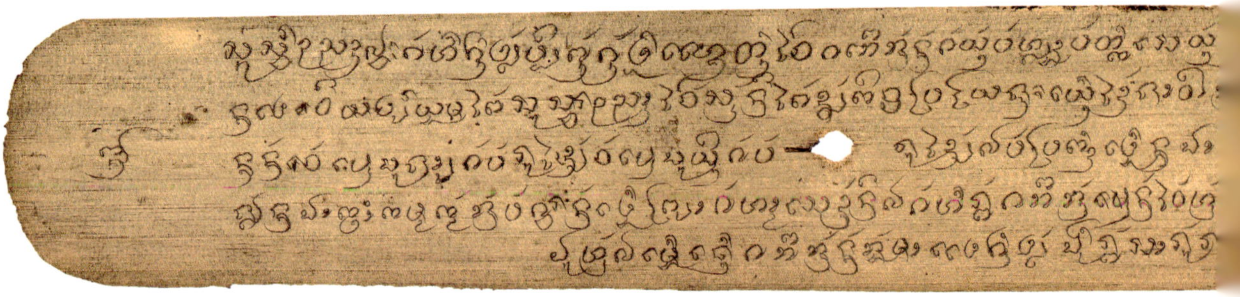

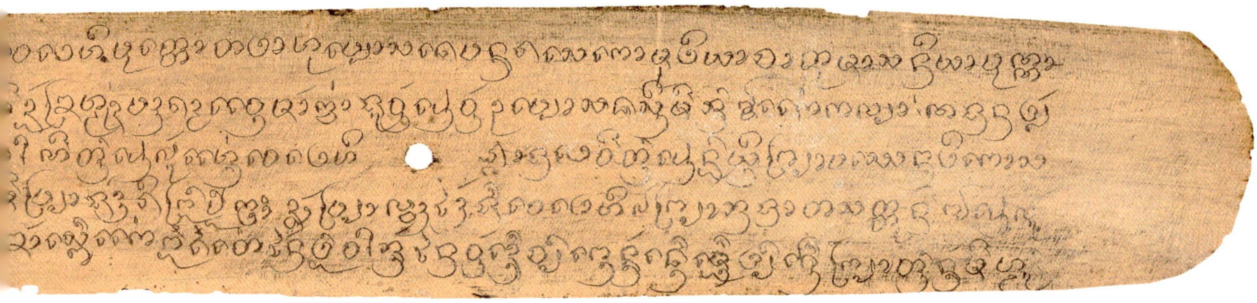

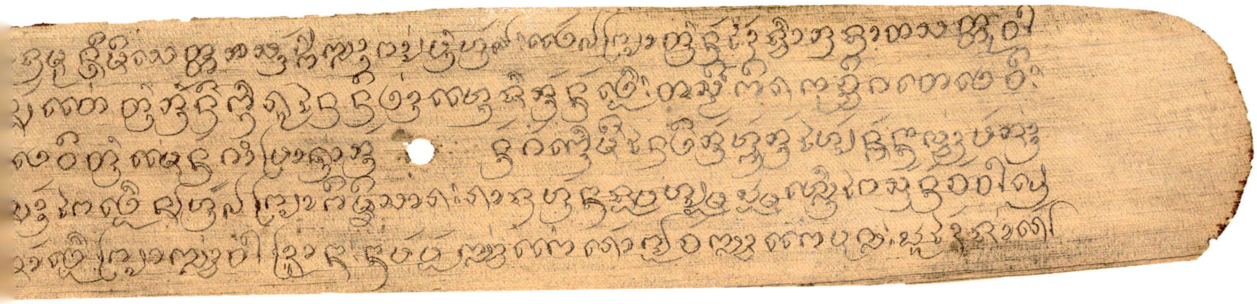

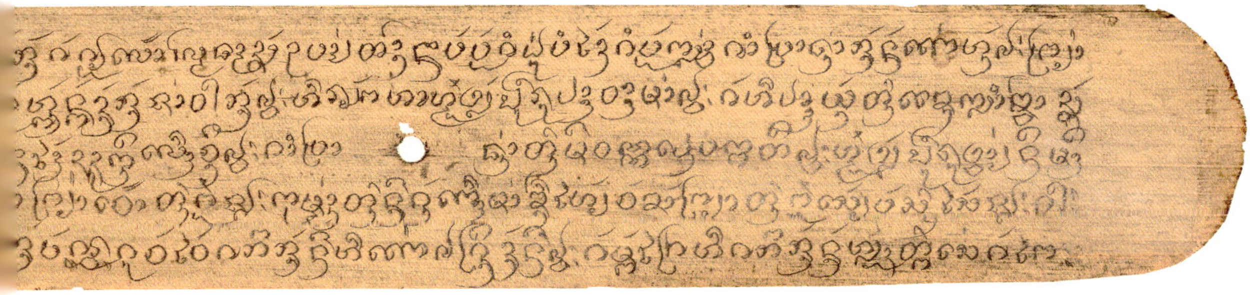

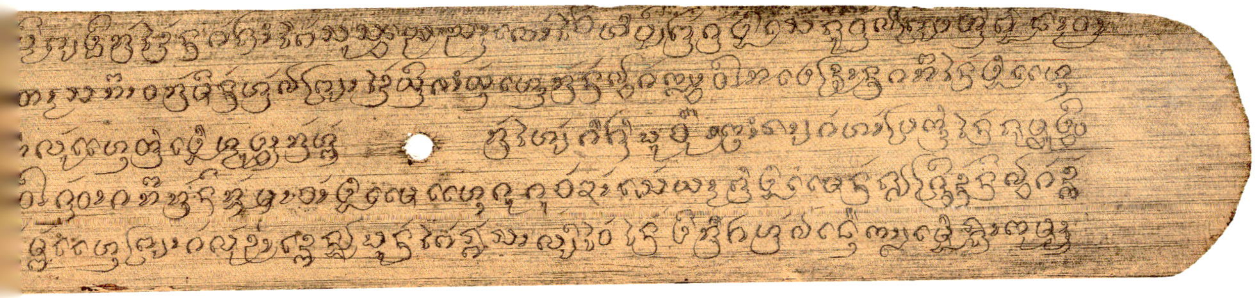

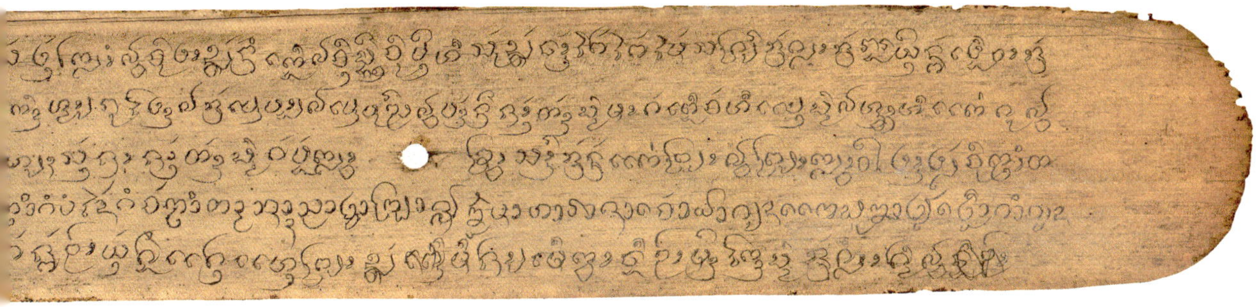

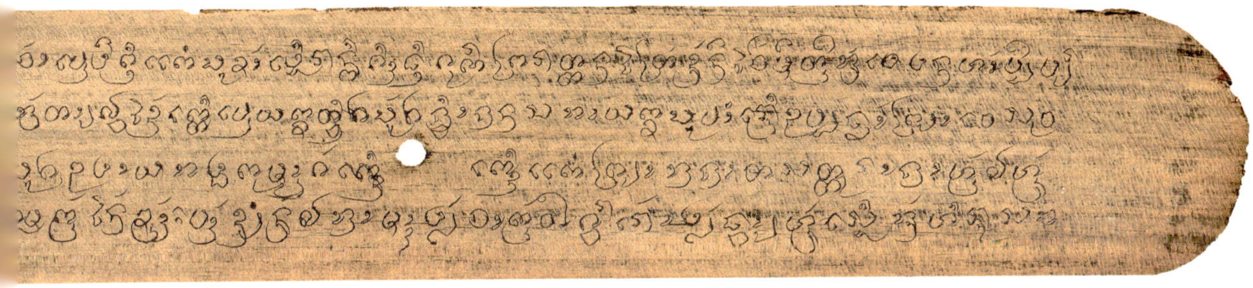

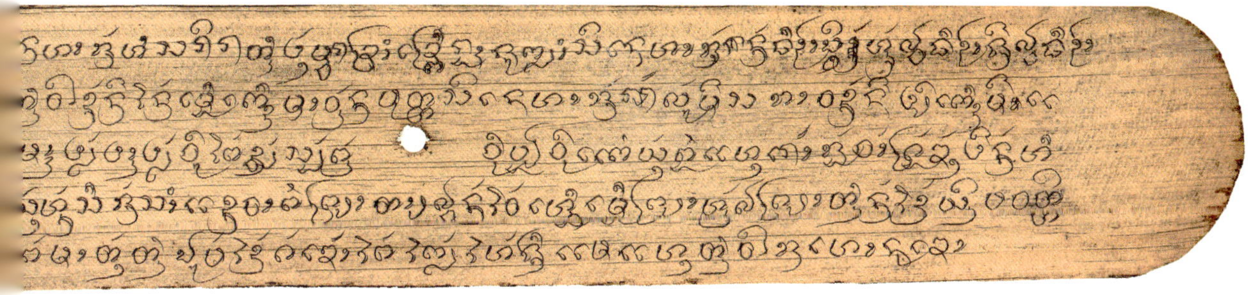

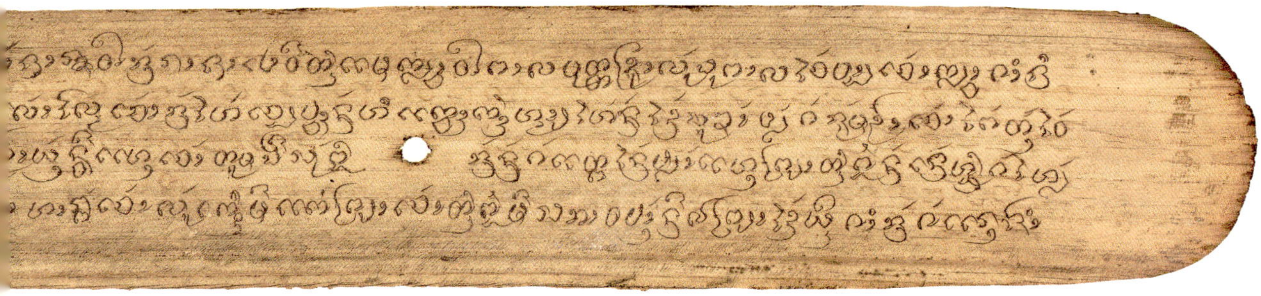

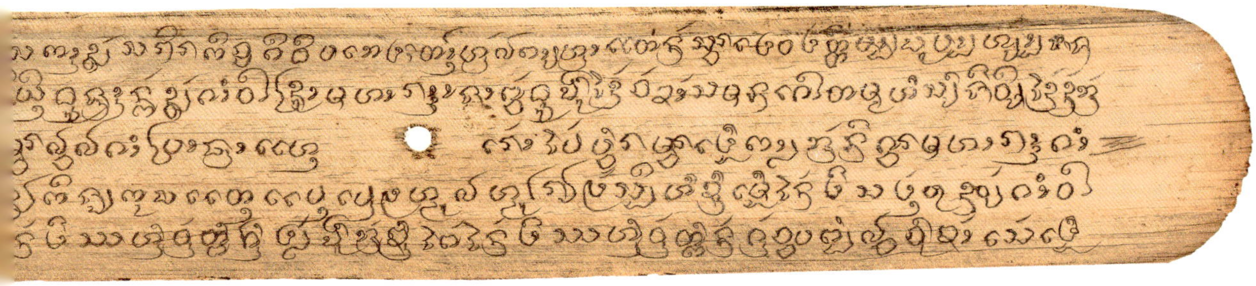

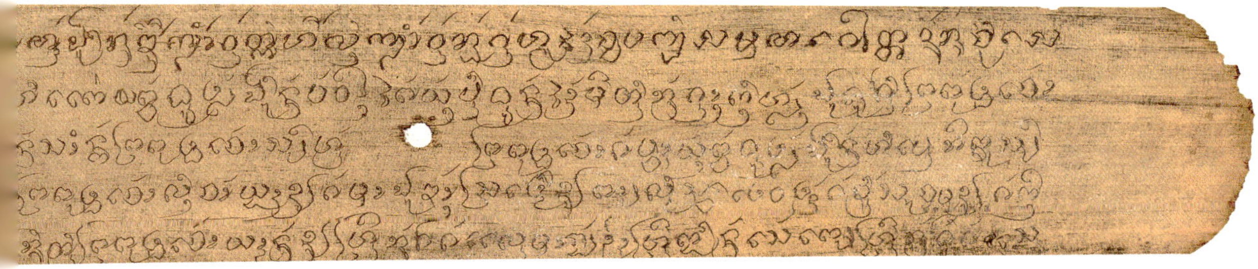

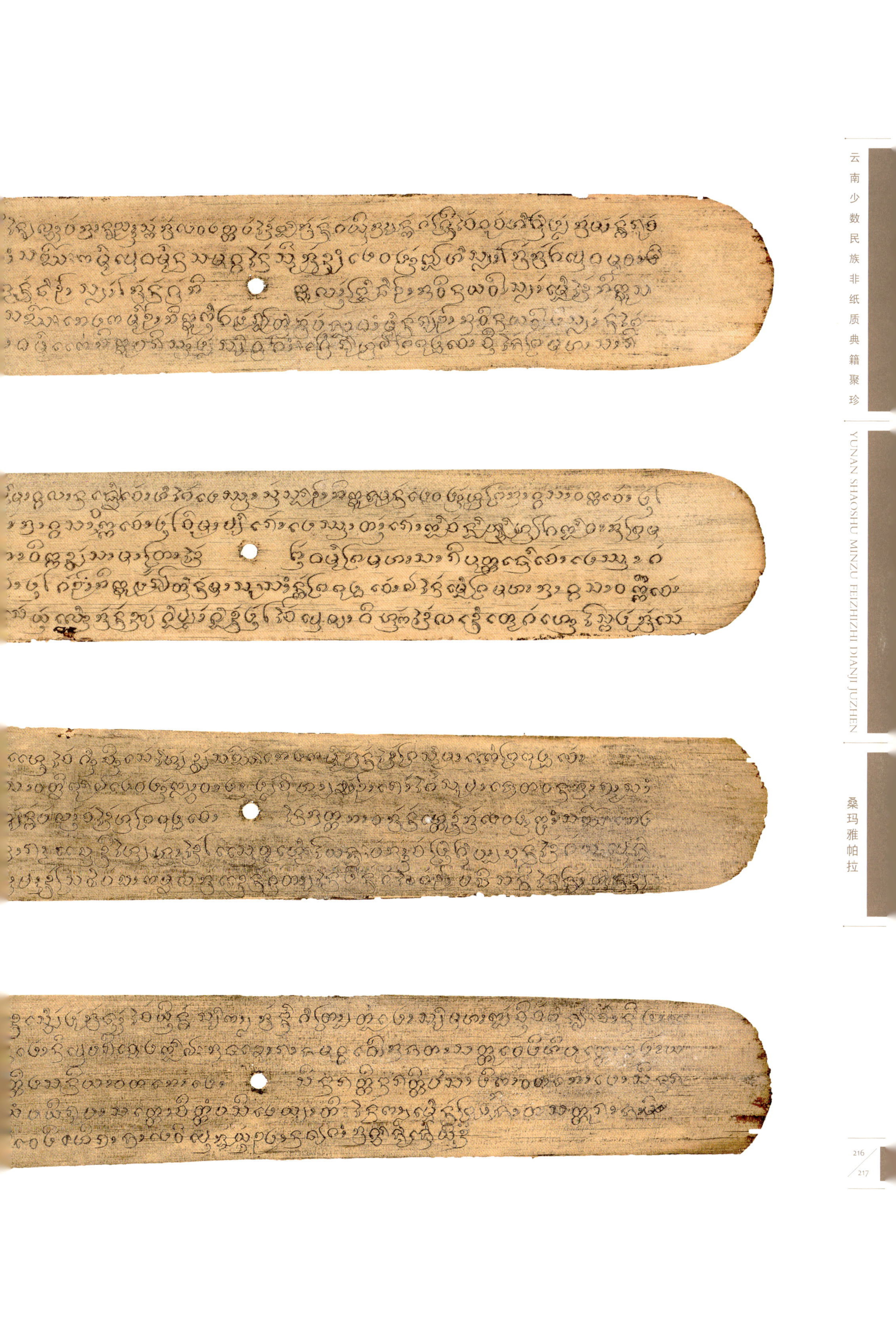

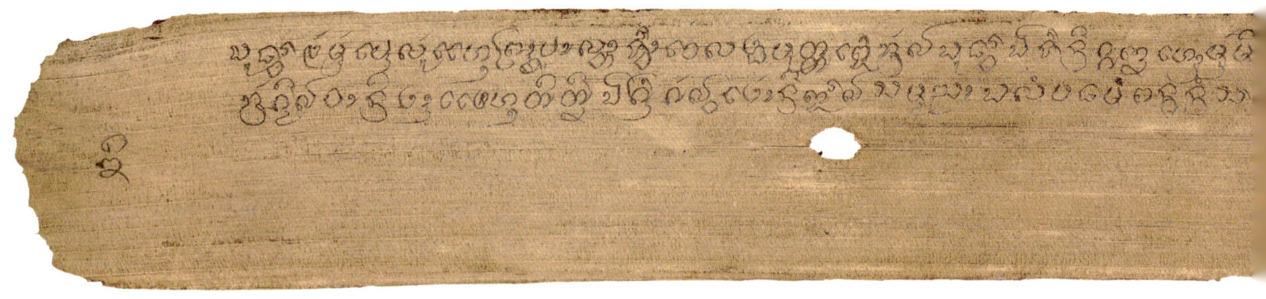

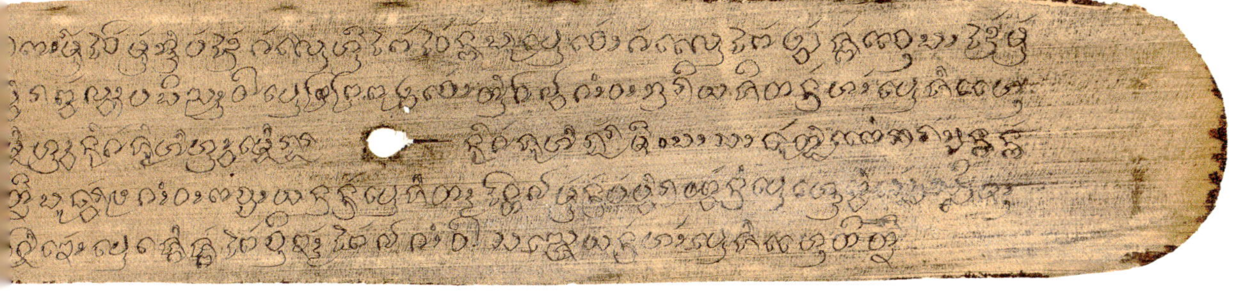

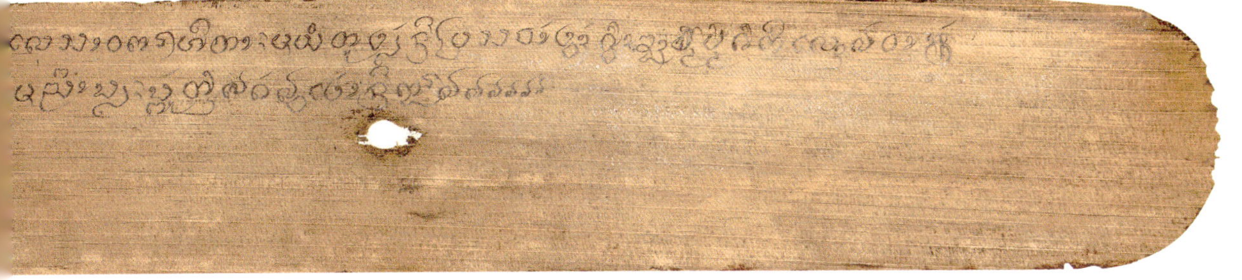

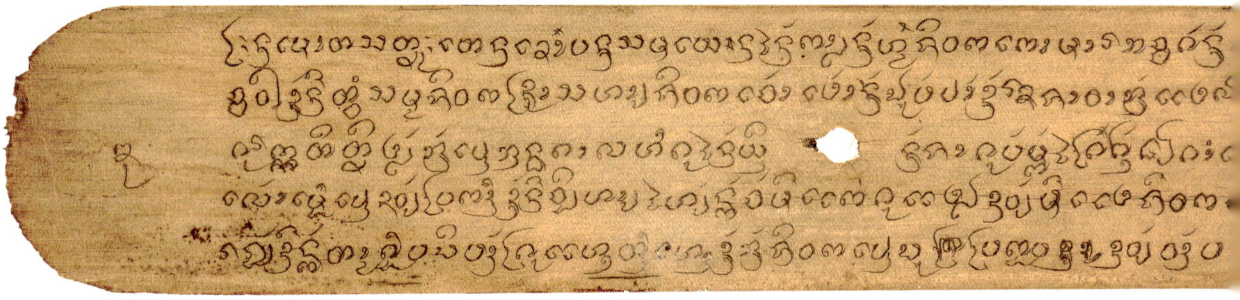

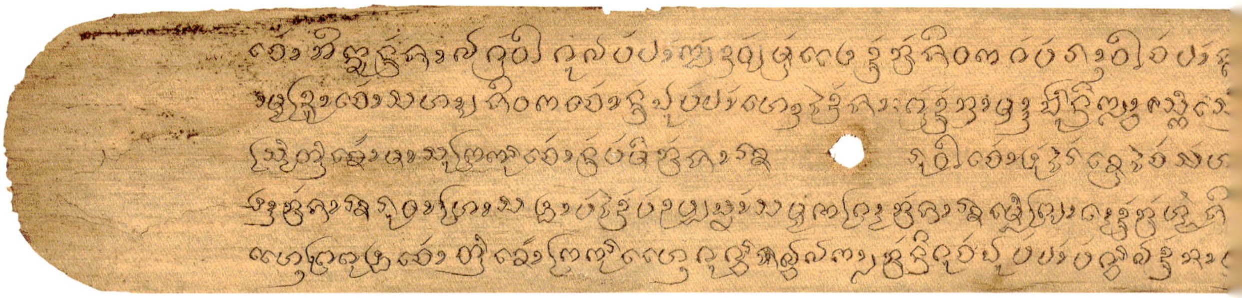

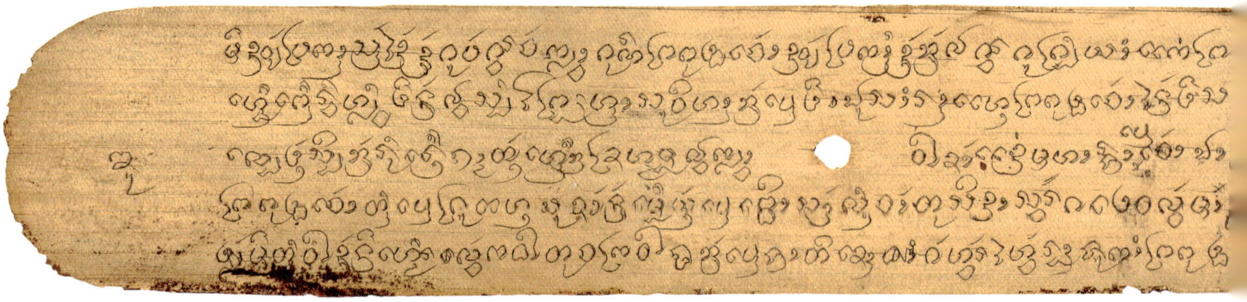

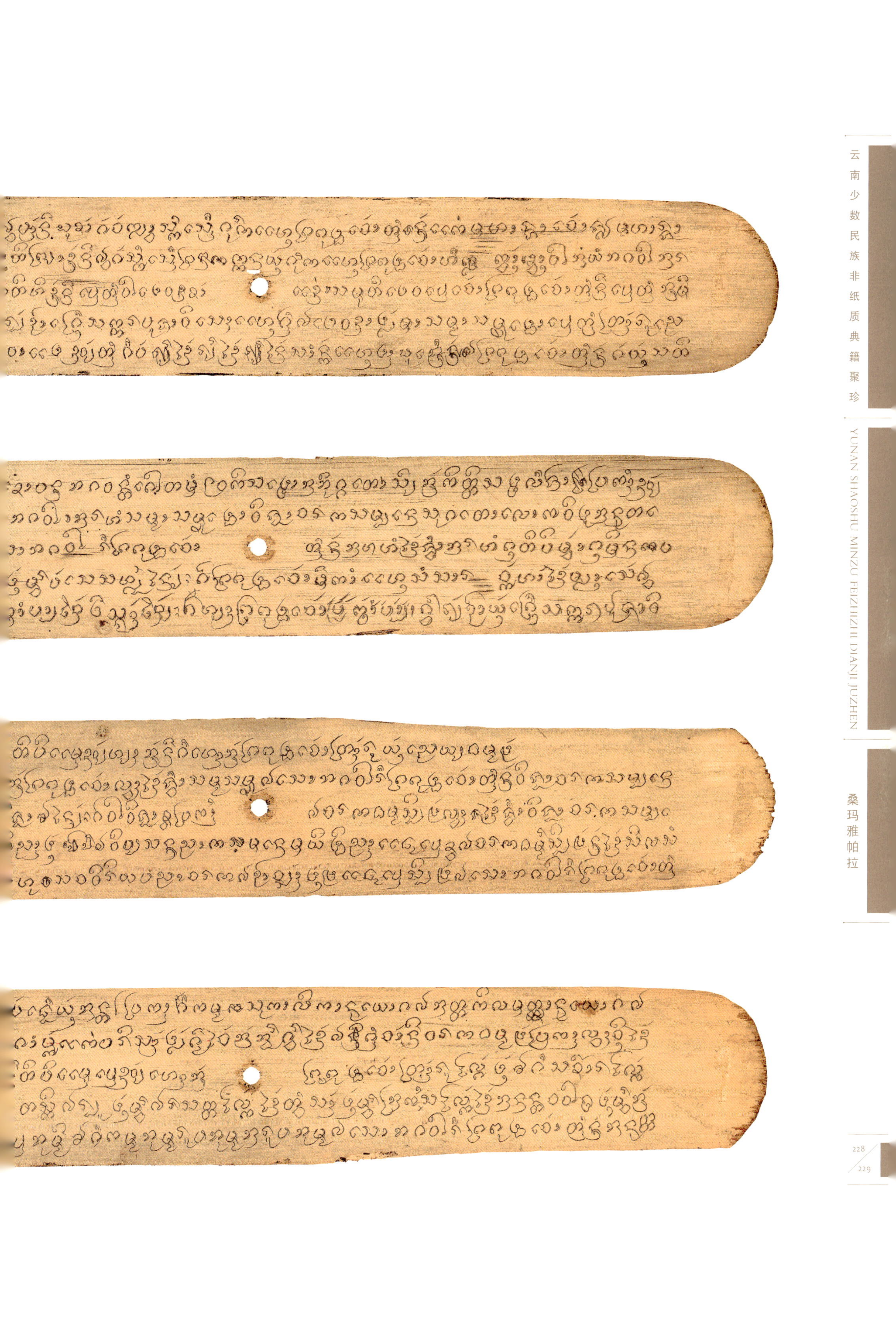

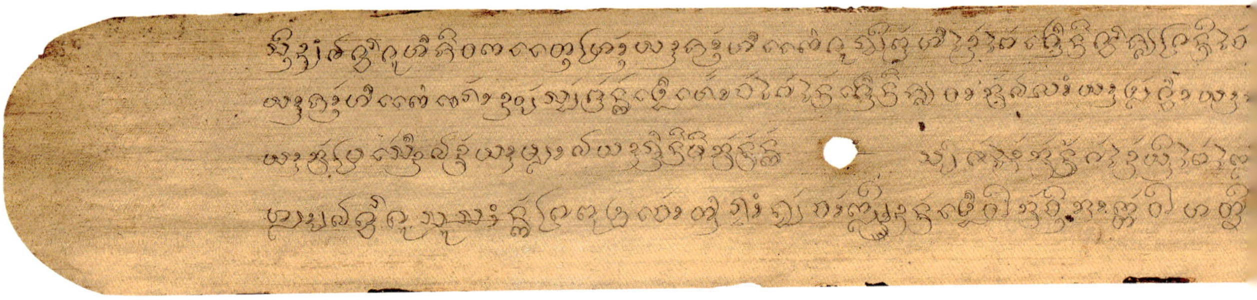

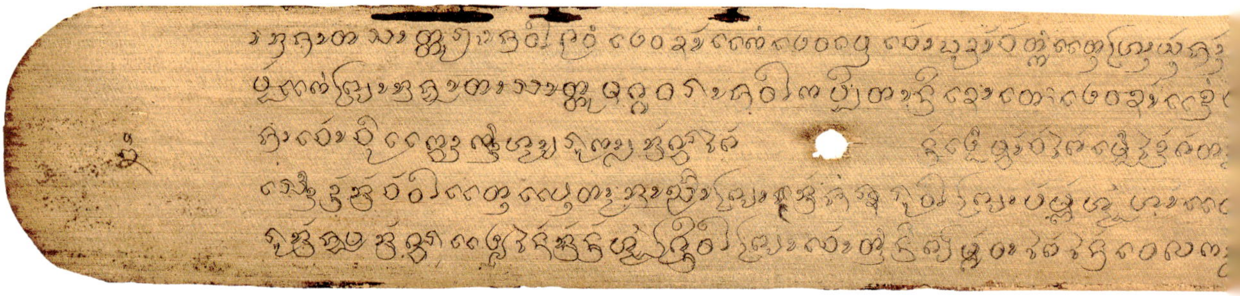

桑玛雅帕拉

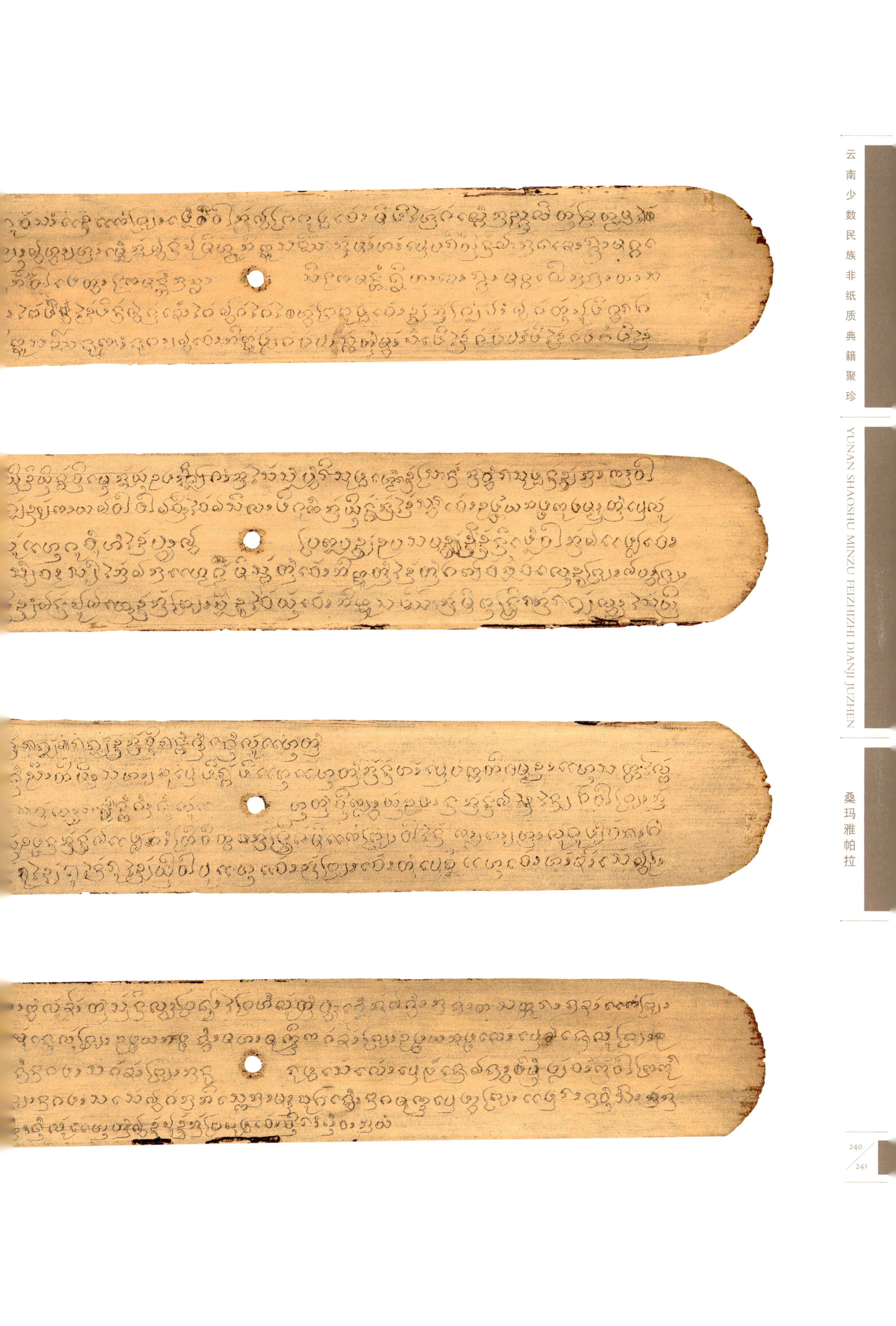

桑玛雅帕拉

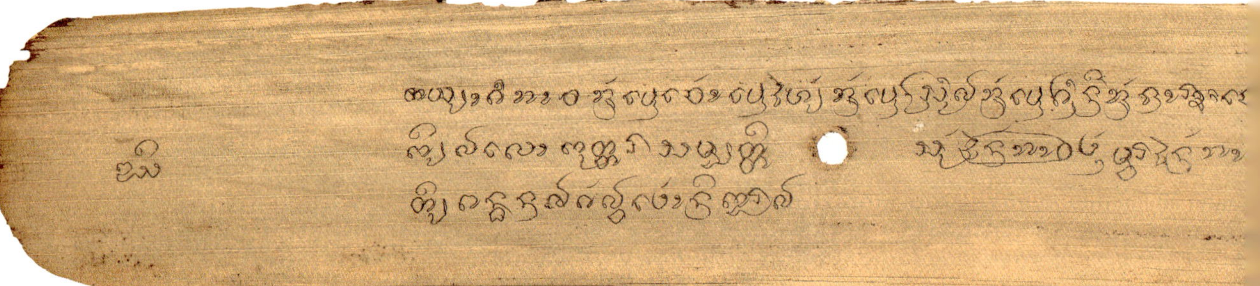

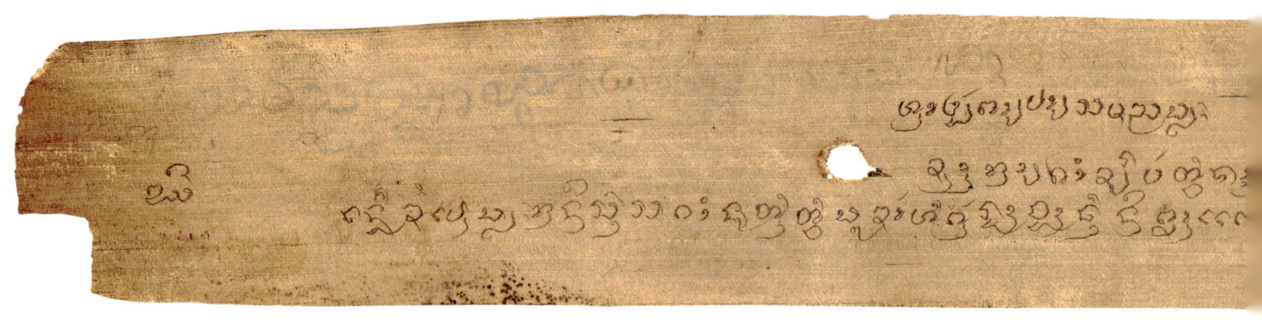

第三册

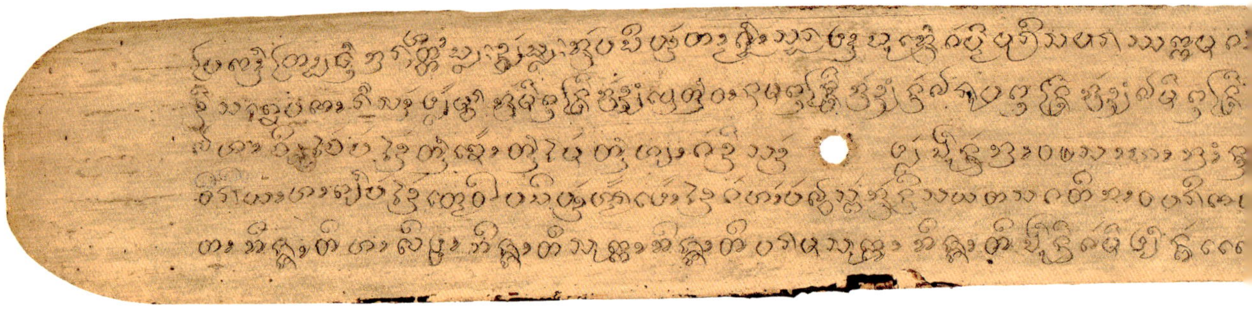

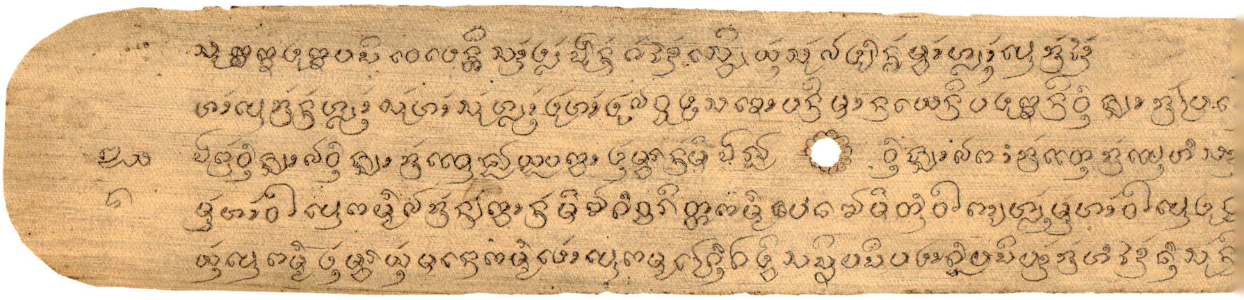

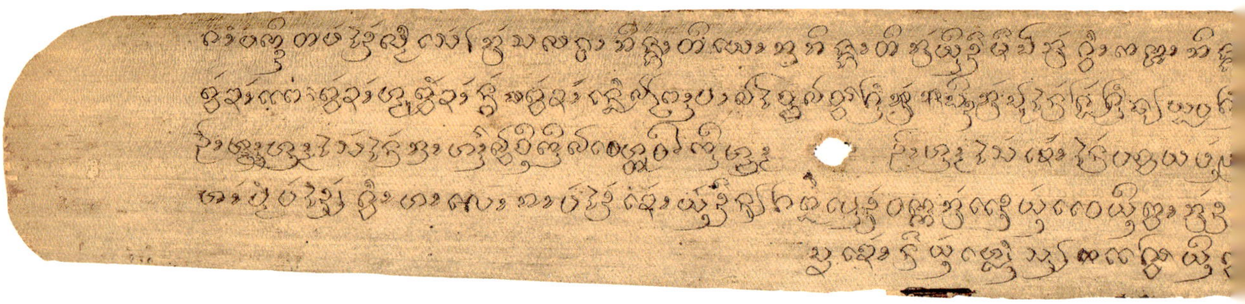

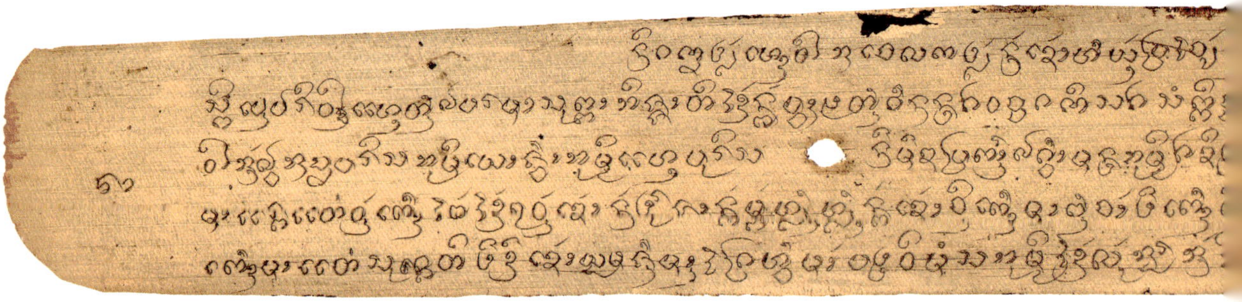

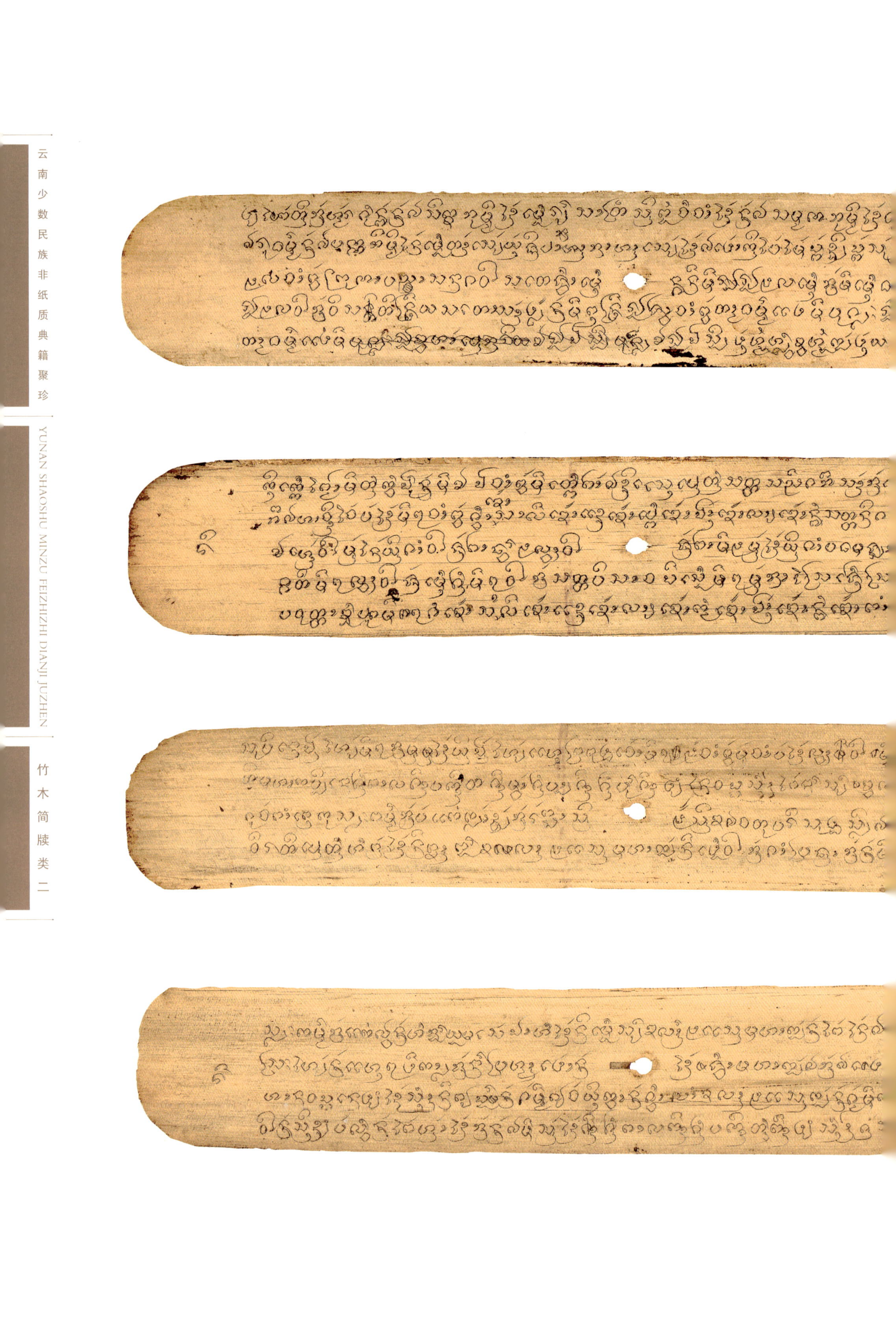

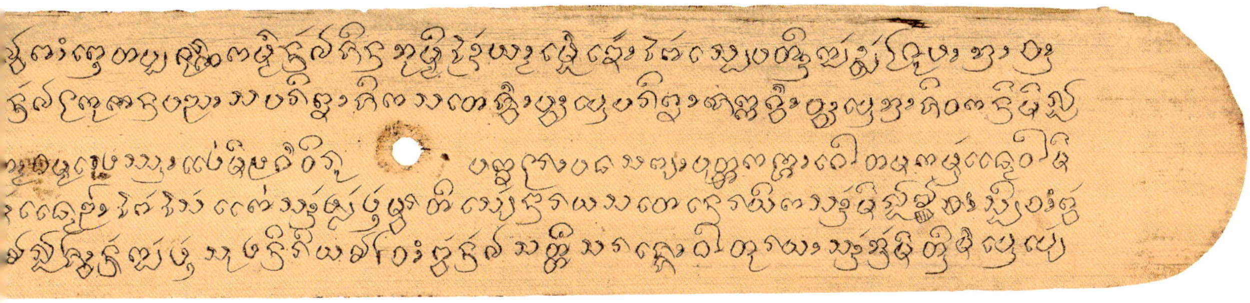

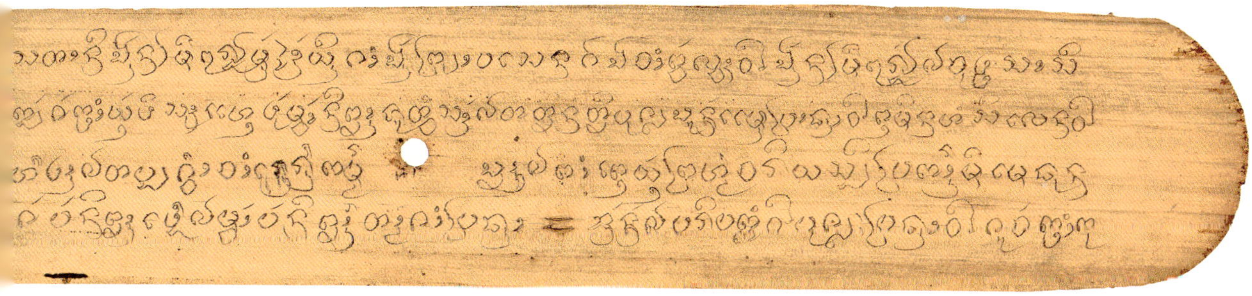

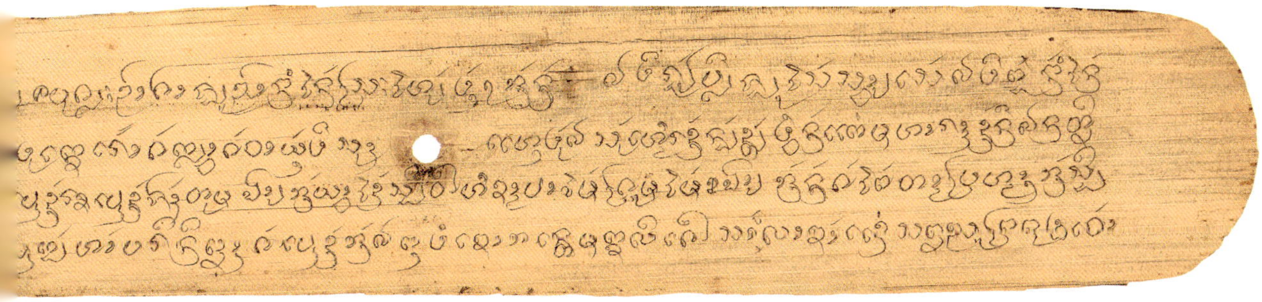

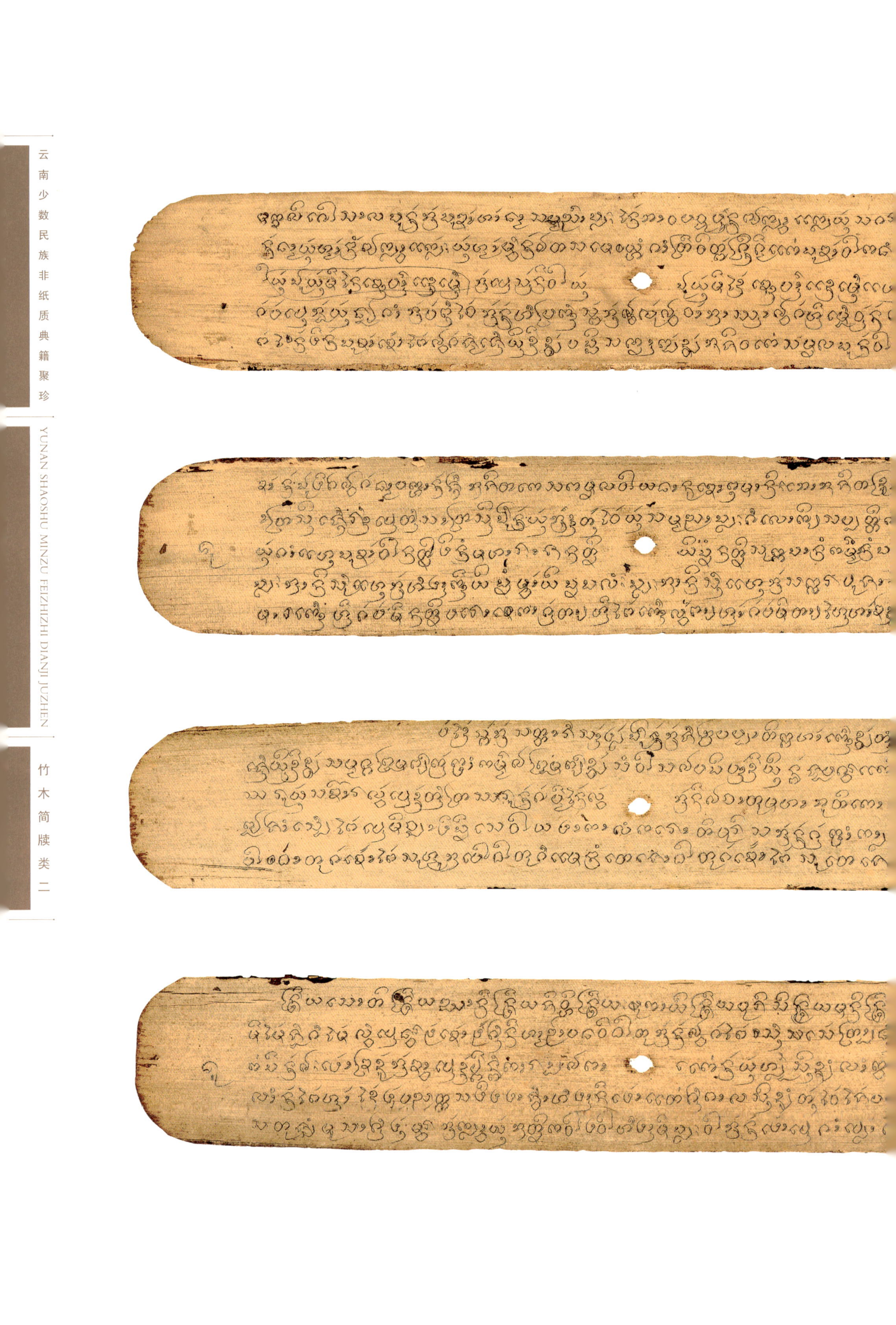

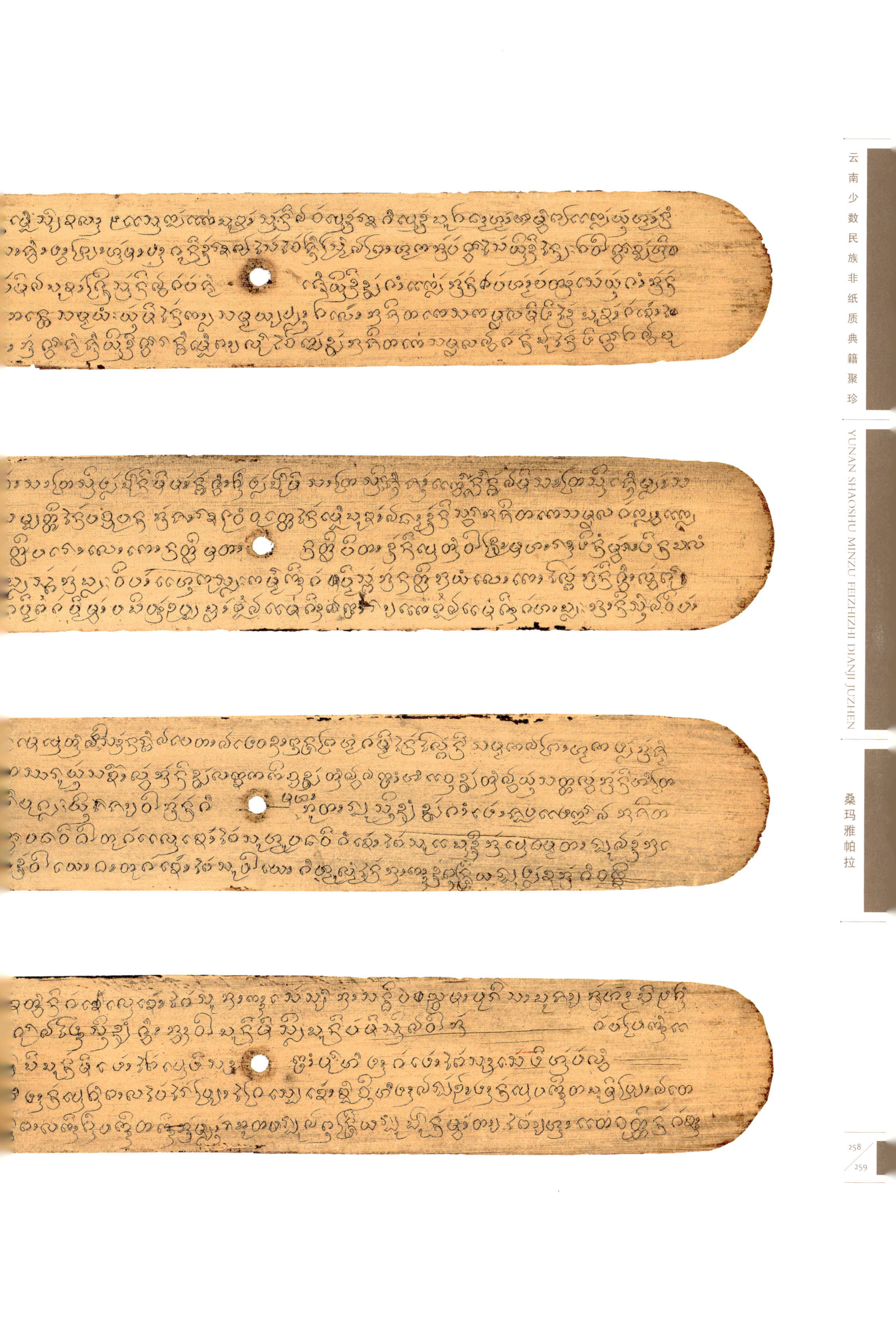

桑玛雅帕拉

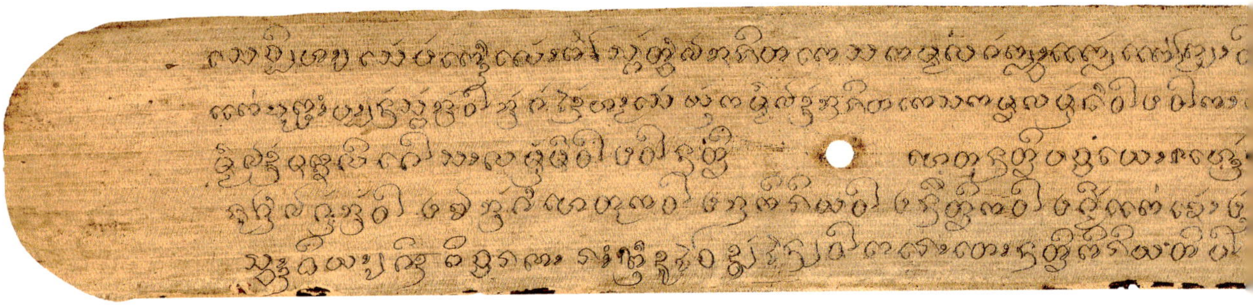

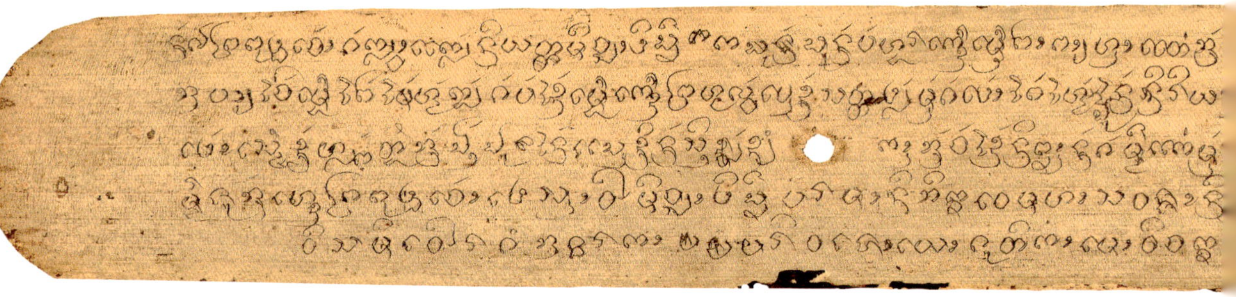

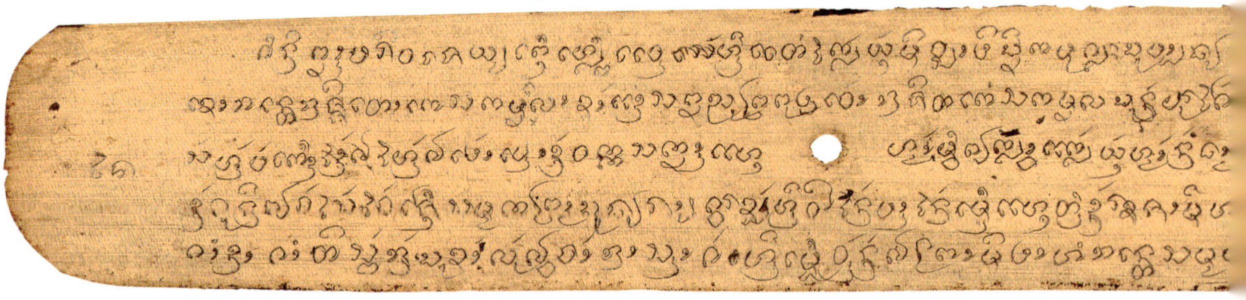

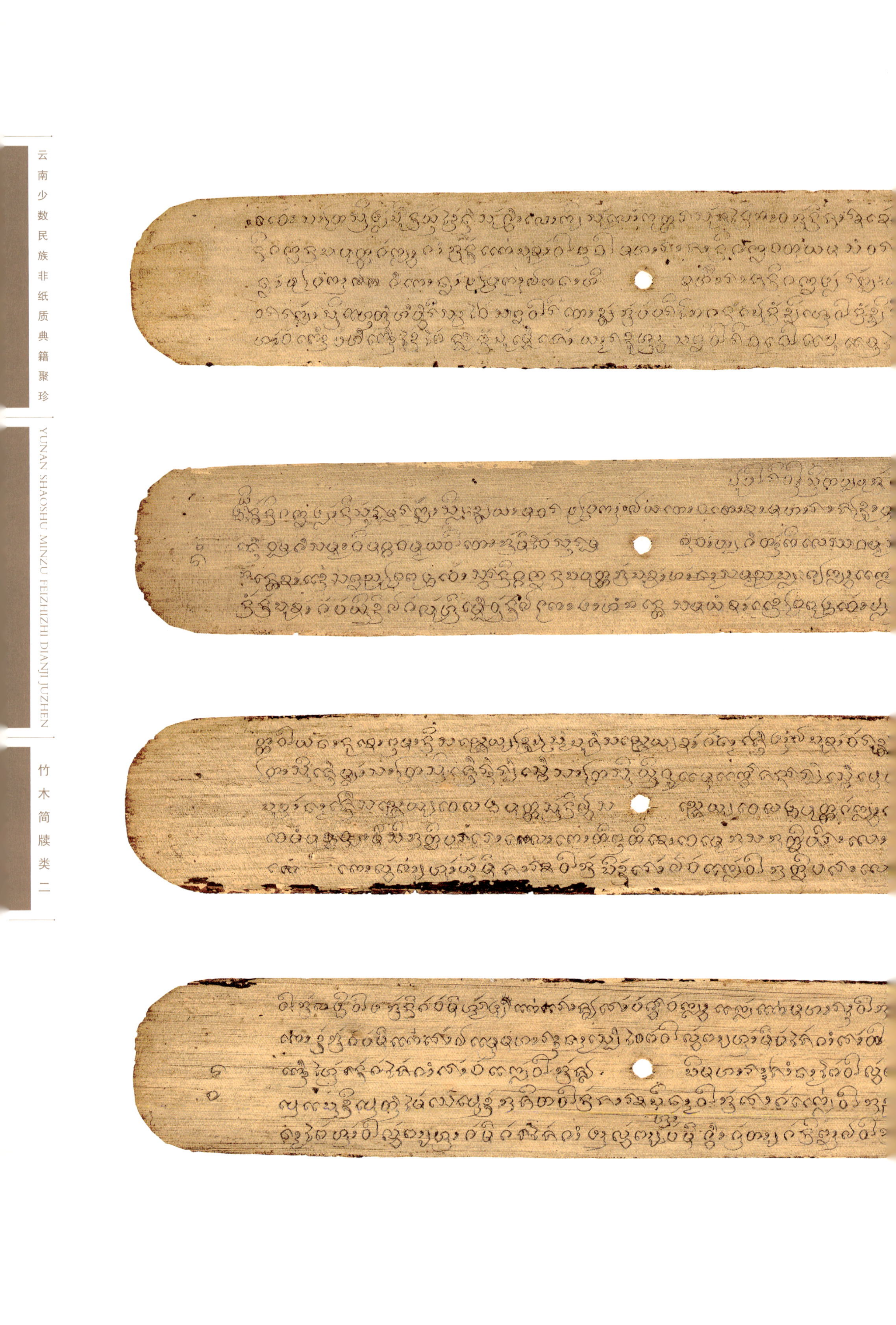

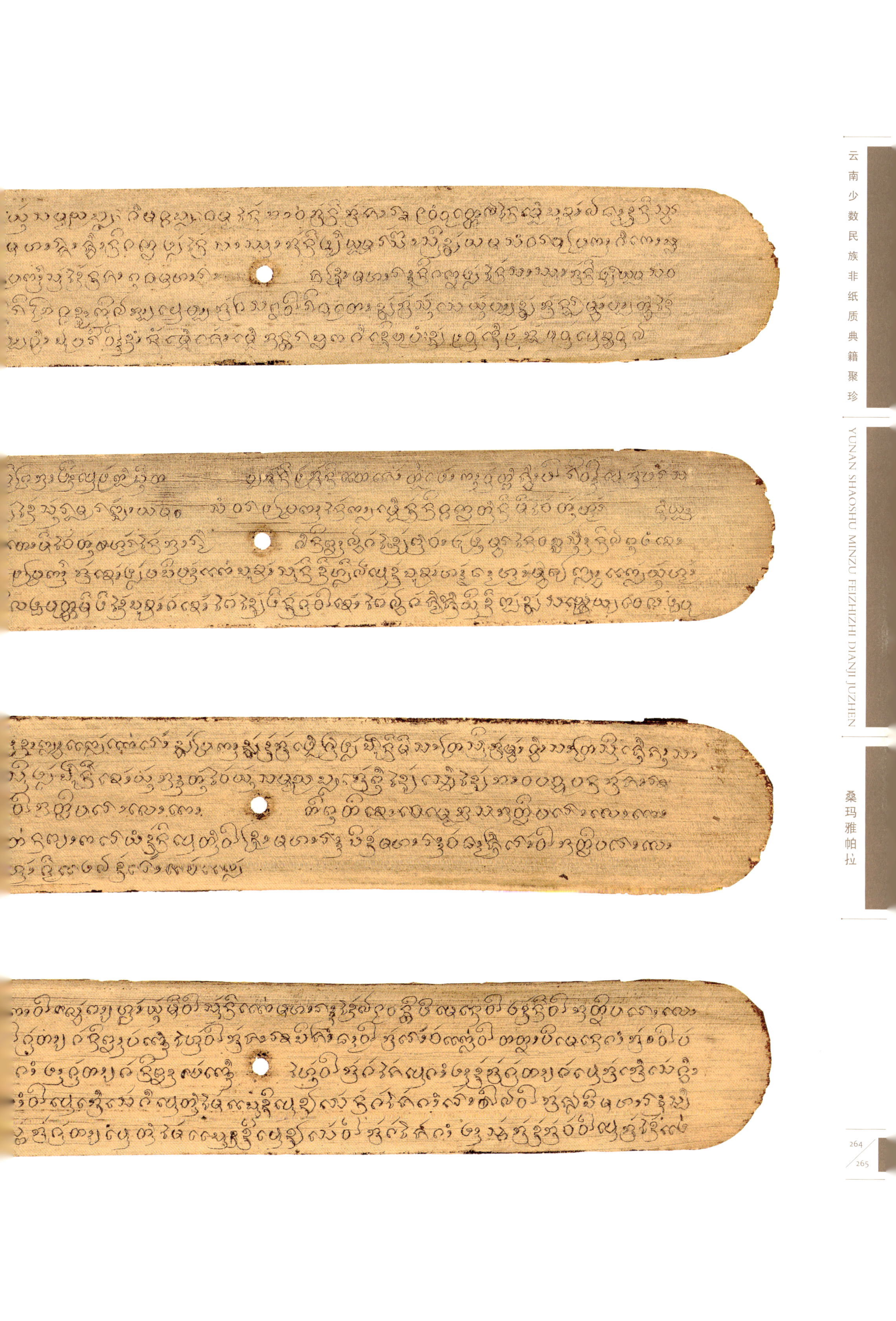

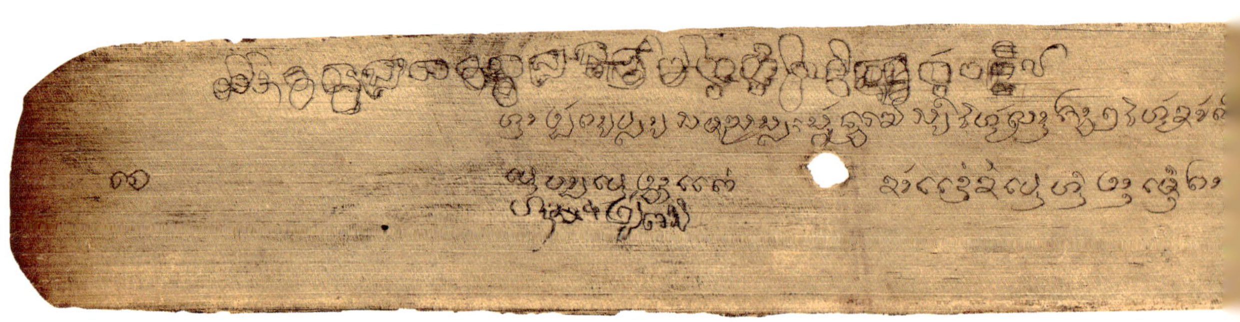

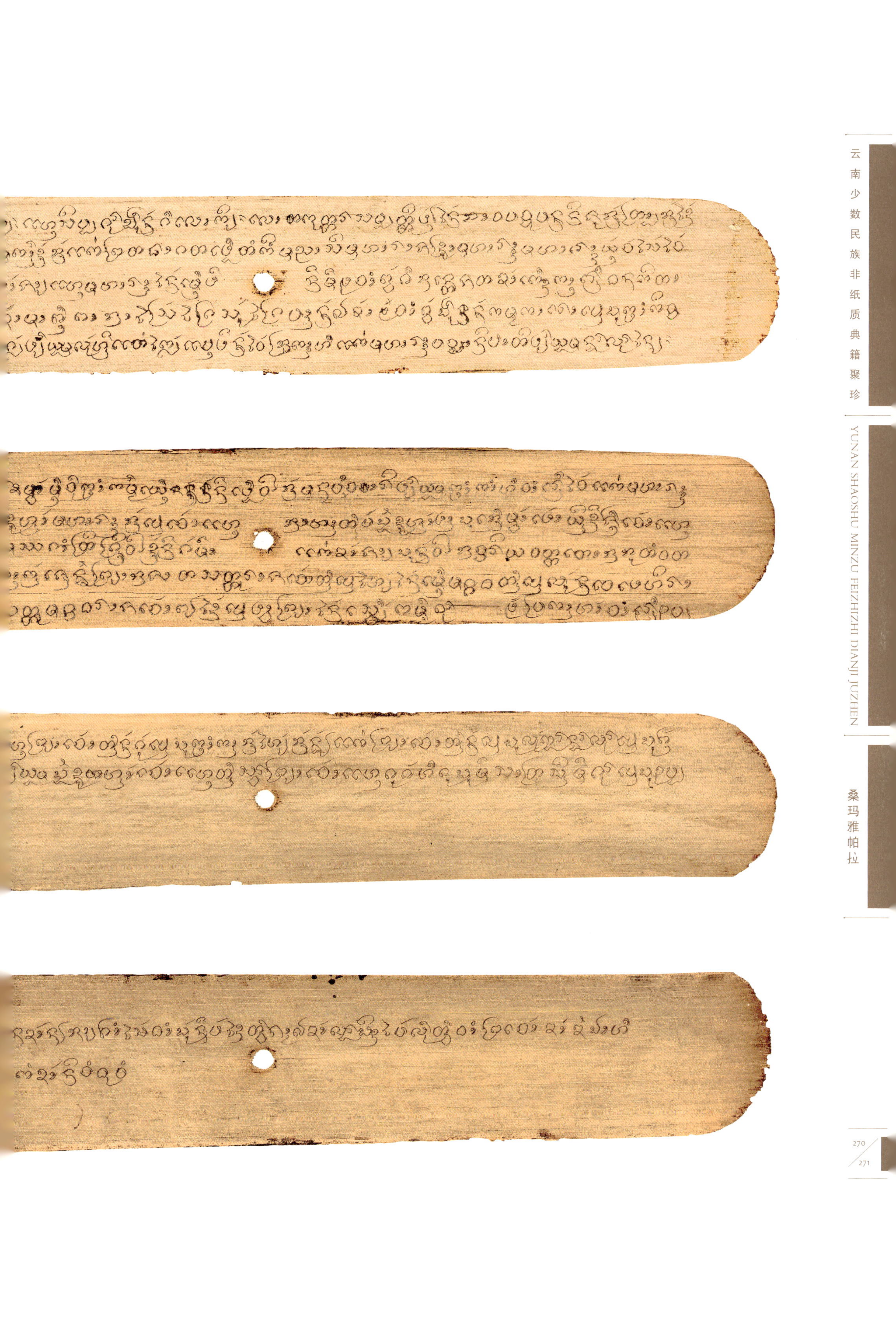

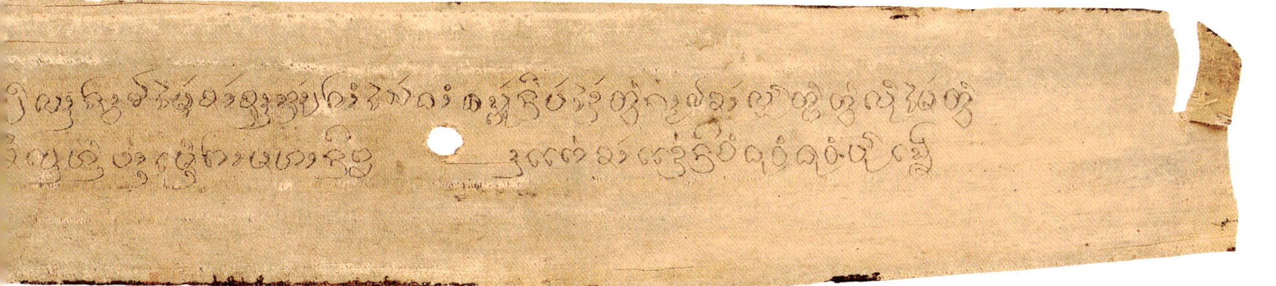

桑玛雅帕拉

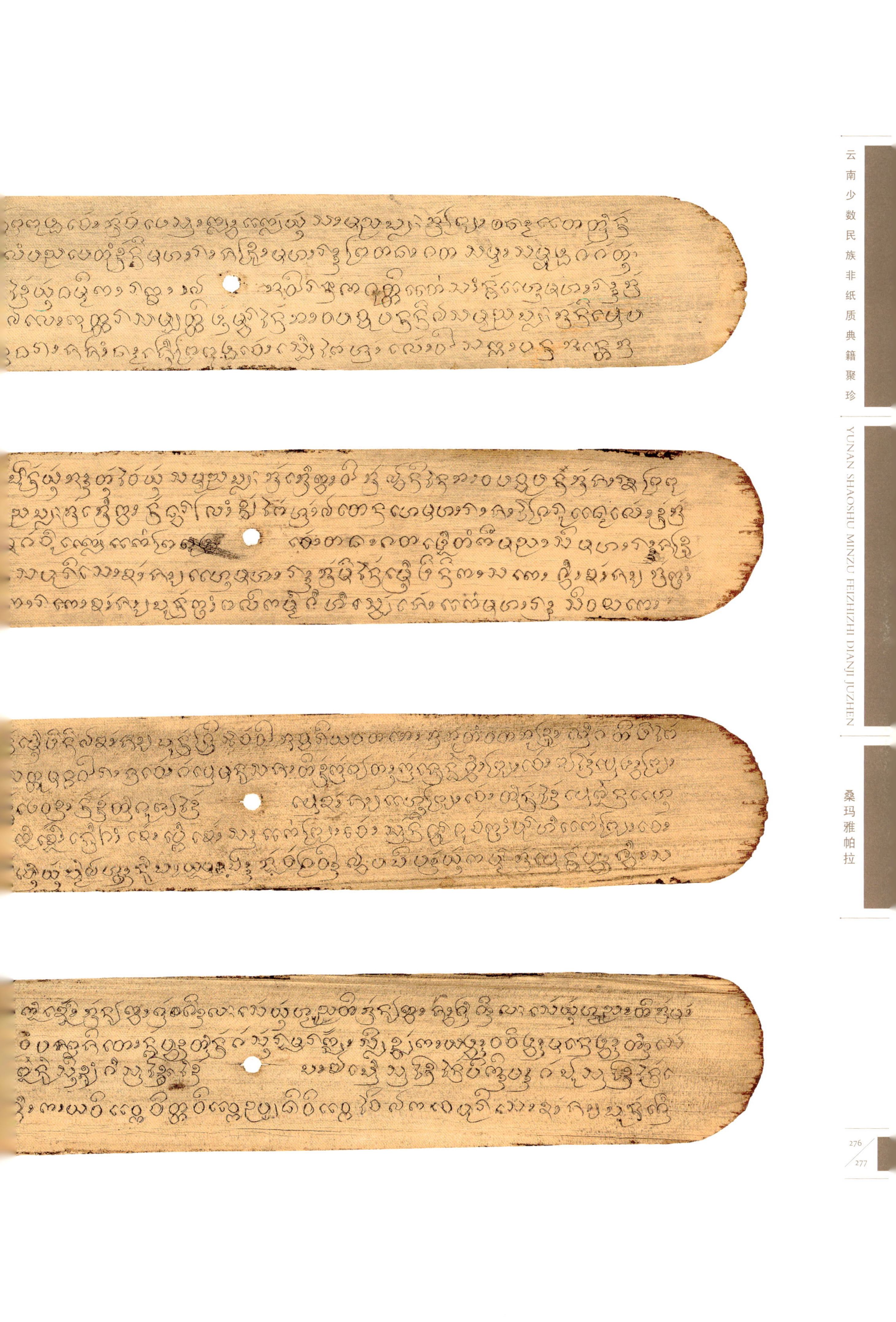

桑玛雅帕拉

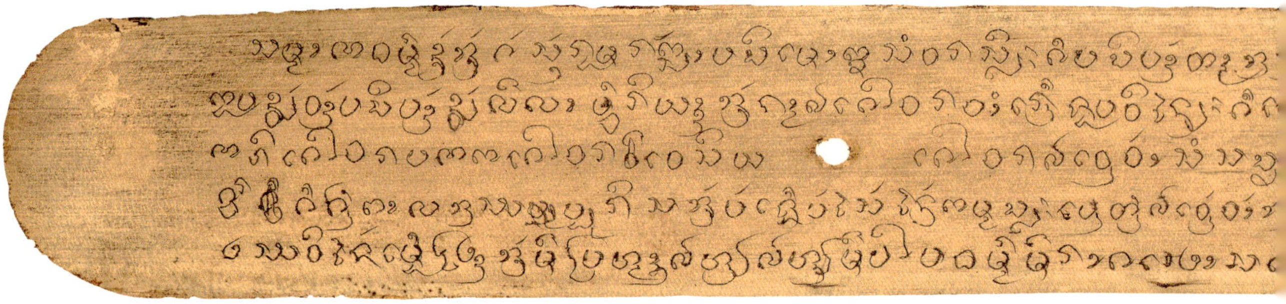

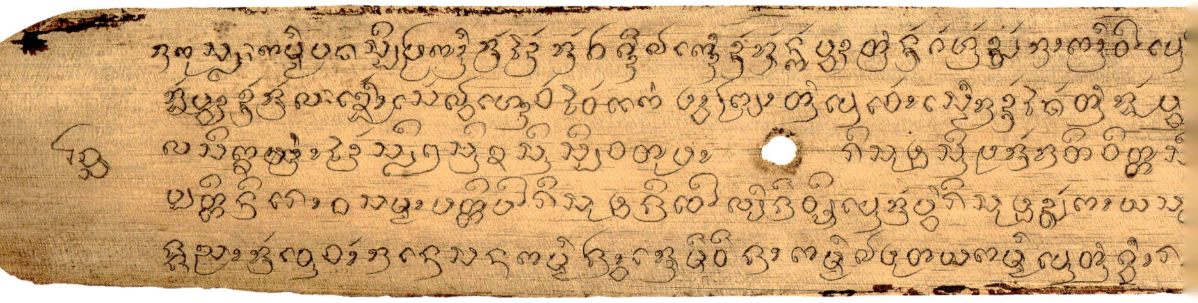

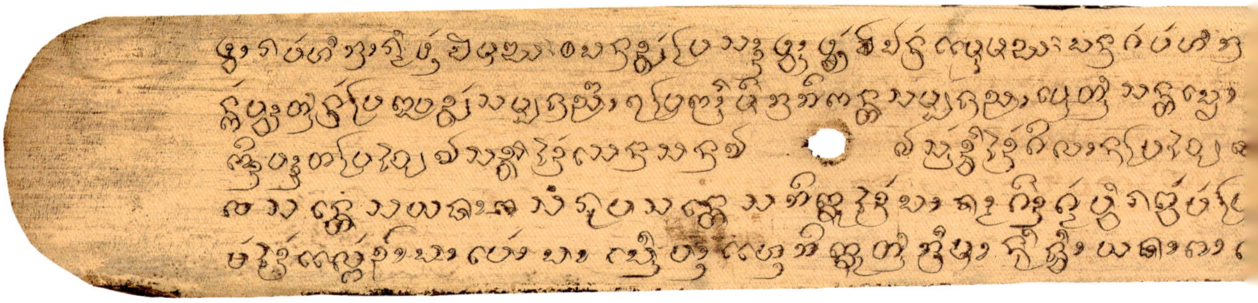

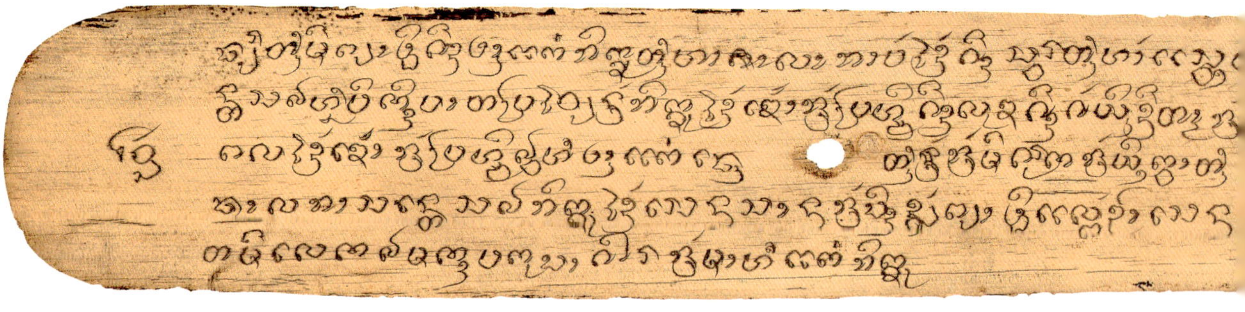

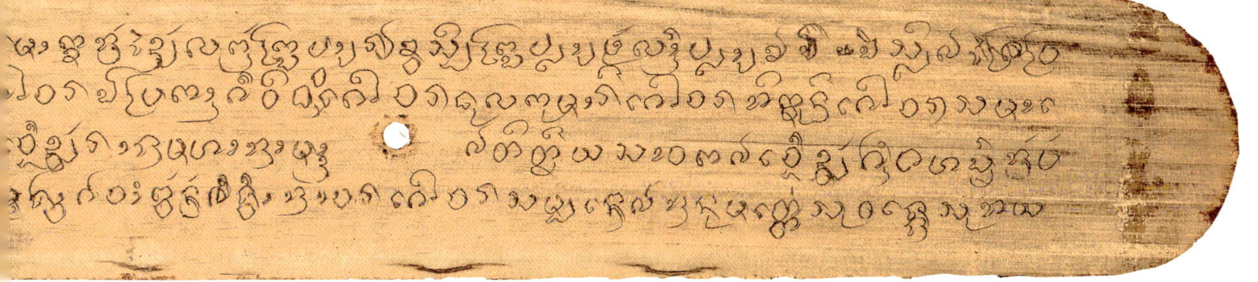

桑玛雅帕拉

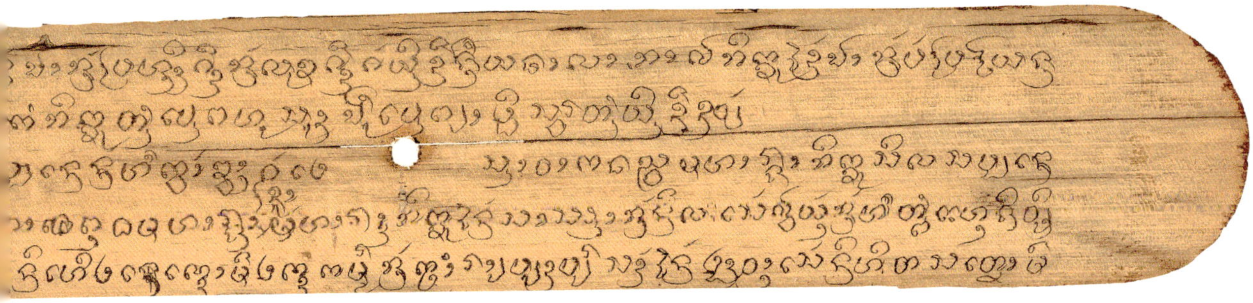

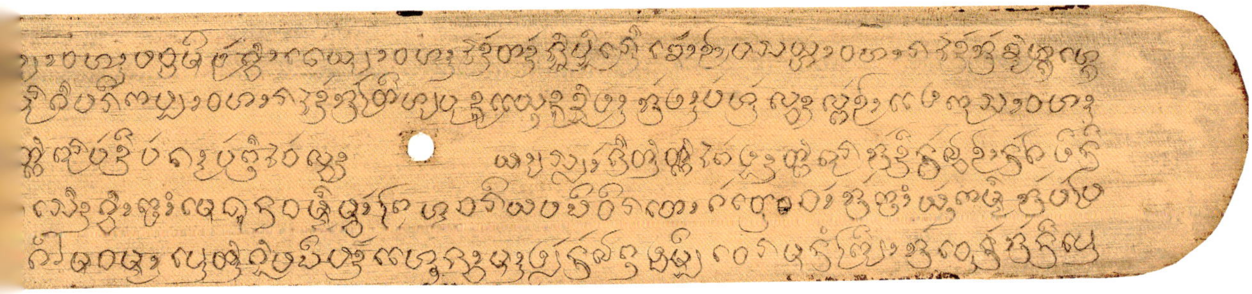

桑玛雅帕拉

桑玛雅帕拉

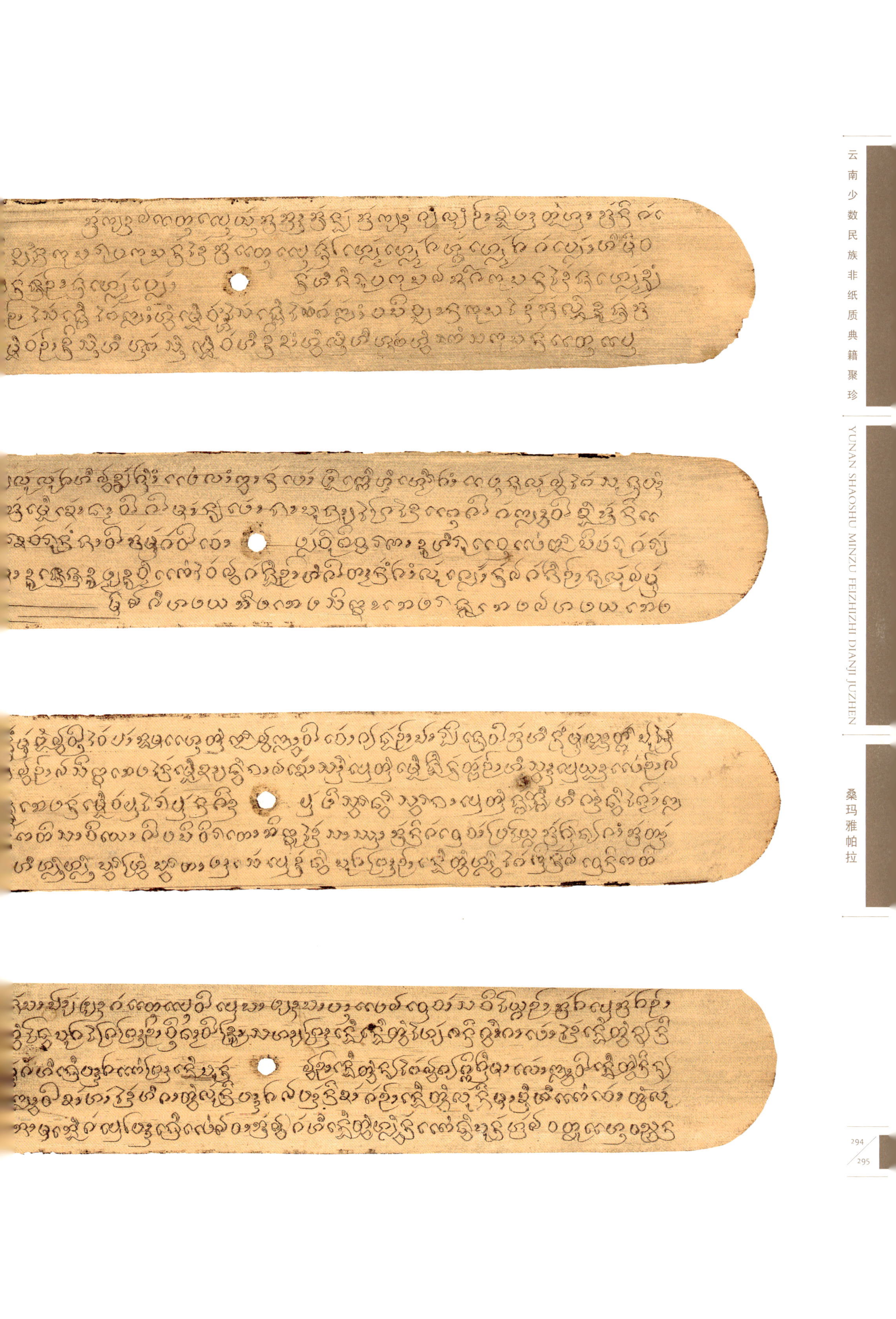

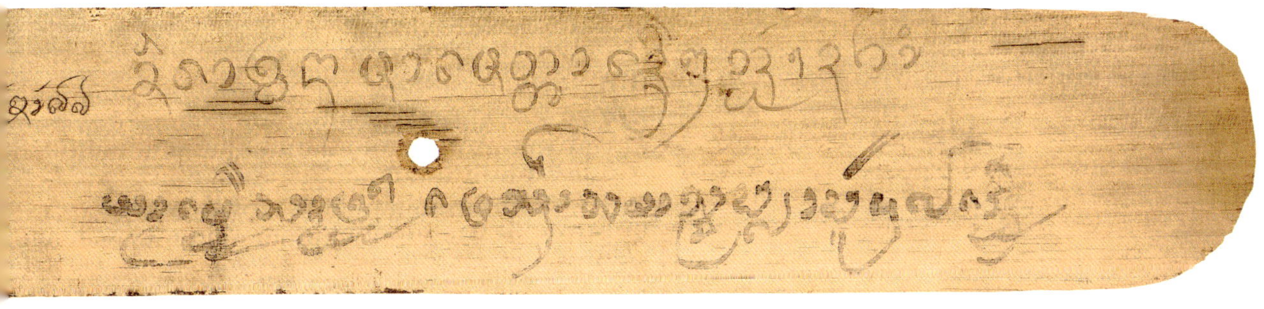

第五册

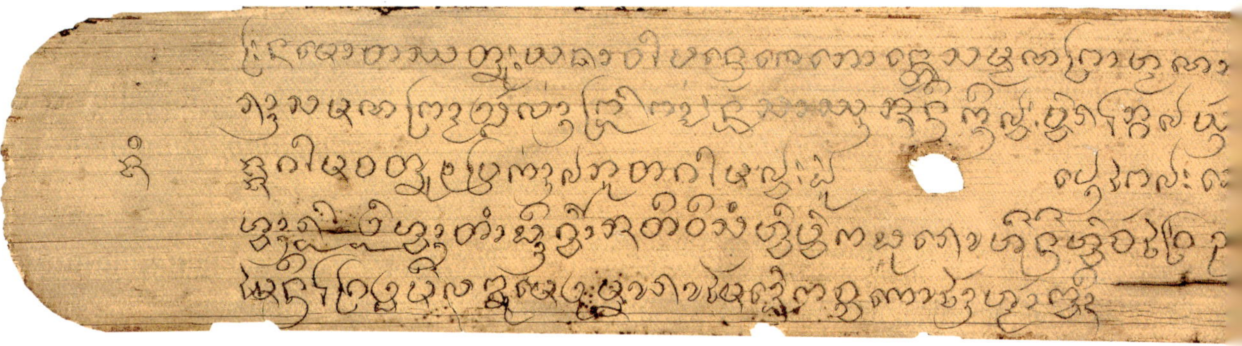

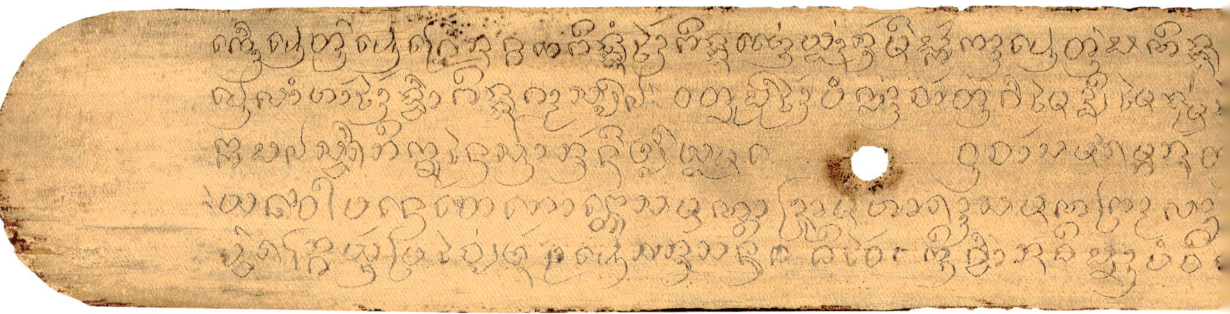

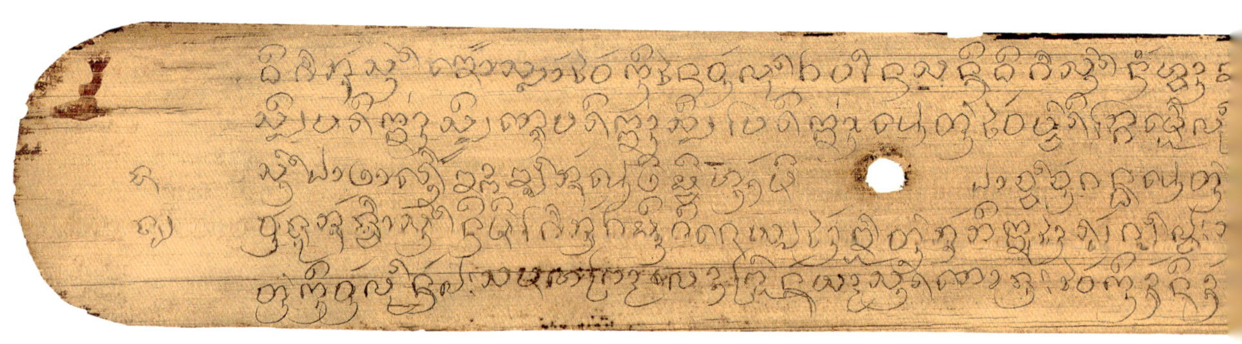

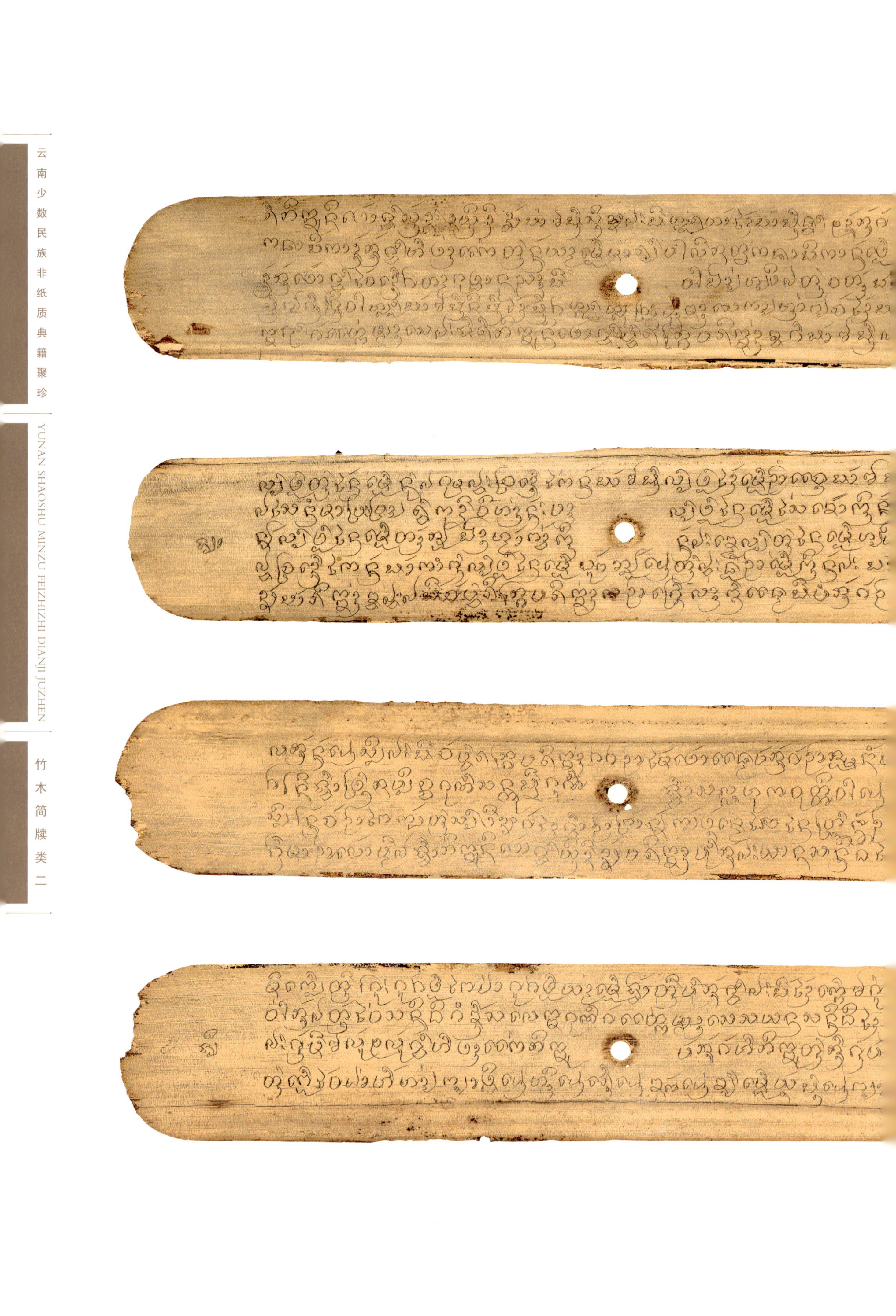

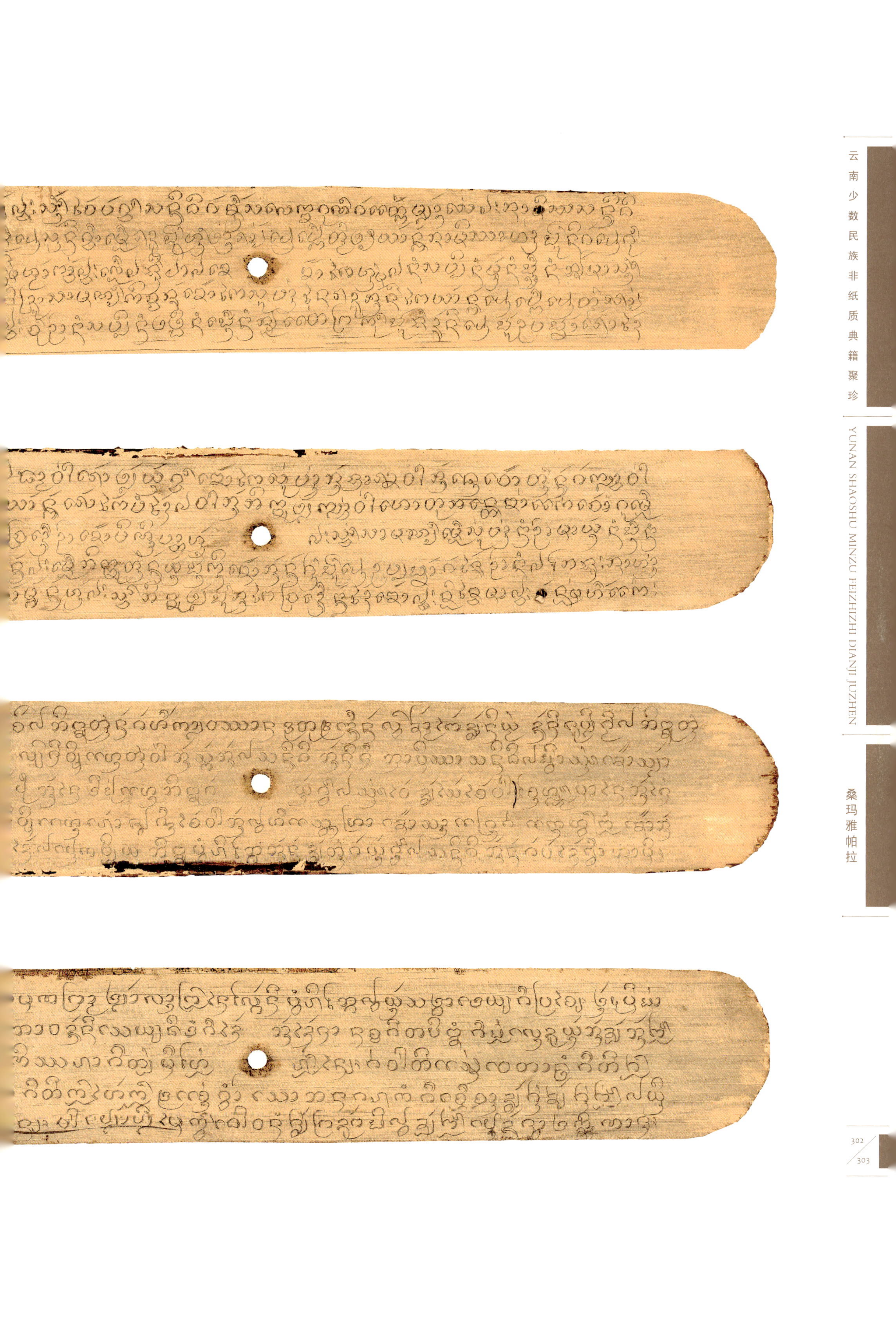

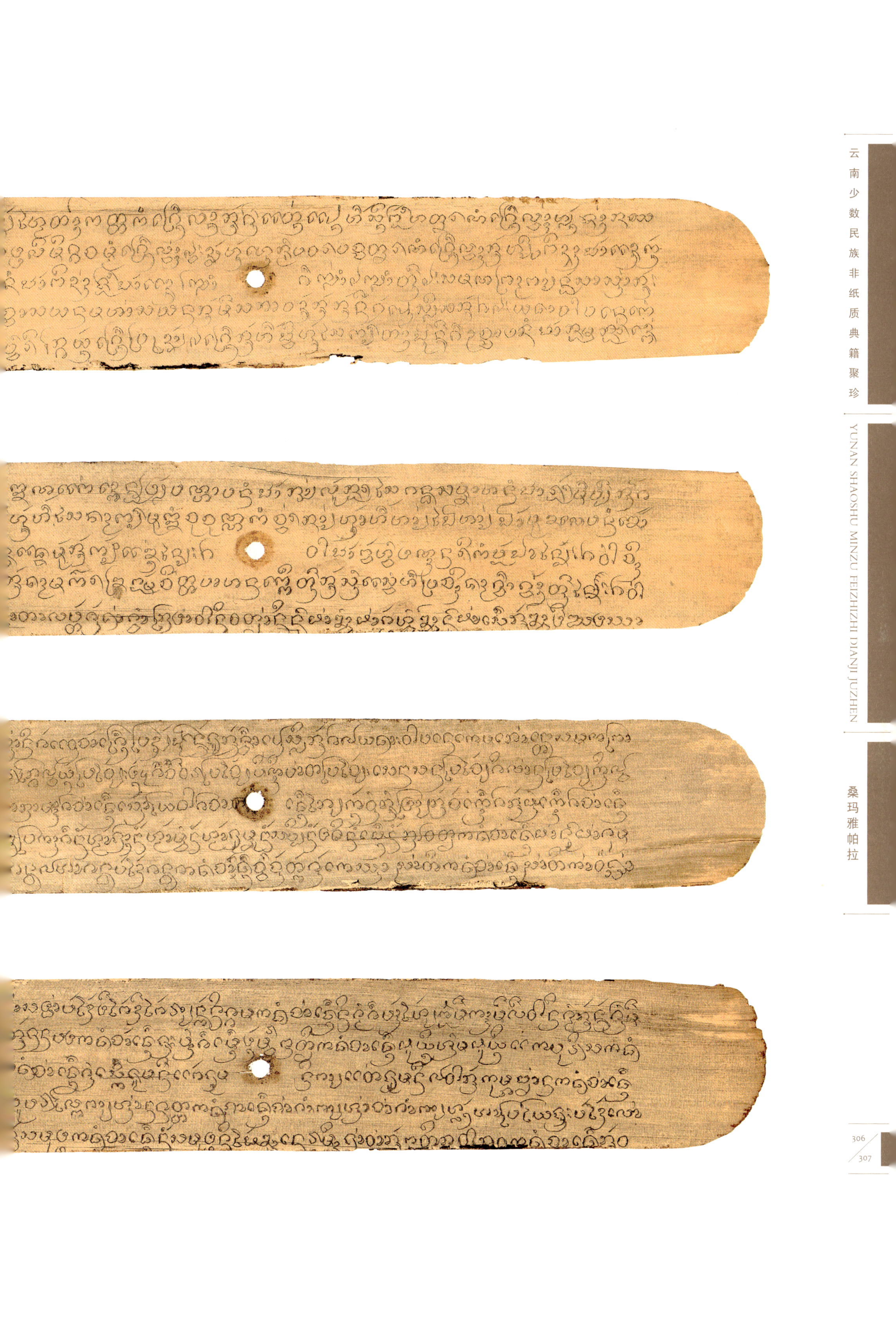

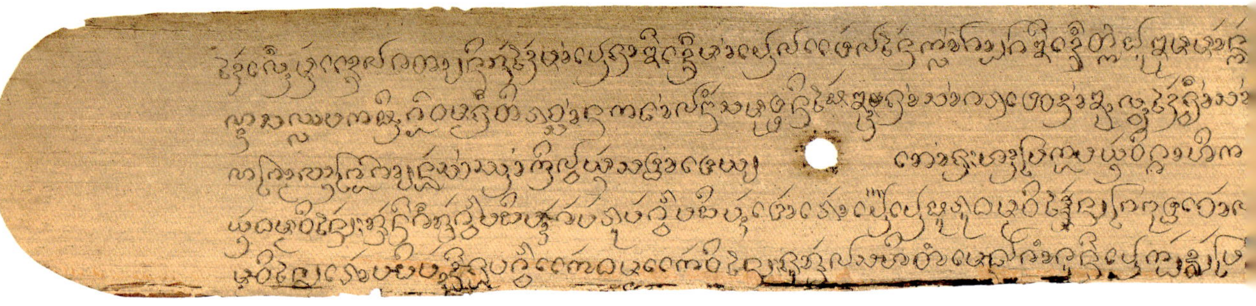

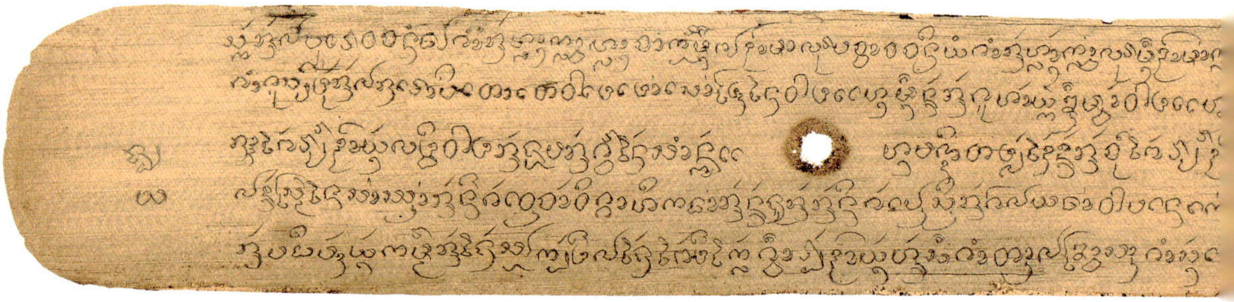

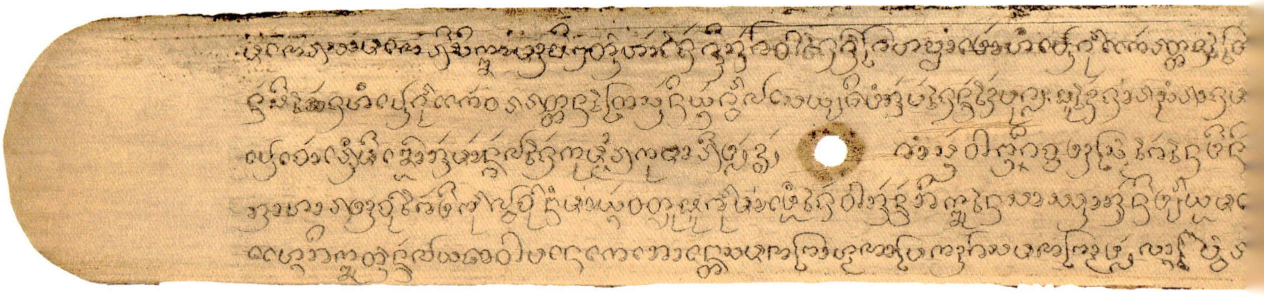

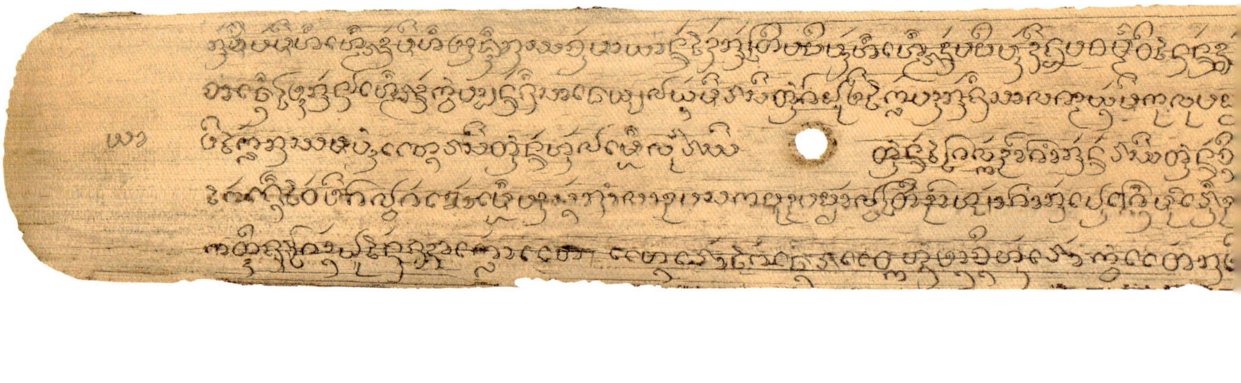

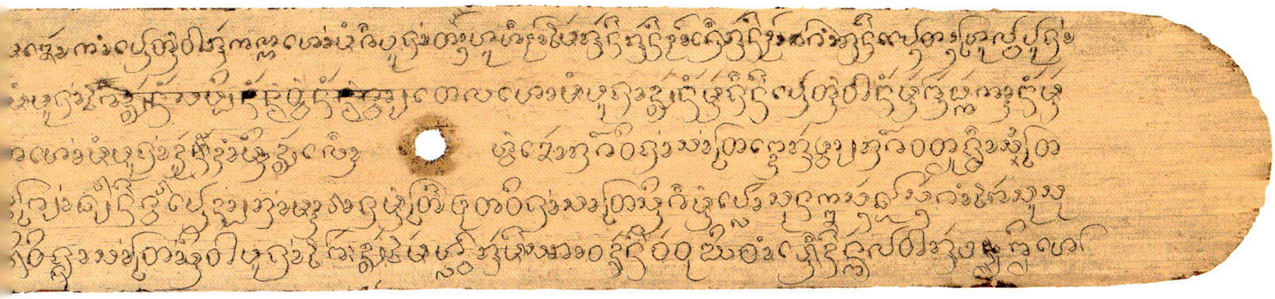

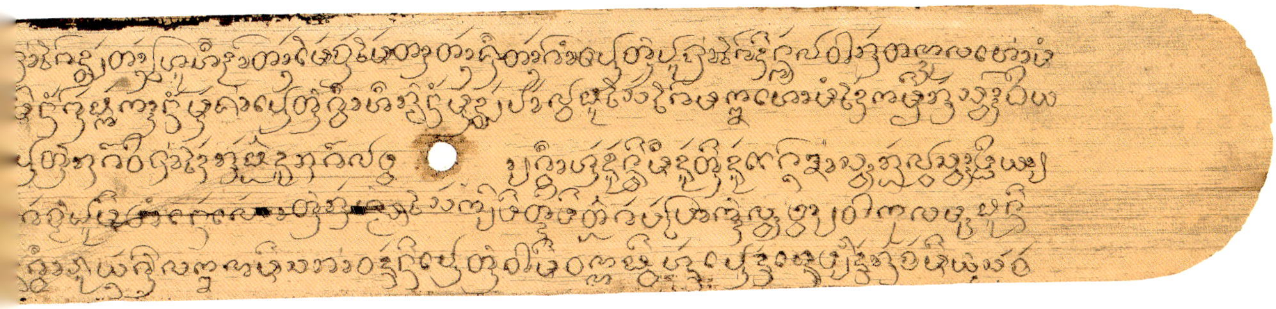

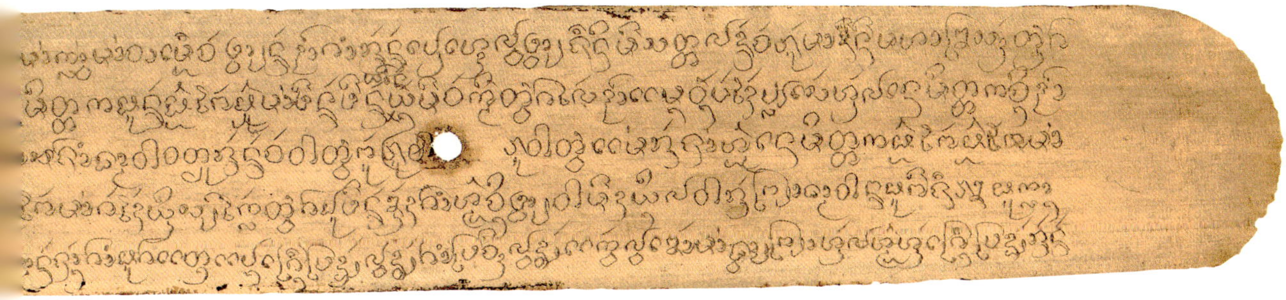

桑玛雅帕拉

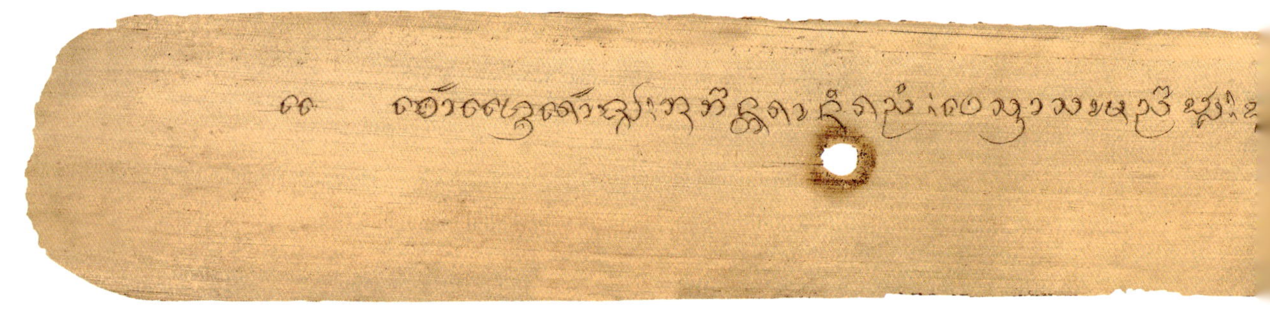

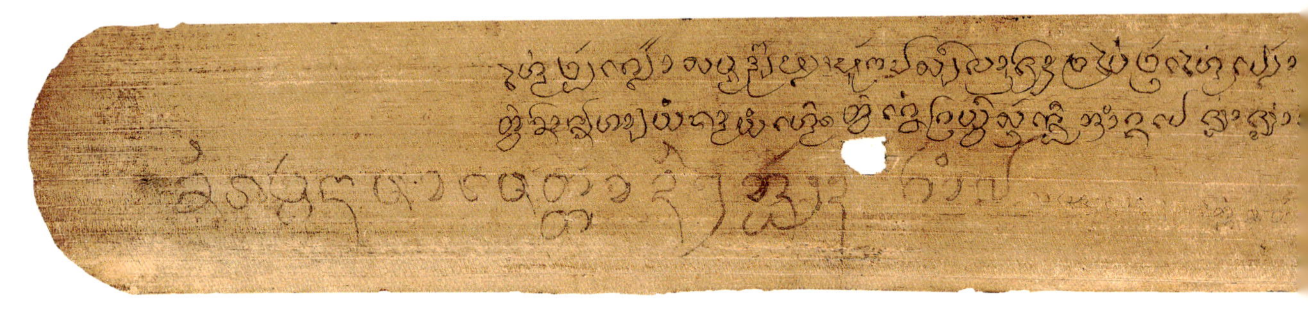

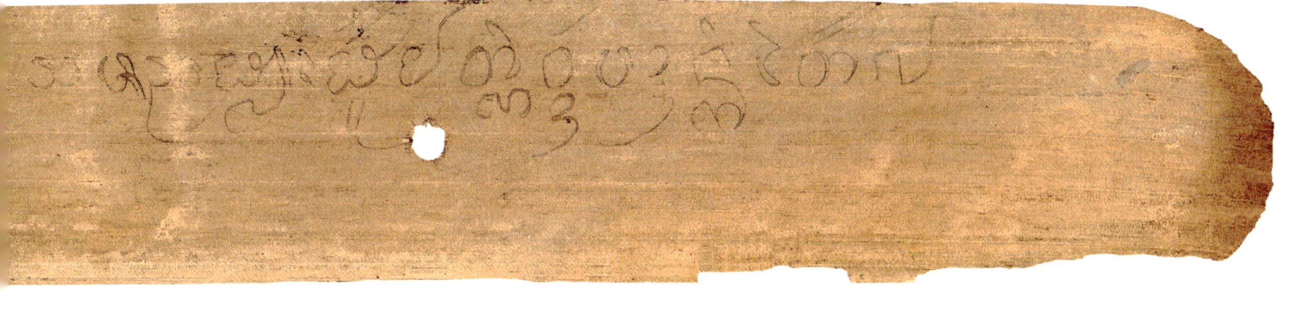

桑玛雅帕拉

桑玛雅帕拉

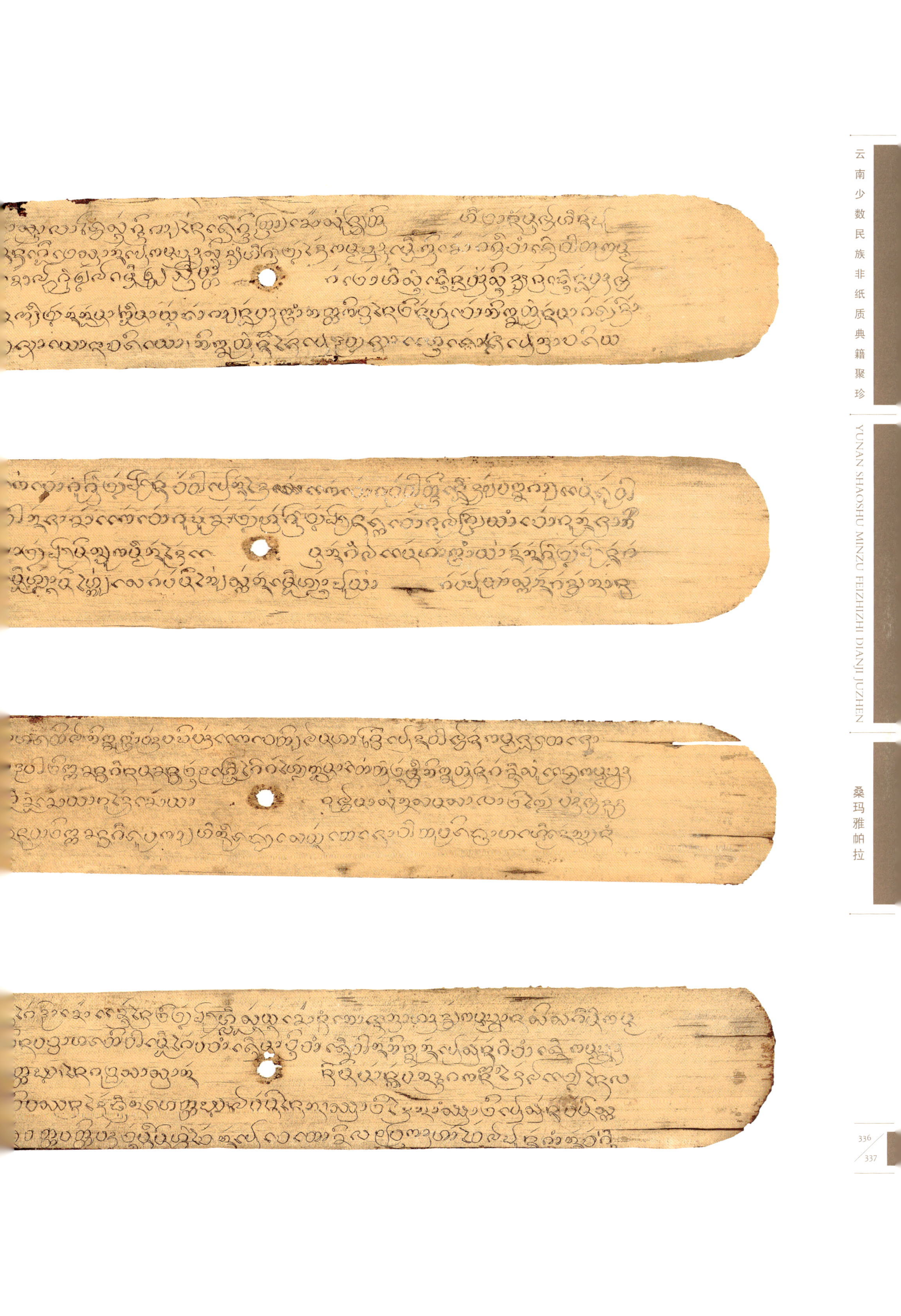

桑玛雅帕拉

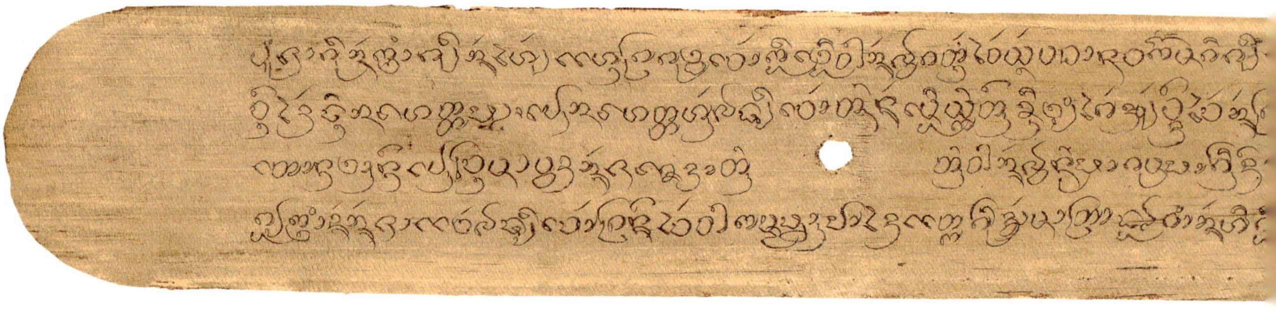

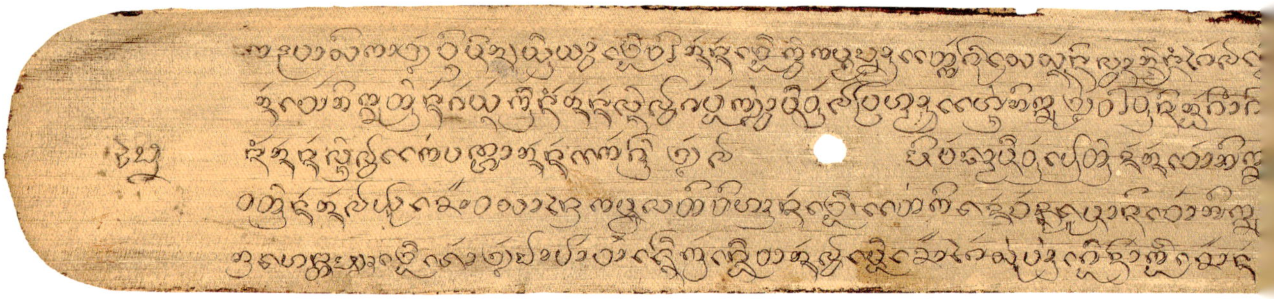

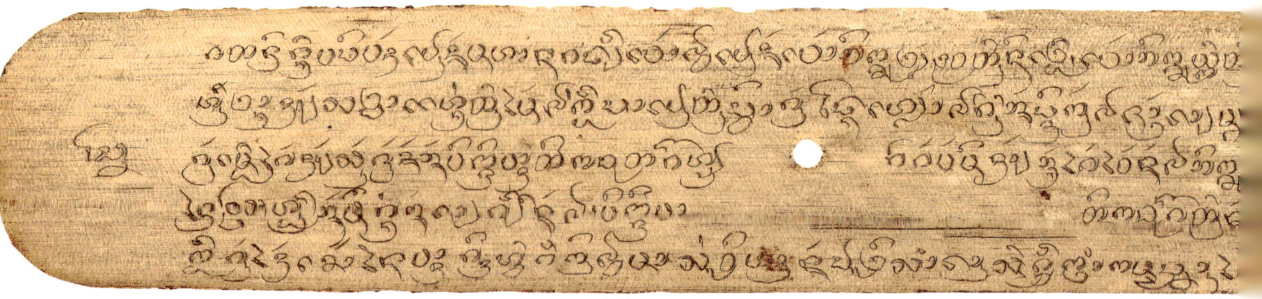

桑玛雅帕拉

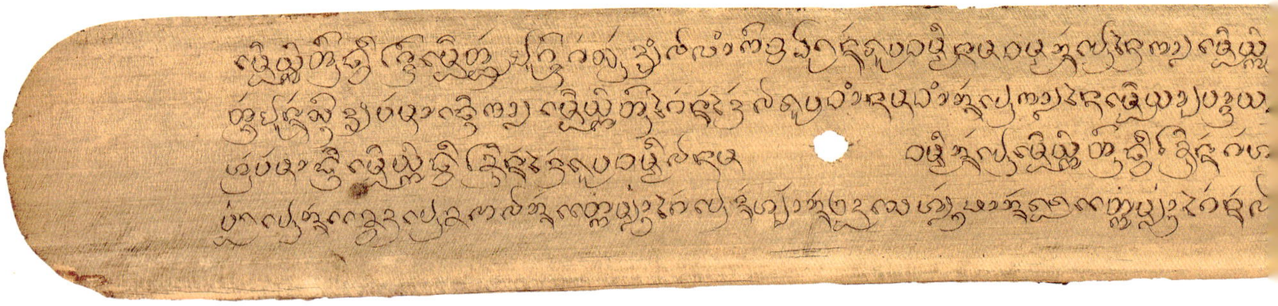

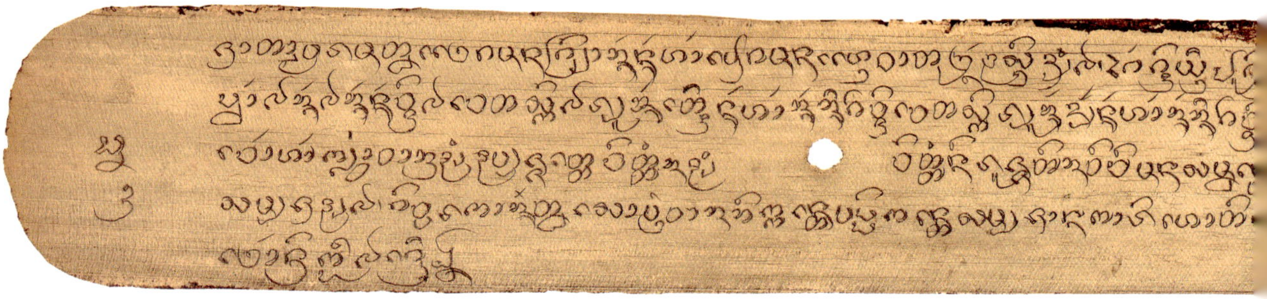

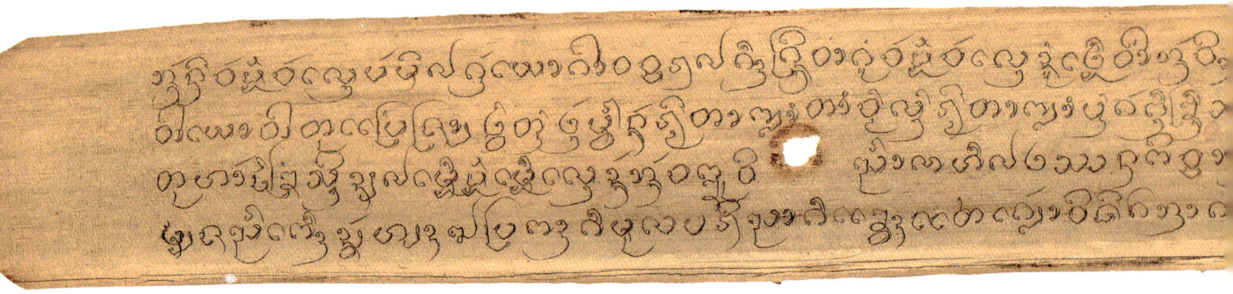

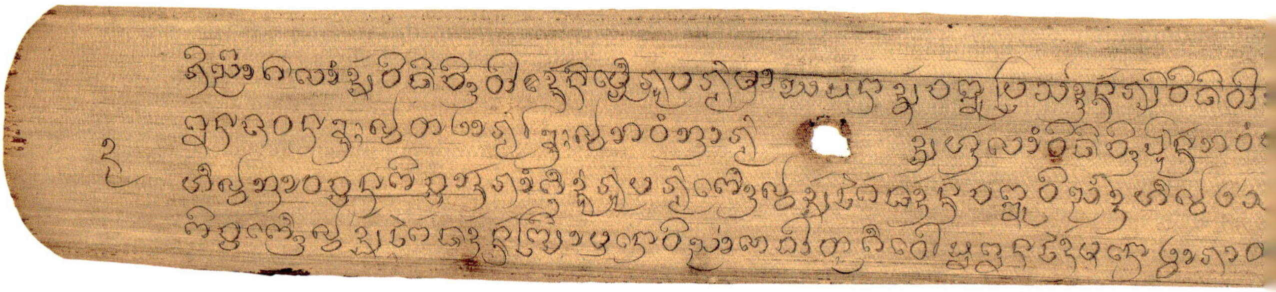

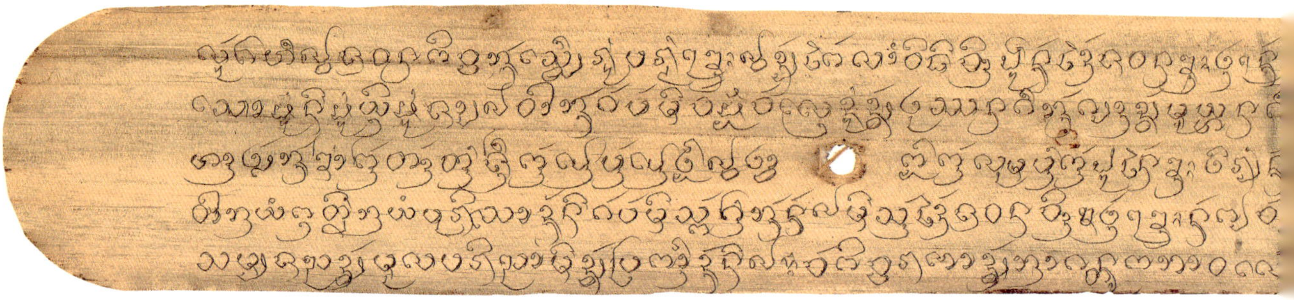

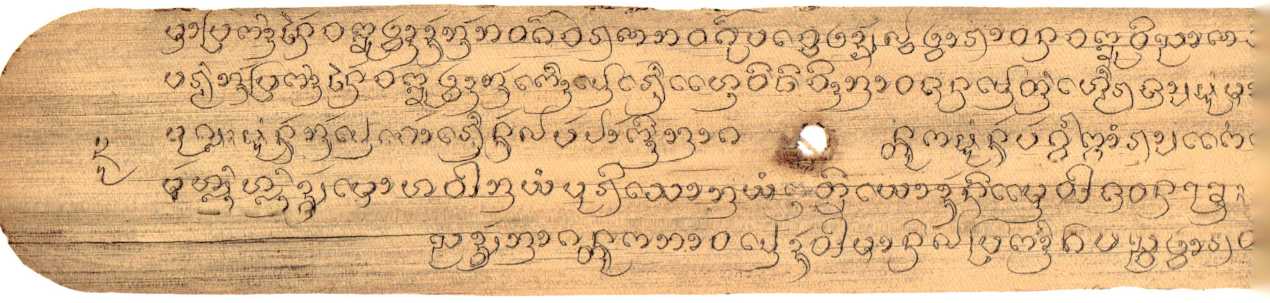

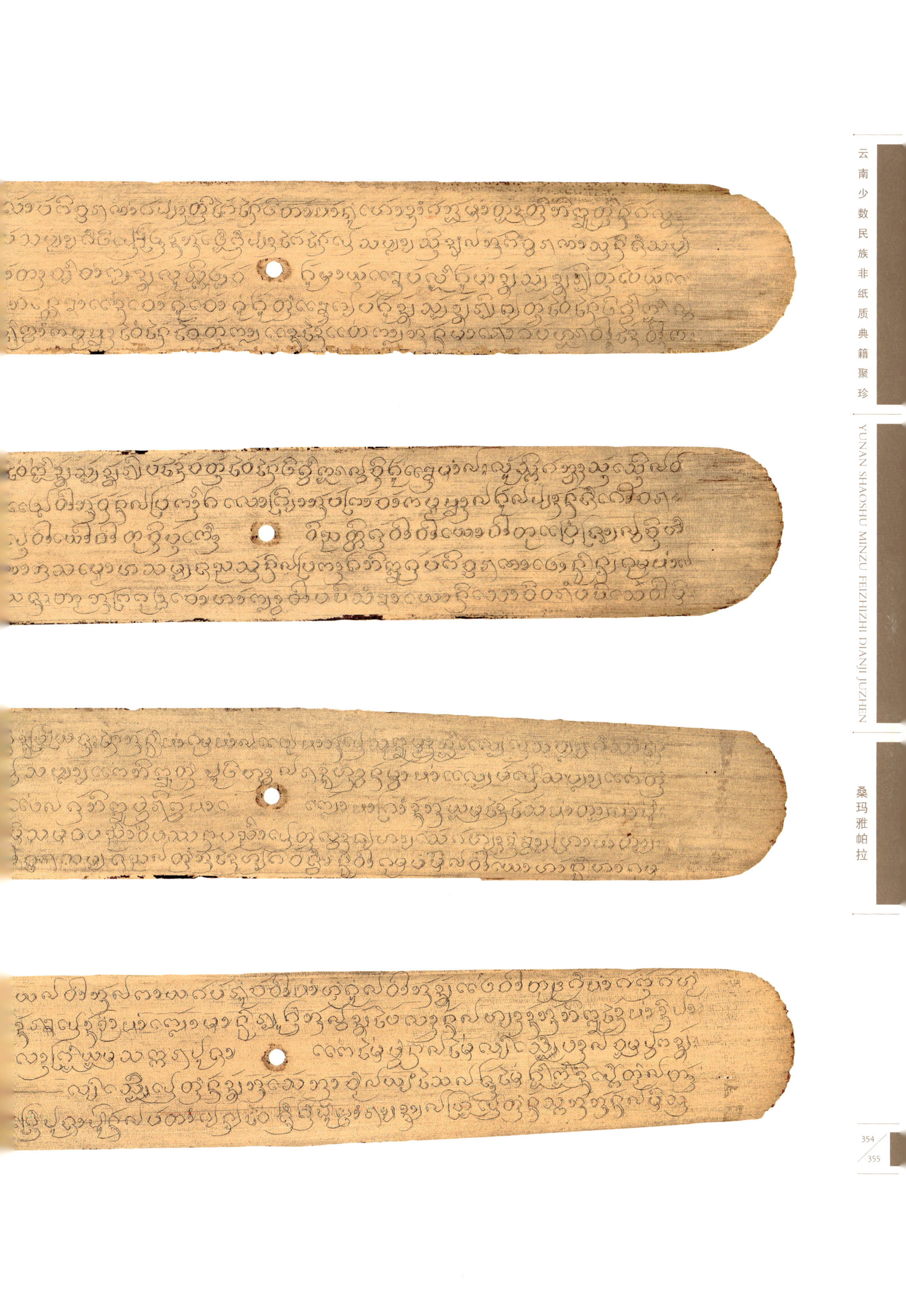

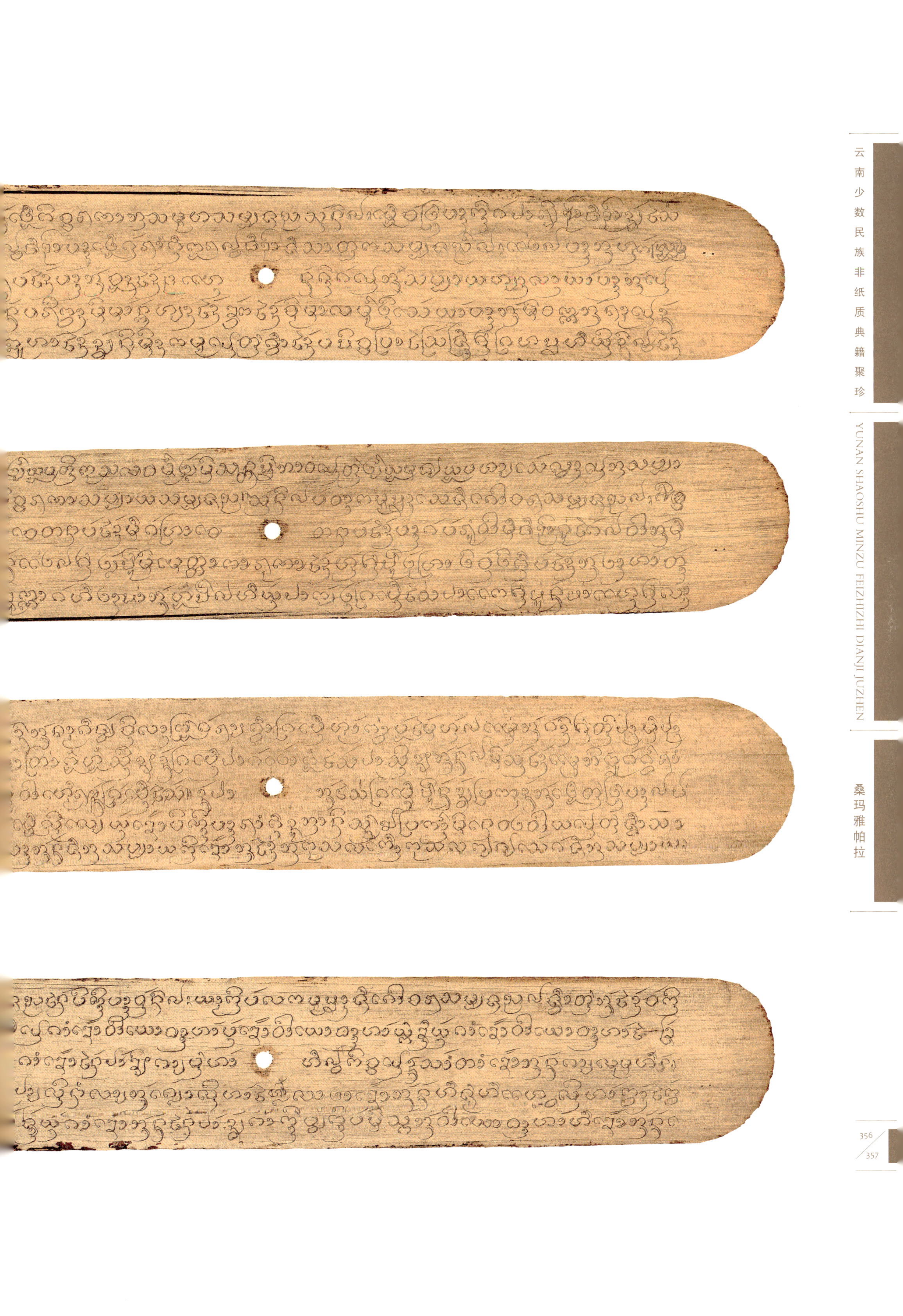

桑玛雅帕拉

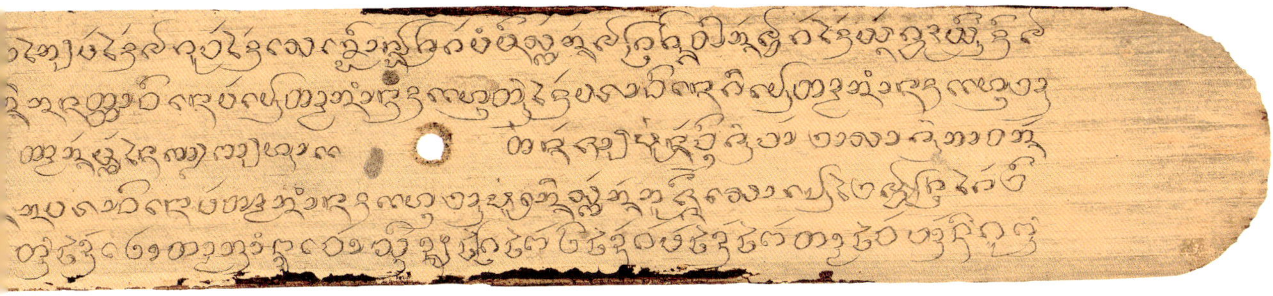

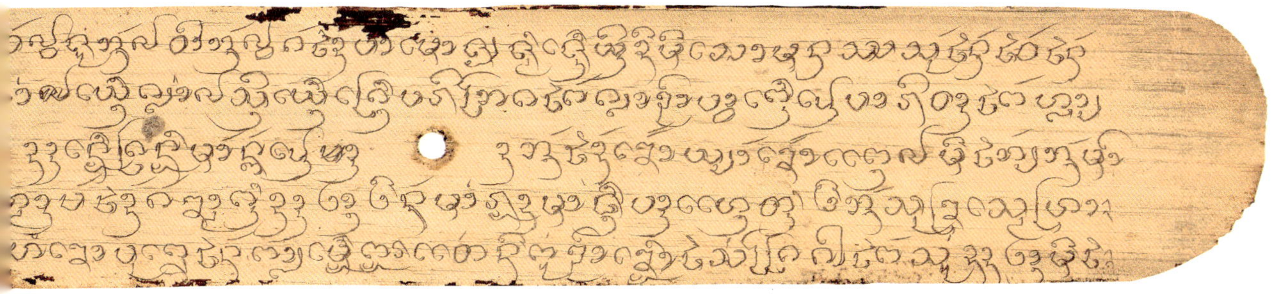

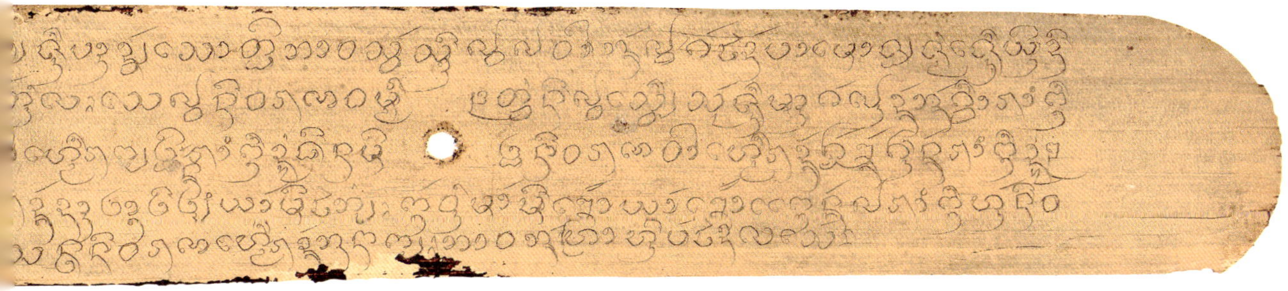

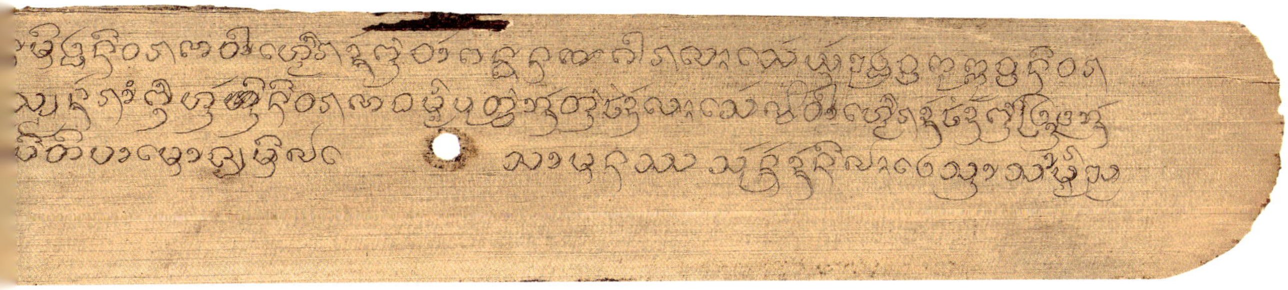

桑玛雅帕拉

第八册

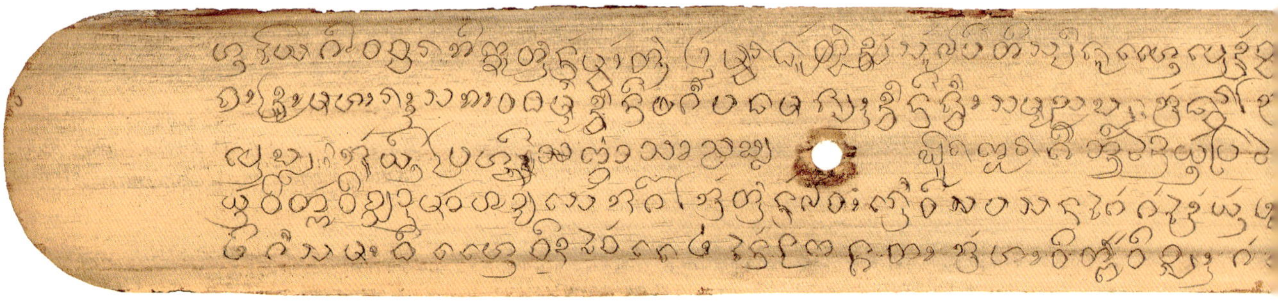

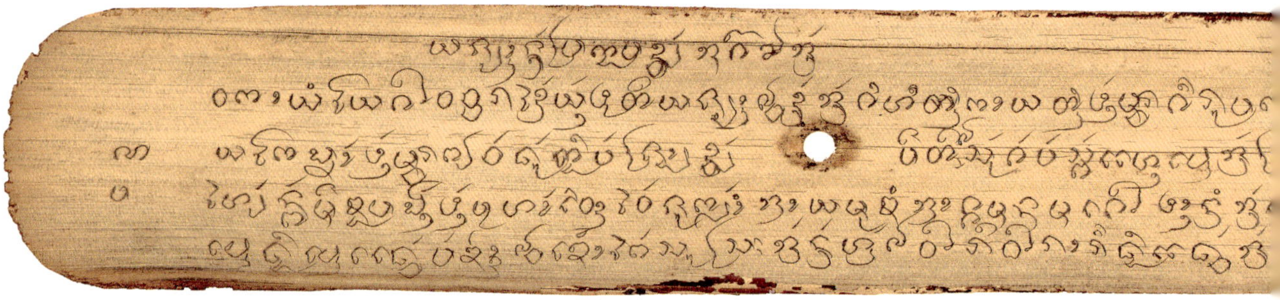

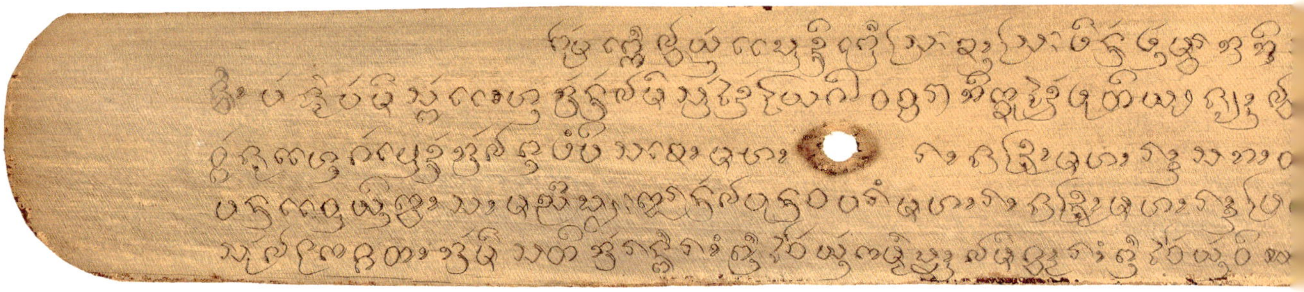

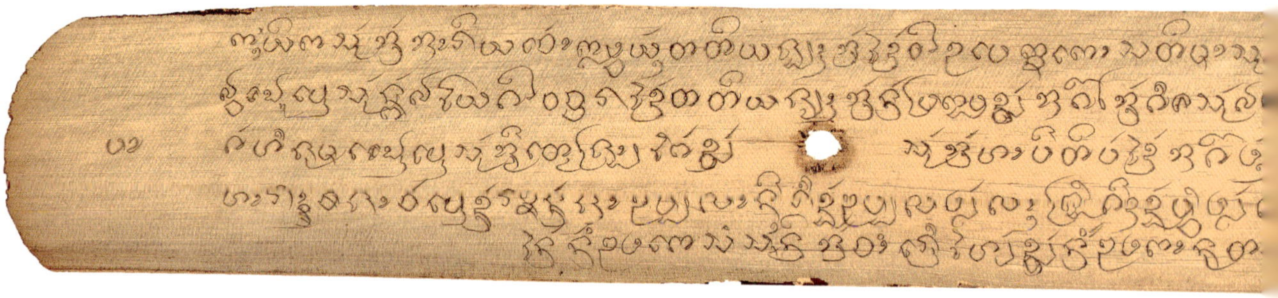

桑玛雅帕拉

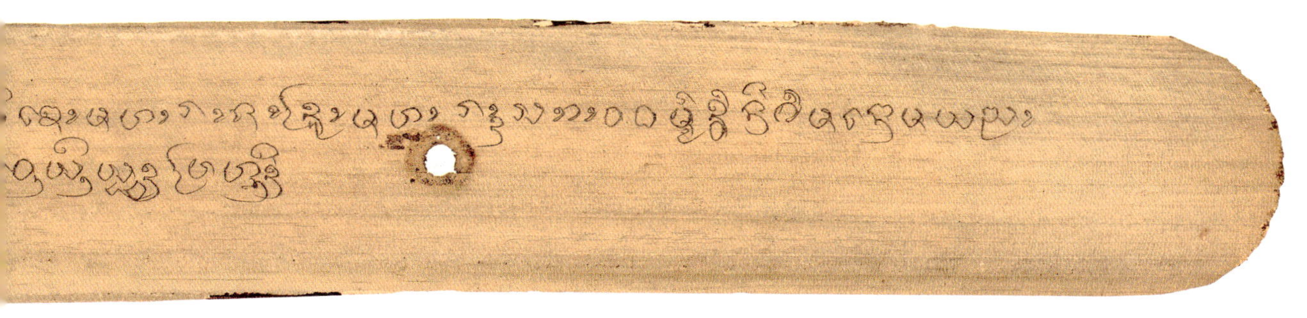

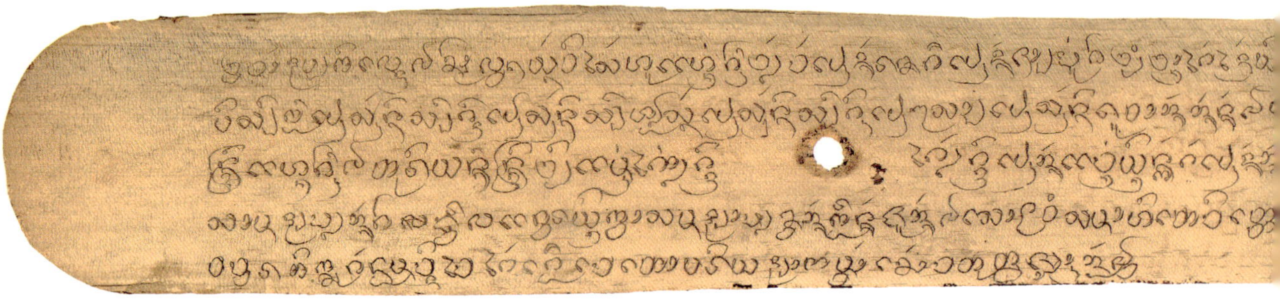

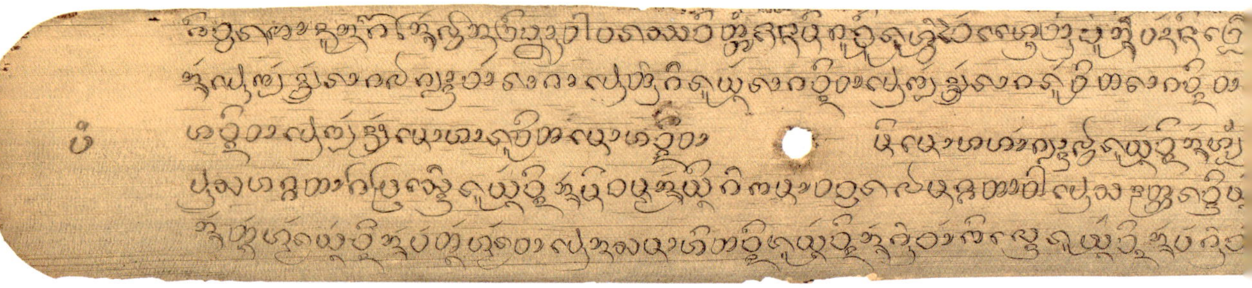

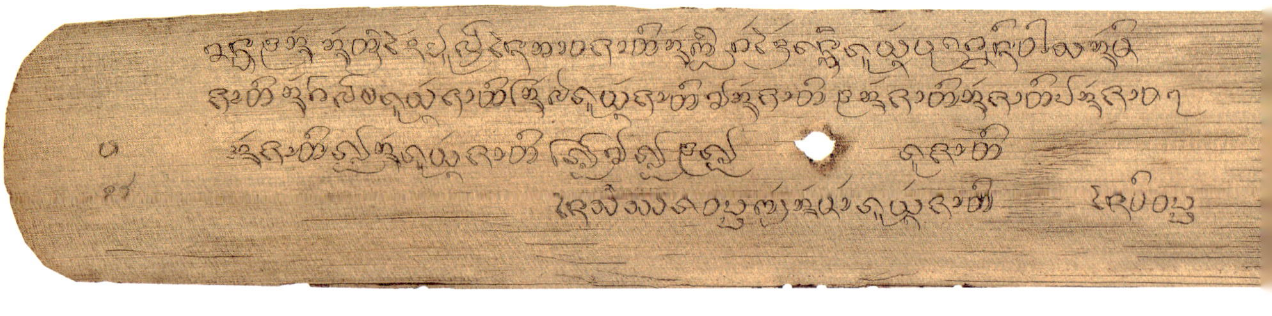

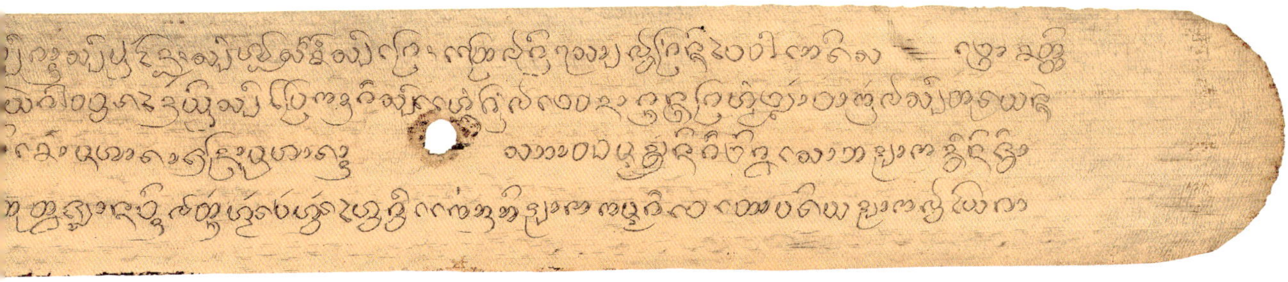

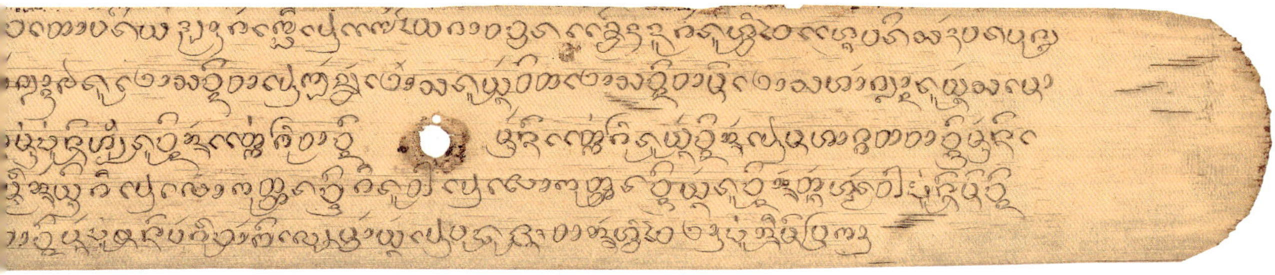

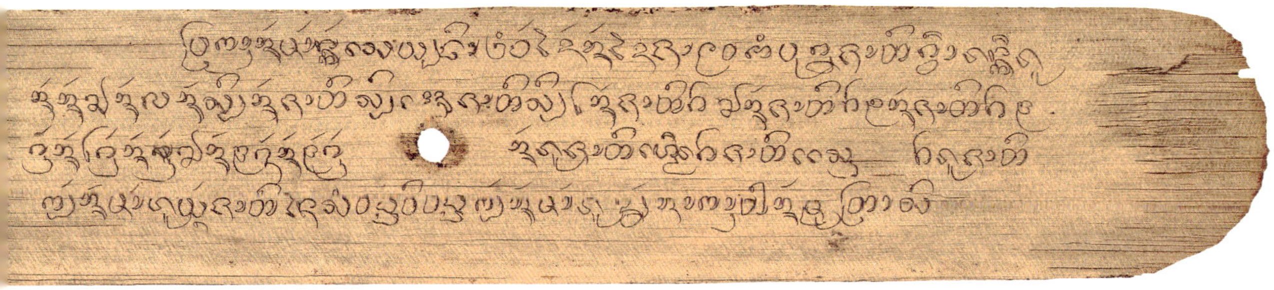

桑玛雅帕拉

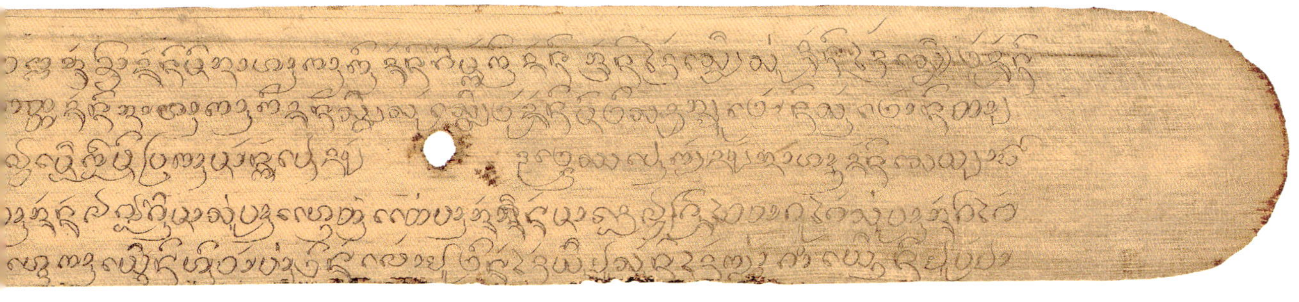

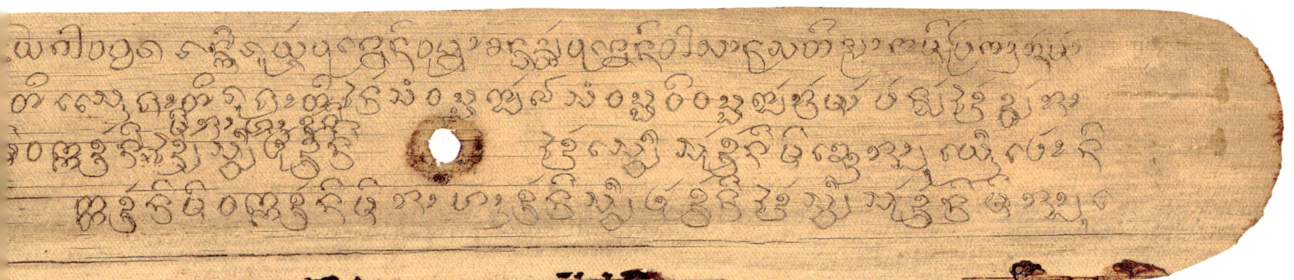

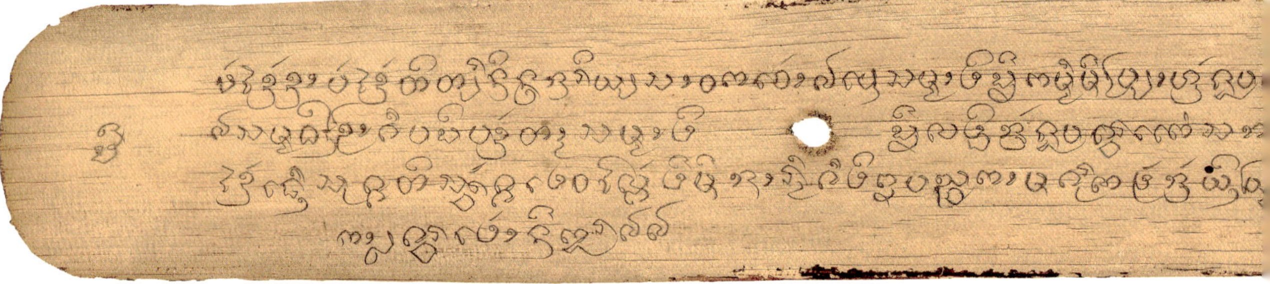

第九册

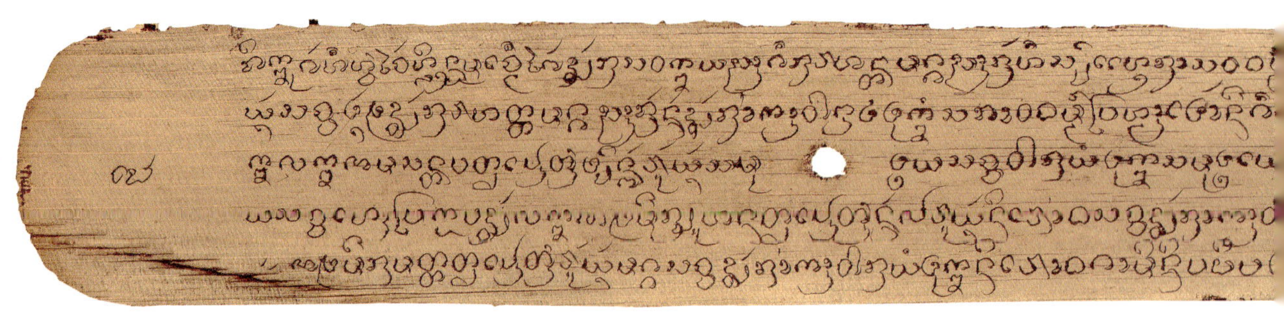

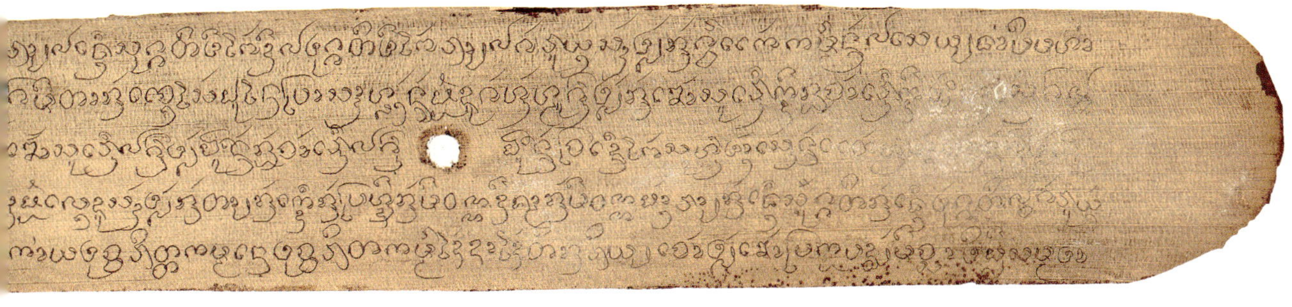

桑玛雅帕拉

桑玛雅帕拉

桑玛雅帕拉

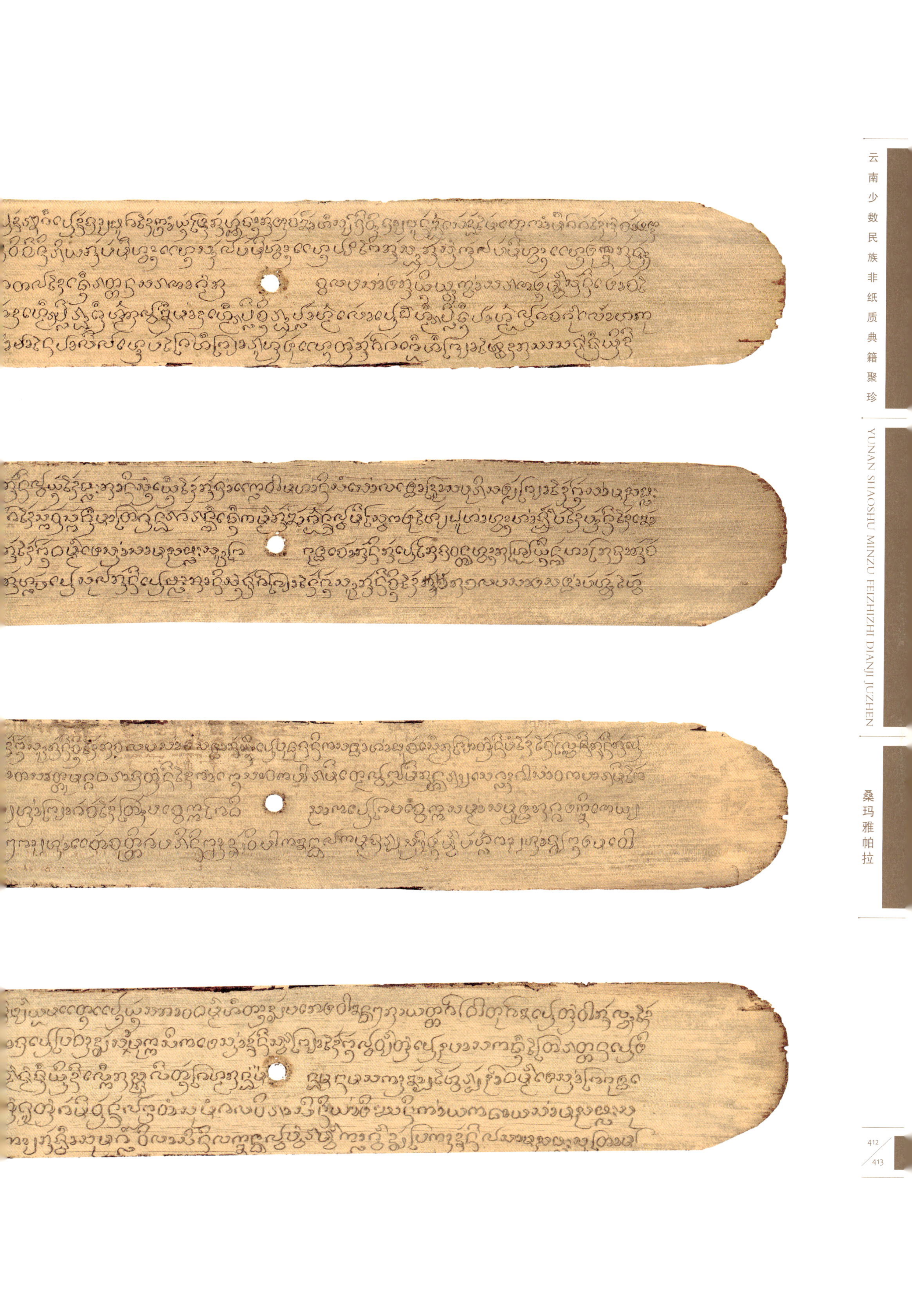

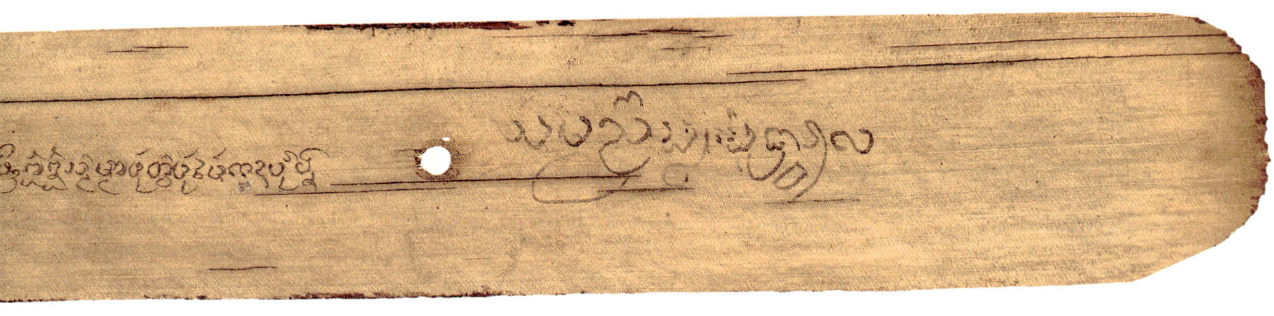

后记

我们长期从事云南少数民族古籍的抢救保护、翻译整理和出版规划工作，对云南少数民族古籍的分布、储量和传承现状有一个基本的了解，发现各民族都拥有或历史上曾经拥有过一些载体独特、形式各异的非纸质典籍，全面抢救保护、搜集整理这些分布零散、濒临消失且长期不被关注的少数民族非纸质典籍是一项具有重要意义的文化工程。

2015 年初，我们便逐步对各民族的非纸质典籍开展专题调查，不断征集线索、采集古籍图片，随着资料的不断累积，便萌生了将非纸质典籍专题影印出版的想法。这个想法得到云南人民出版社的大力支持，经申报入选“国家民文出版项目库”，并获民族文字图书出版专项资金的经费支持，为编纂出版本书创造了有利的条件。2017 年，本书主创团队参与云南大学周琼教授主持的国家社会科学基金重大项目“中国西南少数民族灾害文化数据库建设”，进一步推动了本项目的执行。

抢救保护承载着丰富民族文化内涵的云南少数民族非纸质典籍，具有重要的意义，也是一个充满挑战和未知的尝试。全面搜集云南各少数民族的非纸质典籍是一项耗时费钱费力的工作，这些典籍东一本西一样地散布在全省各地，从线索征集到一一获得授权采集图片确实经历了各种波折。

有的图片在采集过程中受自然条件的限制，采集难度较大。特别是金石铭刻类的图片，有的稍模糊，或缺乏全景图，甚是遗憾。图片如愿采集回来了，要将这些琳琅满目的典籍进行鉴别、释读、分类，更是一项艰巨的任务，没有统一的划分标准可以参照，没有现成的经验可资借鉴，我们唯有摸着石头过河。进入统稿、编排环节，我们既要考虑覆盖云南各世居少数民族，又要考虑丛书的体量、编排等，取舍两难，着实让人困扰。最后，我们唯有以抢救保护、搜集整理少数民族古籍资料为出发点，以云南少数民族非纸质典籍的文化价值作为评判标准，以期为社会科学研究、文化产业发展等提供可资借鉴的材料。就收录范围，我们采用广义的民族古籍概念，适当突破民族古籍学学科的界定和范围，各民族的金石铭刻、骨刻、丝帛素书、竹木简牍等都是我们收录的对象，而结绳记事、刻木记事、树叶信等族属不明、内涵不清、争议较大的暂不作收录。所收录典籍的时间下限一般为1911年，有的适当延至1949年。目前学界对各民族古籍的搜集整理、研究程度参差不齐，对古籍的翻译整理和释读等有巨大差距，这直接影响到我们对典籍的考释和图解。纳西族非纸质典籍的收集、研究起步较早，我们基本可以释读典籍的名称和内容，而彝族、壮族、藏族、傣族等民族的非纸质典籍研究尚处于起步阶段，其典籍的释读、命名尚有难度，如壮族的骨刻书，我们知道是用于历算的，但具体的内涵、使用方法尚未形成统一定论，我们实不敢妄解。所以部分非纸质典籍的文字说明略显简单粗陋。

本项目得到了云南人民出版社的大力支持和配合，特别是金学丽编审在项目策划、调研、稿件甄选、编辑等方面倾注了很多的心血，为项目的顺利开展做出了巨大的努力；吴贵飙馆长、普学旺译审、谢沫华研究馆员、起国庆研究馆员在项目申报、执行等方面给予了切实可行的指导意见和帮助；本书资料的收集，得到丽江市东巴文化研究院、丽江市博物院、丽江玉龙纳西族自治县图书馆、文山壮族苗族自治州民族宗教事务局等基层民族古籍工作部门的全力支持和配合，得到李德静、牛增裕、木琛、李瑞山、王明富、和丽宝、赵庆莲、陆保成等专家的鼎力相助。在此一并谨致谢意。

为较好地呈现这套丛书，我们多方求证、全面搜集典籍、认真编排，确实做了很多切实的努力。但鉴于本书的执行、撰稿人员以青年学者居多，书稿难免有考虑不周和不当之处，敬请读者批评指正！

本书编委会

2018年12月

Postscript

We have been engaging in the rescue, protection, translation sorting and publication planning of ancient books and records of ethnic minorities in Yunnan for a long time, and have a basic understanding on the distribution, reserves and inheritance status of ancient books and records of ethnic minorities in Yunnan. We find that all the ethnic minorities have or once had some non-paper ancient books and records with unique carriers and various forms in history. It is a cultural project of great significance to comprehensively rescue, protect, collect and sort out these scattered non-paper ancient books and records of ethnic minorities that are on the verge of disappearance and have not been paid attention to for a long time.

We began to conduct special investigations on non-paper ancient books and records of various ethnic minorities, and are constantly collecting clues and pictures of ancient books and records since the beginning of 2015. With the continuous accumulation of data, we came up with the idea of photocopying and publishing special subjects of non-paper ancient books and records. This idea was vigorously supported by Yunnan People's Publishing House, and it was selected into the "national project library for publication of ethnic books and records" through application. Besides, it was also supported by the special fund for the publication of the ethnic books and records, and has created favorable conditions for compilation and publication of this book. In 2017, the creative team of this project participated in "the Establishment of the Database for Disaster Culture in the Ethnic Minorities in Southeast China" (Approval Number of the Project: 17ZDA158) which is the major project of the national social science foundation, and vigorously promoted the implementation of this series of books.

It is of great significance to rescue and protect the non-paper ancient books and records of ethnic minorities in Yunnan, which carries over rich ethnic cultural connotations, and is also an attempt full of challenges and mysteries. It is a time-consuming, costly and arduous task to collect all the non-paper ancient books and records of ethnic minorities in Yunnan. These ancient books and records are widely scattered all over the province. Relevant working personnel have experienced various twists and turns from collecting the clues to obtaining the authorization to collect pictures one by one. Restricted by the natural conditions, some pictures are difficult to take. In particular, the inscription pictures are slightly blurred or lack of panoramic images. What a pity! Finally, the pictures were collected as expected. It is an arduous task to identify, interpret and classify these dazzling records. There is no unified classification standard to refer to and no ready-made experience to base on. We have to grope our way. In terms of compilation and arrangement, not only should we consider the coverage of ethnic minorities living in Yunnan, but also we should take the volume and arrangement of the series of books into account. It is really confusing to make choices. Finally, we can only take the rescue, protection, collection and sorting-out of the ancient books and records of ethnic minorities as the starting point, and the cultural value of non-paper ancient books and records of ethnic minorities in Yunnan as the evaluation standard, so as to provide reference materials for social science research and cultural industry development. In terms of the scope of inclusions, we adopt the broad concept of ethnic ancient books and records and appropriately break through the definition and scope of ethnic ancient books and records. Inscriptions, bone carvings, silk books and bamboo and wooden engravings of various ethnic minorities are all included in our collection scope, while the records of rope knotting, wood carving and leaf letters are not included for the time being due to their unclear and controversial connotations. The lower limit of time of the ancient books and records collected is uniformly fixed as prior to 1949. In terms of the interpretations and illustrations of ancient books and records, collection, collation and research on ancient books and records of various ethnic minorities are at different levels, and there is a huge gap in the translation, collation and interpretation of ancient books and records. For instance, due to early start of the collection and research on the Naxi non-paper ancient books and records, we can basically read names and contents of the ancient books and records. However, the research on non-paper ancient books and records of the Yi, Zhuang, Tibetan, Dai and other ethnic minorities is still in the initial stage, and it is difficult to read and name them. For example, we know that the bone carvings of the Zhuang Ethnic group are used for calendar calculation, but no unified conclusion has been reached on their specific connotation and method of use. We don't dare to make improper interpretations. Therefore, some of the explanatory notes on the non-paper ancient books are slightly simple and not so detailed.

This project has received vigorous support and cooperation from Yunnan People's Publishing House. In particular, Senior Editor Jin Xueli has spared no efforts in project planning, research, manuscript selections and editing, and made a great contribution to the smooth development of the project. Director Wu Guibiao, senior translator Pu Xuewang, Research librarian Xie Mohua and Qi Guoqing have provided practical guidance and help in the project application, implementation and other aspects.

Data collections for this book has been completely supported and cooperated by the Research Institute of Dongba Culture of Lijiang, the Library of Yulong Naxi Autonomous County of Lijiang, the Affairs Bureau of Ethnic and Religious Affairs of Zhuang-Miao Autonomous Prefecture of Wenshan and other grass-roots departments of ethnic ancient books and records. We would like to express our gratitude to Li Dejing, Niu Zengyu, Mu Chen, Li Ruishan, Wang Mingfu, He Libao, Zhao Qinglian, Lu Baocheng and other experts.

We have made lots of practical efforts in seeking confirmations from various sources, comprehensively collecting ancient books and records and making arrangements carefully, so as to better present this series of books. However, since the book is mainly collected and compiled by young scholars, it is hard to avoid making incomprehensive and improper considerations. We are looking forward to your criticism and corrections!

Editorial Board of the Book

December, 2018